INDIAN RAILWAYS
FINANCIAL MELTDOWN

INDIAN RAILWAYS FINANCIAL MELTDOWN

A Study in Turnaround to White Paper and Beyond

R.N. MISRA

KALPAZ

Indian Railways Financial Meltdown

ISBN- 978-81-7835-960-1

Published in 2013 in India by
Kalpaz Publication,
C-30, Satyawati, Nagar
Delhi-110 052

E-mail: kalpaz@hotmail.com
Ph: 9212142040

Laser Typesetting: Awadhesh Computers, Delhi

Printed at: G. Print Process.Delhi

Contents

Contents

List of Tables and Figures

Preface

Ever since the publication of White Paper on Indian Railways and its presentation to the Parliament on 18th December, 2009, an interesting but controversial issue was raised about the nature and causes of railways' crises regarding finances and management. The railway was declared as stagnant sector, crushed under its own weight, causing immobility, inefficiency and incompetence. As per White Paper, the traffic growth performance remained below par and railways' contribution to GDP came to a stand still at 1.18. It was complained that the carrying capacity (CC) of wagons had a bearing on the wear and tear of the tracks and the rolling stock. In spite of reduced terminal detention and increased maintenance cycle for better utilization of assets, the railway was far away from the operational efficiency compared to international benchmark. The White Paper harped on losses in passenger operation which grew cumulatively high above several thousand crore of rupees posing as if the paper would bring railways to settle down those losses. The main contention of White Paper centred round 'two' critical changes in accounting norms which, on iterative process, inflated the cash surplus before dividend due to the consultant's imagination, stretching out the amount by more than Rs. 17000 crore. So this amount ought to be retrieved to normal condition by resettling the changes in accounts. The issues primarily before the railways relate to the same as were emphasized by earlier White Papers, Expert Group Report and other recommendations made by railways own committees and working groups established from time to time.

The White Paper, in general, is supposed to be a document of self introspection, indicating infirmities and weaknesses of the organization or the department. It tries to find out solution of the problems which the organization is facing with full transparency and coordination among its workers, staff and the bosses. The White Paper is a cooperative endeavour to improve upon the situation and looking after the possibility of generating better opportunities of work and action. The White Paper at times is issued to clear the misunderstanding prevailing in respect of working, control and progress of the institution. It is an answer to those who demand an explanation from the organization regarding its failure in achieving the aim for which it is established. Normally it is the authority which explains the view point to its people or the general public who has the right to know on the nature and causes of unprecedented happenings or any other serious matter. Since the White Paper goes in depth of the maladies prevailing in the departmental set up, it is not a thing to rejoice or celebrate. The white paper is characterized by its dispassionate approach of analysis, unbiased attitude and neutrality in judgment. Issuing White Paper is like presenting a reality show which explains true situation - the condition as it exists.

But the White Paper on Indian railways issued in December, 2009, does not justify its basic character and approach to introspection and self analysis. It is confined to a particular period of study and directly comes to the controversial situation of judging a particular regime, its leader and the activities which have been performed. Although care has been taken in not naming the person or the achievements, but viewing the entirety of the situation one can never fail to understand the reality behind the White Paper.

The present study provides an exposure of the reality – a case of counteracting the White Paper on Indian Railways as well as their financial meltdown. It is a well known fact that the White Paper expresses the inner feelings of being proud of creating an intensive study of the past five years 2004-2009 which belong to the regime of the person known to be the leader of turnaround. No White Paper has ever been presented so partial in approach as the present one. White Paper is never kept confined to a particular case, event or defined to serve only personal plan or action. The White Paper presents a historical analysis of the subject, bringing past and present together, frequently passing the boundaries of such period to produce unbiased results. But this White Paper has unprecedentedly attacked the individual, the group of people and the regime as a whole.

The present analytical study, therefore, puts forward an anti-thesis of White Paper – a critical account which does not only assess it on its merits and demerits but also presents a counter picture relating to such a lopsided paper. The subject under study has been introduced basically to explain the conflicting ways of two stalwarts of the railways - one the predecessor and other the then incumbent of Rail Bhavan. The predecessor had a full period of five years from May 2004 to April 2009 and the successor had her stint from May 2009 to May 2011 - a period of about two years only. The net result of such changes in administration brought the financial meltdown of the Indian railways.

In second and third chapters of the present study, the White Paper was viewed as an attempt to thwart the turnaround and an instrument to subdue the spirit of the railways. The chapter on counteracting the White Paper (fourth chapter) provides an answer to the faulty findings – the main analytical part of the study – linking overrated elasticity with the potential rate of growth of the railways' elasticity and judging the real situation. Here a correct potential growth rate has been calculated depicting the real percentage of increase in expected elasticity as against the percentage of shortfall as per expected elasticity shown in the White Paper. A sensitivity index has been added for making comparison and to show how even a bit of increase in elasticity generates a great expected rate almost an unachievable phenomenon. The concept of cash surplus has been misconstrued by the White Paper; as a result it has been highly distorted and played like a shuttle cock by the present incumbent of the railways. Still one finds that the predecessor has been the highest scorer of the railways' innings so far played. Two chapters viz., sixth and seventh have been added to highlight in general terms the financial and managerial syndrome and diagnostic analysis of the railways' failing health. In eighth and ninth chapters, the White Paper has been put to test to find out in historical context how it is relevant when the railways have already experienced a glut of White Papers after liberalization and how it stands face to face with turnaround event of the railways which has become a historical fact. There is no denying the fact that reforms and changes are needed for railways as discussed in tenth chapter, but neither restructuring nor privatizing them is the real answer. Chapter eleventh brings an analytical study of the present changing situation i.e., 'White Paper and Beyond'. It provides a situation to understand how dangerously the railways have sunk into a quagmire. The railways require transformation but a surfeit of White Papers and other such reports have strangulated them making them ineffective to respond to any change. Chapter eleven relates to the present period of great neglect creating financial meltdown and administrative deterioration. In the end, conclusions have been drawn interrelating railways moving from Turnaround to White Paper and their aftermath.

This brings out an entire thesis - an answer to the questionable assessment of the period which has formed the basis of the White Paper and ultimately became the cause of railways meltdown. The author has not used names of the players in the game of issuing the White Paper to keep them away from appearing repeatedly in the entire text. So the reader has to judge the sequence of the facts and happenings according to the 'predecessor' and 'successor' who are well known persons and have worked during their stint within the period of study i.e., 2004-09 and 2009-11 respectively. The study has analyzed the situation to find out how the White Paper stands in justifying its case in projecting a particular period or regime in the larger context of the railways' transformation into a world-class system. The author takes the responsibility for anything offending appearing inadvertently in this analytical work and apologizes for the same in advance. A corrective measure is always open if some such facts are brought to notice. The author offers all success to his readers and keeps follies and faults as a part of his own share of assessment. It is personal but necessary for the author to express his thanks to his wife Smt. Nirmalesh Misra for going through the entire text and providing valuable suggestions and also his daughter Kirti for the cooperation and support provided for finishing the work in time.

New Delhi **R.N. Misra**
Sept, 2012.

Acknowledgements

The author is obliged to the ministry of railways, government of India, for using extensively the extracts of the publications 'White Paper on Indian Railways' and 'Vision 2020', issued in December 2009. There appeared a lot of material in the media - print and electronic - regarding the White Paper and the author feels obliged to such persons and institutions for the help provided including the organizers of the Dailies, namely *Times of India, The Hindu, The Economic Times* and *Business Line* and the relevant material made available through other important news papers and the magazines - weekly and fortnightly. The author is obliged to the insiders of the railways who from time to time helped in organizing the material for the study. The author is profoundly indebted to Prof. Ram Deo Bhandari, ex-Member of Parliament, who made available to him the copies of White Paper and Vision 2020 when these were presented to the Parliament as the publications were not priced for sale (now available on internet). The author expresses deep sense of obligation to the members of Railway Board and other staff, specially the academic, linked with the railways' institutes and study centres. The author came in contact directly or indirectly with important employees of the railways who encouraged him to write on the subject as it was timely and needed to be explained for the Indian people, in general, and railway-staff, in particular. Shri N. K. Gupta, Dr. N. C. Satyawadi and Dr. Ramanan were of special help to him. The author's elder brother Shri S .N. Misra, who served the Indian Railways in several capacities from station-in-charge to the researcher at RITES, had directed him to link up to several bosses who in their capacity had power to drive and direct the railways' policies and programmes. The author shall be failing in his duty if he does not mention the learned and highly experienced ex-employee of the railways, Shri A .V. Paulose who retired as the finance commissioner (Member Finance), Railway Board, and is still active in study and research concerning railways' finances and other policy matters for useful discussions with him.

The Genesis

It was on 18th December, 2009, that the White Paper on Indian Railways was presented to the Parliament by the then minister of railways – Mamata Banerjee. This was brought out in retaliation against the achievements of the preceding minister – Lalu Prasad who created turnaround of Indian Railways, generating unprecedented profits.

The appearance of the 'White Paper on Indian Railways' created an impression that the turnaround process of the railways was much hyped than real. This raised a controversy rather disbelief in the minds of the people in general and railways' staff in particular about the earlier achievements of the predecessor.

The present work is the outcome of the situation where an analytical study has been made to provide an answer to the faulty findings of the 'White Paper' and has established an anti-thesis of the same. This study thus protects the concept of turnaround of Indian Railways and its transformation from loss bearing to profit generating organization.

Hereafter the 'predecessor' will stand for Lalu Prasad and 'the then incumbent of Rail Bhavan for Mamata Banerjee' in the entire text in order to avoid names appearing repeatedly. The years of analysis of Lalu Prasad belong to the period from May 2004 to April 2009 and that of Mamata Banerjee to the period from May 2009 to May 2011. The name of Lalu Prasad has been substituted in several ways like leader of the turnaround, the ex-minister or the former minister, the old guard of the railways etc., and the name of Mamata Banerjee has been substituted almost opposite like the new incumbent or the then incumbent of Rail Bhavan or the then minister for the railways or the successor etc. Mamata Banerjee left the railways portfolio in May 2011. Since then the ministry of railways went into three more hands (The Prime Minister

Manmohan Singh; Shri Dinesh Trivedi and Shri Mukul Roy) but it is Ms. Banerjee who still dominates the railways with de facto power to handle the organization. One can relate the names according to the period and the situation as they appear in the text.

1

Turnaround to White Paper: Whither Indian Railways?

In the present political scenario of India, it is a rarity that the successor agrees and carries forward the initiatives of the predecessor. The doubts raised on the eve of the (former) minister's departure from his office at Rail Bhavan in April/May 2009 have proved true.[1] How would the turnaround process of the railways be sustained in the long run if the new incumbent of the railways or the successor tries to dig in the very roots of the change? The suspicion has come home to the roost. (Kumar, 2009b: 25)

Under the multi-party democratic system as we have, the governments come and go and so do the ministers. This is the essence of democracy. During the changing regimes, our leaders must behave in public gracefully and act gently without any malice and prejudice towards each other. The new incumbent of Rail Bhavan[2] and her predecessor[3] belong to two different states and constituencies of India with separate ideologies and there seems to be no occasion for their clash of interests and moods. But the new incumbent finds in her predecessor a formidable opponent in sharing the power game of politics which is why she is bent upon downsizing the image of her predecessor to whatever level he has achieved during the last five years of his stint as the railways minister from 2004 to 2009 (Ibnlive, 2010). Both the stalwarts of these two states-writing the story of political non-alignment - have set to perpetuate disharmony in their behaviour as an anti-thesis to what presently the lead characters of one of the best sellers '2 STATES'[4] forge to unite two cultures, states and the lives differently.

Conflicting Ways

The predecessor who left the railways in April 2009 and the new incumbent of Rail Bhavan who joined in May 2009 belong to the same genus and both politically are the products of deeply agitated movements prevailing during their youth in their respective States. However, they have come of age when they can with great care and sobriety look at their own affairs without any attempt to malign each other. As the successor is in the position of power, she holds greater responsibility to keep her cool, get her work done even in a better way than her predecessor and show her mettle to bring about a 'second turnaround' for the railways. She should not drag the prestigious department of the railways and its officers into controversy on the basis of issuing White Paper only to prove that her predecessor was full of odds and manipulations and did nothing positive for the railways. In fact, it is an exercise in futility on her part by doing so. She may be the victim of the same situation as and when she leaves the office. Retaliation and undoing the work of the predecessor breeds contempt. The ex-minister (the predecessor) had held the view that the success story of the railways was the story of the hard work and cooperation of all the 14 lakh employees ranging from the top bosses to the lowest rung of the workers like points men and coolies. If the new incumbent — the Trinamool chief - chooses to downgrade the image of her predecessor, an internal rift among the employees is bound to be created and the organization would be the worst sufferer in the long run.

The then incumbent of Rail Bhavan or — the chief of Trinamool Party—knows it well that every accusing finger is accompanied with an equally accusing counter finger. There is no use of creating controversy over turnaround process of the railways. The figures don't tell lies and all the achievements can't be the product of manipulations. The figures showing surplus have been generated by the railway staff in consultation with finance commissioner and the revenue so collected is deposited with the Reserve Bank of India (RBI). If there is any conceptual difference of putting an item from one particular pocket to another, it is an internal matter and does not require a White Paper to expose it publicly. However, the concept of turnaround was used by the railway board and its staff for achieving greater revenue and the process of change was ultimately set in motion. The predecessor simply acted upon, and Indian Institute of Management, Ahmedabad (IIM-A), analytically highlighted the same on behalf of the railways. The ex-minister (2004-09) is not alone in justifying turnaround. There is a vast spectrum of intelligentsia and institutional support for him — nation and worldwide.

The Railways-Chair

By withdrawing the prestigious chair from IIM-A, the then incumbent of Rail Bhavan has not shown her magnanimity.[5] It is an act which brings disgrace to the railways' authorities. Suppose, for example, Obama administration breaks away with the nuclear deal finalized during Bush's time, how would India feel? It is just a matter of intellectual propriety, honesty and integrity. A chair is an academic honour to both the parties and must be duly maintained. The then incumbent of Rail Bhavan should have learnt the lessons from the West where government and corporate work together for the betterment of the society. If corporate has a social responsibility, the government too has an intellectual debt to be paid to academics. At times, when internal assessment fails to bring results, one has to consult outside experts. With the creation of the chair at IIM-A, a constant consultative service was generated just as R/D was carried on in a production unit. The railways were free to accept the analysis produced by the institute or reject it. It was a known fact that Nitish Kumar too had commissioned the Rakesh Mohan Committee and ultimately it was he who gracefully shelved it. Even during that time, the incumbent of Rail Bhavan had joined the railways as a minister for a short intermittent period and she had kept the working of the Expert Group in abeyance.

When (the former) railways minister visited IIM - A, in September 2007, he had promised to set up a 'railway chair' at the prestigious B-School for research in railways infrastructure and management. The minister was obliged to do so in the wake of 'turnaround of the Indian Railways' projected and presented before the nation as a hallmark of the railways' potential to change and develop through an in depth study made by the institute IIM - A declaring railways as a sunrise sector. It was in contrast with the earlier study made by The Rakesh Mohan Committee Report 2001 in which Prof. G. Raghuram was included as a member. He had proclaimed that nothing could stop the railways to become world class, achieve their target and develop into a profit earning undertaking. While presenting the budget for 2007-08, the minister announced the setting up of a Railway-Chair at IIM - A with effect from April 1, 2007. The institute had already signed a formal Memorandum of Understanding (MoU) with the Indian railways about the setting up of the chair and a provision was made for a sum of Rs 11 lakh to 15 lakh annually (consecutively for five years - increasing Rs. 1 lakh every year starting with Rs. 11 lakh initially) for carrying out research programmes on the railways.

It was a debatable point whether the 'turnaround' study submitted by Prof. Raghuram of IIM - A was a genuine or just a paraphrase of the railways' own study material, statistical statements and analyses, but the highly trained and qualified cadre of Indian Railways Services did not appreciate Prof. Raghuram's intrusion into railways' 'internal affairs' because it would silently and craftily try to corrode and vitiate the functioning of the railways, converting it into a 'private concern' much like a worm in the bud, eating softly from within. The mystery of corporate capitalism is that what they cannot achieve directly, they try to acquire it through intrusion and infiltration. IIM - A is the cauldron of capitalism in India like Harvard Business School (HBS) in US. What they 'teach' and 'don't teach' form the main basis of their ideological thrust and intensity. A person from such a committed school of thought would be more a 'corporate man' than an exponent of public policy measures of government sector as the railways is. The presence of such a person would not benefit the railways, as a public sector, in any form. Perhaps Prof. Raghuram's focus on 'organizational structure' of railways and The Rakesh Mohan Committee Report 2001 ran parallel in contents and he very subtly tried to keep the Railways Report 2001, alive for all practical purposes. The Railways' cadre therefore sharply reacted and attacked the very purpose of the study and the ministry said, "Productive ideas have not come. The chair has been scrapped, as the Railways can ill afford such wasteful expenditure". It was a point to be noted that the study[6] made by Prof. Raghuram which contained sixty-five A4 size pages, only nineteen pages were relevantly drafted by him (and his associates?) and rest of the study, developed purely as exhibits, like appendices, to the study almost a borrowed material from Railway statistical and financial sections located at different corridors of Rail Bhavan. Many of these exhibits were irrelevant like the list of the Railway Ministers, Chairmen of railway board, zonal offices and their details, and sample of super fast trains and their routes etc. (thank God no inclusion of the 'Time-Table - Railways At A Glance - 2007' as an exhibit was made). One would not find any questionnaire at the end of the study, so it was presumed that no primary investigation was done by the researcher. The whole study was based on secondary data on the railways own collected statistics.

With the coming of the new Railway minister[7] in 2009, the scenario was changed abruptly and the legacy of the predecessor was blown to pieces. It was almost a total upturning of the decisions earlier taken by the past regime. And the first step in this direction was to scrap the Railway Chair. It was a hurried decision because in the globalized world no institution could survive in isolation and one of the causes of railways deterioration was that it had developed a habit of making an island of its own - just living in the 'make-believe world'. This narrowed down the horizon which was reflected in many aspects of the railways thinking and the worst could happen was that the railways started losing its hold over generating innovative ideas and creativity in commercial and operational practices. As every institution needs an institutional support; a department requires an organizational push up and a system develops through well knit and planned set up; so the railways too need such a support; standing alone will not do. Only working together and collaborating with each other is the need of the time. The Indian Railways were no exception to it. It needed the support of the ever growing and developing technology, managerial system and financial techniques. Where from the railways would get them? It must link itself with IITs, IIMs and international rail-road associations and traffic and transport consortia. It should get linked with international B-Schools and technology institutes also. The railways chair at IIM- A had the basic aim of introducing innovative practices for the Indian railways. It was also to develop strategies and create a network for infrastructural growth and remodeling the railway traffic. Since taking over the charge, the new incumbent has been systematically dismantling the predecessor's regime. There were certain other allegations made against the predecessor and a Central Bureau of Investigation (CBI) enquiry too was suggested to bring the past minister (the predecessor) in the dock. The politics of the railways over shadowed the academic advancement which was developed through the programme of research and case studies at IIM, Ahmedabad, during the past regime. The Railways were the sufferers, not the B-Schools; an opportunity was lost; a systematic degeneration took place within the organizational set up of the railways.

Spending a paltry sum of money on the sponsorship of turnaround, IIM-A, the faculty and the railways chair, is just a minor act of academic pursuit as a research programme for such a mammoth organization as the Indian Railways is. The railway should honour its commitment, cooperate and learn from the institute which is not ordinary in its name and fame. For example, Late Prime Minister Nehru gave political asylum and honour to Dalai Lama amidst dangerous situation. Any new incumbent after Nehru might have reversed the decision. But no: this is not our tradition. We have allowed him to stay and all the PMs including Manmohan Singh have reiterated that Dalai Lama is our honoured guest. Likewise, the present incumbent of Rail Bhavan should not falsify our tradition and must retain the chair as an honourable commitment. The cultural history of India is replete with such instances when the king used to go to the Rishis in their Ashrams for consultations. She should feel elevated by showing her generosity in retaining the chair, considering that by doing so she is coming nearer to the temple of learning like Gurudev's Shantiniketan. IIM-A is one of the dignified institutions of India and the railways must show its generosity towards academics.

What is more surprising is the comment made by a few insiders of the railways that they could not get anything substantial in return from IIM-A. All the figures and facts used by them were generated by the railways. They have added nothing new to the analysis. Perhaps the critics fail to understand that an analytical enquiry does use the figures provided by the 'subject' of study itself. What makes the study important is the methodology, tools and models which are used in enquiring while analyzing the study to come to the correct conclusion. The railway has to generate facts and figures as it deals with business, finance, marketing, sale and production along with customers and a large work force attached to it. The work of tabulating figures, charting them out and creating balance sheet, as done by the railways, is not enough. The railway is capable of generating a vast variety of statistics but it cannot have objective mechanism of testing hypothesis, analyzing facts and figures, projecting and forecasting demand and supply of services, concluding cost benefits, implementing manpower planning and adopting input-output analysis of productive process including intermediate and final demands and calculating growth pattern. Nobody is questioning the competence of the professional cadre of the railways; it is perhaps the best in India. But we are living in the times of interdisciplinary approach of the study and research. There is no harm if an institute of management is attached to the railways. The railways after all had two chairs established in the 'areas' of bridge engineering and dynamics of rail vehicle system at IIT, Roorkee. What is the harm if a new chair is established at IIM - A, for managerial and financial studies? Would the railways be poorer by spending a small sum of money on such a project? The railways still require a body of experts and an intellectual support. The Indian railway does not have such an expertise. It has to borrow services from outside and pay for them. What wrong has the predecessor done?

Funding Research

Coming to the point of investigative journalism using Right to Information (RTI), working as sleuth and a member of some secret service and finding that 'turnaround' is a paid project is nothing but a prejudiced process of reporting, totally divorced from objective expression, views submission and exchange of ideas. The railways have nothing to hide. It maintains total transparency. It is railways' process of funding for research activities. As already explained, the railways had to get facts and statements verified, tested, analyzed and brought forward for ascertaining strength and weaknesses. It is like a doctor testing a human body. The body belongs to the patient but various tests are performed on and within the body to come to the diagnostic conclusion. As for a serious patient, it requires an 'Apollo - the hospital', so the body of the railways requires, at times, the help of a B-School (like IIM/A/B/C/ or Harvard) for diagnostic analysis. Who else would declare the positive results of turnaround to the public authentically? Only a paid expert would do the job. Thus, turnaround was certified as a potential force generated for bringing the railways to the path of initial change and progress. And this was done by the super specialty B-School of India i.e. IIM-A. The present incumbent too has appointed a committee headed by Federation of Indian Chamber of Commerce and Industry (FICCI) Chairman, Amit Mitra, to seek report on land use, public private participation in the railways and other related matters. Will it work without any charge or expenses?

Shift in Accounting Process

Taking up the case of shifting of accounting convention and rules and other fixed system of book entries, one has to keep in mind that the whole of accounting process is based on traditional pattern of rules followed by changes brought through convention committee recommendations. But the reform has to be brought initially to the notice by those who need such changes and it is a long run process. Sometimes, the change is initiated immediately, breaking the convention and adopting a new pattern of accounting. But all changes are not brought about at a time. The CAG (Comptroller and Accountant General) approves or disapproves the change. But the process of reform is carried on with the hope that the CAG would approve with minor changes and after the compliance report submitted to them. The CAG is not a body for not allowing changes. It certainly puts question mark and doubt over such changes. However, the convention committee puts forward the changes as desired and as addressed according to their needed reforms. The CAG approves the changes which are not extremely out of tune. The changes, approvals and putting forward new changes are normal activities of accounting process. The auditor's brown pencil signs up everywhere on the books of account like punctuation marks which are meant to show that a cautious approach is needed for the accounting system. It also means for compliance of their suggestions and removal of doubts. The CAG is a type of speed breaker in financial matters to avoid head on collision. Sometimes, it goes beyond its scope and works as a combined force of an auditor and an investigating authority i.e. CAG and CBI put together (CAG, 2006, Report 5). But it should not be treated as a 'stop' at the traffic lights. One has to cross the bumps on roads cautiously without feeling any jerks within a time frame. But side by side the CAG has also to change its style of working, interpretation and instructions to the institutions to which it is attached for auditing. Its old fashioned system of analysis has to be changed paving new ways according to financial aspirations and needs. It must modernize itself in the wake of new democratic values. The whole set up of administration and bureaucracy has to accept the changing order and CAG should not feel shy of getting itself transformed into a new model of financial accounting, standards and values. The railways have not kept any secret of the changes which they adopted in the accounting process.

There are three changes made in accounting process by the railways during the period 2004–2009. They are the part of its long going reforms in financial standard. They are:

- Change in lease charges payable to Indian Railways Finance Corporation (IRFC).
- Change in interest accounting in railways fund balances.
- Changes in the calculation of losses on strategic lines.

The Indian railways has been adopting the process of accounting reforms and addressing them according to the needs. The railway has appointed a consortium including French Railways SNCF and Ernst and Young, among others to work on its accounting reforms programme. The government of India needs service-based revenue and cost data from the railways to support existing government reporting requirements, according to the Economic Survey. The railway, thus, has to address various issues for business orientation including changes in lease payment accounting process, rate of interest according to fund balances and concessions of loss making branch lines.

There has been a paradigm shift in lease accounting nationally and internationally. So the Indian railways is not an exception to this process. There are two approaches to lease accounting - risk based and reward based. The lease obligation may appear to meet the definition as a 'liability' under operating lease if it is risk lease. Similarly, right to economic benefits under operating leases may appear to meet the definition as an 'asset' if it is reward base lease. When such changes are internationally (IFRS - International Financial Report Standard) adopted, how can Indian GAAP (Generally Accepted Accounting Principles) remain away from these definitive changes?

The controversy over the railways shift in lease accounting process comes under IRFC to which the railways pay lease charges. There are two components of lease charges - the expenditure component and the asset component. Earlier all lease charges were recorded as 'expenses'. Now the interest component is regarded as expenditure and the principal as an asset or a capital form of lease. In 2008 out of total Rs 2153 crore lease charges, the principal or income part was only Rs 1677 crore and was added to the receipt or surplus and so was the case in 2007 when only Rs 1720 of the principal amount was added. But it should not be said that all surpluses are due to shift in accounting policy or they are not legitimate surpluses. Since IFRS is adopting a change, the modified lease policy in the Indian railways has to come to stay as the approved accounting principle. Similarly, there is very little depth in arguing against the case of deciding interest on fund balances to be brought into 'miscellaneous' receipts as well as losses on strategic lines to be deducted from working expenses. Why the re-imbursement of losses should go to reduce excess of expenditure and not to reduce dividend liability? In 2008, Rs 637crore amounted to this head and interest on fund balances amounted to Rs 1175 crore. As a result of all such changes the railways' income increased to Rs. 3489 crore in 2008 and Rs 2690 crore in the year 2007 in which Rs 1720.90 crore, Rs 660 crore and Rs 309 crore have been shown as the lease charges, rate of interest and losses on strategic lines respectively. But there was no stoppage of the turnaround process of the railways as substantial surpluses were created year after year.

Turnaround: Resurgence of Railways

It was officially declared in 2006 when the budget for 2006-07was presented to the Parliament that the railways have got tremendous success in achieving the turnaround i.e., changing the situation from loss bearing enterprise to profit earning organization. It was not done suddenly; in fact it took about two years of constant efforts to bring about such a change. When the new minister took charge in 2004, it seemed to be a difficult proposition. The fund balances of the railways had gone to their minimum, at the level of Rs. 358.75 crore in 2000-01, and the years 2002 and 2003 could not add any significant amount for investment, though earnest efforts were made to increase revenue. The operative ratio had touched the highest point - more than 98 percent. Had the dividend liability not differed in 2000-01, the ratio technically would have crossed 100 per cent meaning thereby that earning one rupee would cost more than a rupee — almost a self consuming economy was generated. This created a terrible problem and the mood of the railway men - the employees, staff, and workers of railways' unions was marked by anxiety, fear and hopelessness. The situation could not be allowed to persist any longer and drastic steps were needed to eradicate the symptom and the disease.

During the years between 2004 and 2008, a multipronged attack to cure the financial illness was taken up. A proper diagnosis was performed and the curing process had started. When one desired to earn revenue in competitive transport system, increasing fare or freight would not help to derive expected results because growth of transport remained shy of increasing prices. It had to find some other ways of curing the disease. So the basic fact what not-to-do was made clear. Increasing fares and freights were not only politically sensitive but supposed to be economically weak steps to adopt because of the greater responsiveness of relationship between price and traffic demand.

Therefore, two important steps were taken up: one, reducing the cost of transport and other, increasing the volume of traffic. There were many more traditional and innovative practices added to boost up the traffic and enhance revenue. All these processes were continued for two years and started bearing good results. The cash surplus before dividend increased from Rs. 11051.29 crore in 2004 to Rs. 25006.17 crore in 2007-08 and fund balance stood at an all time high of Rs. 20500 crore in 2007-08. During the regime of the predecessor (2004-05 to 2008-09) a total amount of Rs. 88668.77 crore of surplus was created. How this happened and what steps were adopted to bring this specific change was the story of success termed as 'turnaround of the railways'. It was real, innovative and historical event. It was the story of railways consolidation and improvement - a show of solidarity and rallying point - an expression of enthusiasm and unity among the workers. This was the resurgence of the railways brought about with a new mindset and a new agenda for railways transformation.

To grasp the story fully of Indian railways, one has to begin with the strategy adopted. It was to generate volume of traffic by forming 'longer, heavier and faster trains'. The attention was diverted from increasing fare and freight to reduce cost and enhance productive efficiency. The idea was shifted from unit cost to 'per train cost and benefit'. The idea to change 'tare to pay load ratio' came as a powerful strategy. The old formula was practiced which allowed the lowest load per wagon. The regime of the predecessor (2004-09) had picked up the right chord to change the system on two grounds: first, it was dormant or dead formula and second; the wagons were already overloaded, more than the formula had permitted. Why not change it to the benefit of the railways? And it was done, though Board members initially were reluctant to adopt such change. The loading of wagons thus was changed from 20.32 T to 22.9 T and for specific routes to 25 T per wagon.

Some traditional steps were taken to improve the revenues. Here the strategy was to bank upon the available resources and utilizing them fully. "It was like milking the cow fully or else it would fall sick". Two steps were important to mention in this connection: one, reducing the wagon turnaround days from 7 to 5 and second, decreasing the train examination time or mileage. These steps were taken to rationalize the existing system for better utilization of rolling stock. No higher science was needed to understand the process, but it required only 'will to change'. There prevailed very complicated classification of commodities system in the railways ranging up to 4000 item groups. This group classification was reduced to 400 and then to manageable 18 groups only. It was the part of freight classification and rationalization scheme. There were other zonal and divisional administrative reforms adopted. All these programmes augmented the carrying capacity (CC) and tuned up the tariff policy with the result that within the period of turnaround, from 2004 to 2009 the railways registered incremental originating loading of over 230 million tonnes.

The above principles were extended to the passenger business also. Since the railway is a public sector unit, it has to carry with it the social obligation to provide efficient and affordable mobility to a large section of the populace. The strategies adopted in the sector of passenger traffic during the turnaround period consisted of the following:

- The fare of the premium classes where the competition existed with airlines were adjusted according to competitive theory.
- The second class fares were kept unchanged on the basis of the principle of affordability.
- The length of the popular trains was increased from 16-18 coaches to 24-26 coaches.
- The speed and upgradation of the trains were reviewed within the existing constraints.
- Participation of private operators in passenger related non-core areas such as parcel and catering was encouraged. The losses incurred by the railways in this part of activity were halved by this process.
- IT technology was made accessible in case of ticketing and reservations to homes and offices.
- In order to accommodate wait-listed passenger upgradation from lower to higher class was done without any extra charges.
- The middle class or lower middle class passengers were given the facilities of enjoying the luxury of air-conditioned train with nominal extra expenses. The Garib Rath (fully air conditioned train) was introduced on the principle of 'the economy of large scale' and 'decreasing cost'. Greater the number of AC coaches attached to a train, lesser would be the maintenance cost', was the principle applied to Garib Rath.

The total turnaround process was based on: 'play on volumes, reduce cost, reduce tariff, improve market share and margins and earn record profits'. The underlying philosophy was to improve yield per train as against the earlier obsession with tariff i.e., rate per passenger or tonne.

In this process the Indian Railways were able to create additional capacity without increasing number of trains or adding to congestion on the saturated corridors. As a result, though the cost of inputs like wages and fuel increased, the unit cost and rail tariff came down. While in the past the traffic growth trailed GDP growth but during the turnaround period, it exceeded that of GDP. This renewed the public confidence in the railways ability to respond to the challenges of our rapidly increasing economy as well as strengthened the self belief among the railway men to look ahead to the future with optimism. The railways thus laid the solid foundation through the process of turnaround to develop several initiatives to launch to transform Indian Railways into the best among world railways. The following initiatives were important to be noted:

1. Construction of Dedicated Freight Corridor.
2. Capacity augmentation.
3. Railways technological modernization.
4. Outlets for farmers.
5. New manufacturing units.

The principles underlying Turnaround of railways were based on honesty, strong will, willingness to change, adopting strong leadership and strategies like optimism, utilization of rolling stock, dynamic freight and fare policy along with the basic business approach and social obligation.

White Paper: Dispiriting the Railways

Immediately after the turnaround was achieved and finances of the railways were improved as a result of reform and change, during the predecessor's regime, some people not able to digest the success story of turnaround had started a whispering campaign against the leader and his achievements. The human relationship among the railway men is very peculiar. They say it lasts only up to the 'outer signal'. The moment the person is out of sight, he goes out of mind too. This is the sense of their professionalism and the predecessor and turnaround are no exception to it. A few of them have started doubting the pace of development during the period; others have focused on much hyped position of turnaround. They also have criticized it merely as a populist propaganda. But what has been missed by all of them is to recognise that a good beginning has been made; a dashing start has taken place.

In May 2009, new minister for railways took over the charge replacing the leader of turnaround. Best known for her tantrums and mercurial nature, she tried to create her impact by overthrowing the programmes of action and achievements of whatever level they were made by her predecessor. The Indian railway as a public sector department was quite open and accessible for these kinds of activities. Most of the professionals of Rail Bhavan did the same as the time demanded them to do. They started writing a different CV of the predecessor to gain the favour of the present boss. In July 2009 at the time of the presentation of rail-budget, the minister announced that the White Paper would be issued regarding the assessment of the period of the predecessor i.e., 2004-09.

This announcement was neither needed nor desirable. Those who wielded power and occupied position never swayed with the flow of the wind but she allowed herself for this to happen. And the rest of the task was taken up by a few 'favourites' at the Rail Bhavan. The statistical wing was ordered to supply spicy material and an outside agent was asked to analyze and submit the draft report known as White Paper. It was later refined and re-written and a ghoulish foreword was added to put an official stamp on it.

What is this White Paper? Why has this been issued and presented to the Parliament without approval of the cabinet? It is difficult to answer, but the author of White Paper i.e., railway ministry has the blessings of the minister as well as of the ruling party's high ups. The White Paper perhaps means to scale down the criteria so that at the time of comparison after the minister leaves the office may stand at a level above or in worst scenario at par with her predecessor. The White Paper is meant to kill the spirit of railways. The hard earned confidence, self esteem and progressive ways generated through turnaround during the predecessor's period have been nullified. The human face of the railways has been tarnished giving an impression that it is all hard iron frames and rough and tough institution devoid of any feelings of hope, love, sacrifice and human sympathy. The railways thus were made dispirited institution showing degeneration, defeatism and decadence.

White Paper has been issued to generate disharmony between the believers and non-believers of turnaround. Wrong statistics and non-comparable data have been put together to derive erroneous conclusion. White Paper is a self defeating document, full of contradictions and inconsistencies. It lacks coherence and clarity of thought and suggests no innovative ways for development. The paper has been issued purely to bring the past regime in disrepute so as to start afresh the game on the newly laid turf without any hang over of the past.

White Paper: A Ghost Story

White Paper was issued to frighten the nation and its people for the pitiable situation which the railway was passing through and to create dreaded ghostly image of it in various ways and forms; hues and styles. Grim and fearful ideas were propagated like - the railway had ceased to be a commercial organization; it had bleak past and going to have bleaker future; nothing concrete was done during the past regime and turnaround was a fake concept etc. White Paper was an awful story about the past and projected dull, devastating and ominous future for the railways. It presumed railways as a 'lost case' putting challenge to the workers and staff to accept it and reconcile with their fate. White paper seemed like an elaborate obituary written on railways stretching pages after pages with highly pathetic notes spread all over it like wreaths placed on the grave stone. It was a ghost story meant to create terrifying situation about the railway and its working.

The story starts with awful note from the minister showing 'infirmities' as a result of analysis. 'The biggest concern was the health of the railways'. She also mentioned 'financial turnaround' as a topic of 'discussion and debate' and considered White Paper as a 'dispassionate study'. But it seemed to be neither objective nor properly researched paper. White Paper was made-to-order report to put the past minister (predecessor) in the dock. It had a clear intention of discrediting the past regime for its achievements.

The White Paper is a flawed report. It has accepted over rated elasticity in making a comparative study of performance with two different levels of elaticities and has concluded that the period (2004-09) has been below par. It has frightened the readers to know that the rail GDP has hovered around 0.79 and that railways industry has not added beyond 1.18 to national GDP. Such statistics are not worth mentioning from macro economic point of view without knowing their real implications. In developing economy like India, the transport elasticity especially of the railway has to be within 0.8 to 0.9 or less than 1 or else it would cease to be a developing economy and its impact will be of a different kind. As far as railways' contribution to national economy from GDP point of view is concerned, it is still following the same pattern and does not promise any greater contribution. It will require decades for transport economy to change this pattern. The period of the predecessor (2004-09) is not exception to this. Although the growth of railways performance was associated with the growth of GDP at national level but it did not happen automatically. The railways had strived hard to achieve the growth rate during 2004-09 and it should not be 'seen' in the backdrop of the high growth rate of the Indian economy. Various examples may be cited when national economy flourished, but the railways could not achieve considerable progress. The growth during 2004-09 has been meaningful and should be appreciated. There had been considerable growth in traffic, infrastructure, safety and general financial performance during the period of turnaround.

White paper has created fear psychosis (as does every ghost story) of 'wear', and 'tear', of tracks owing to increase in carrying capacity (CC) but has never paid attention to already overloaded wagons being carried in a corrupt manner. It forgets to mention that the formulà used for CC was as old as the history of Indian railways and while the tracks have been renewed, no change in the formula to increase load pattern has been adopted. Actually in 21st century we are following 19th century formula of 'tare to pay load ratio'. In the same way the SWOT analysis performed by the White Paper does not suit the pattern of a public sector like that of the railways.

A highly dreaded and horrifying episode of 'change in accounting norm' was added to please those who love ghost stories and keep the suspense for more engaging sequences. It was statistical 'sleight of calculation' done by the consultant. It was unbelievable, but happened like 'an image disappearing before the camera', the body melting before the naked eyes, the figures evaporating like camphor in the air. The revenue earned by the predecessor got reduced to one third of the original! It was not reduced in RBI account books but through a funny situation created by the consultant from imaginary accounting system — a ghostly presentation of a phantom accounting process.

The story then takes you to still further terrifying world trip without any expense, but brings you back at the end to more horrific situation. Indian railways are compared to all other railways of both the hemisphere - North/South and East/West as if the predecessor or UPA (I) regime had promised to launch a campaign to make Indian railways look like an American, Chinese, Russian, Canadian and Japanese Railways just to mention a few of them.

Railways– 2009-12: Years of Great Neglect

When the railways moved from bankruptcy to turnaround - the efforts were made in two stages: first, it was done in slow and subtle manner - a background was created and second, when a drive for turnaround was rigorously followed. Nitish Kumar was quite aware of the fact that there was something wrong with the railways but he wanted to be sure of the causes and the quantum of the deterioration. He commissioned an inquiry through the Expert Group and waited for their analysis. To his astonishment, the Expert Group reported 'deadly situation' for the railways and if nothing was done urgently the organization would meet its doom. The method suggested to recover from the deteriorating condition were very extreme in action and approach. The report therefore was shelved, but it was an eye opener for the present and future organizers and policy makers to think deeply about the financial, managerial, operational and commercial problems of the railways and find out suitable working solutions. Nitish Kumar did his best, but his period was short lived as a minister. He consumed two years to settle down and the 14th Lok Sabha elections changed the scenario.

Then there came the stage second, when legendary leader of turnaround with all fanfare, determination, confidence and innovative approach joined as a minister. As a grassroots leader, he had his own out of box thinking and his brashness has made it more accurate and specific to take quick action. He acted upon effectively and changed the course of events and railways' working. He generated new mindset to bring revolutionary change. He was a whole time minister and did not waste even a day to work out his programme. All this had been made clear in the story of the 'resurgence of the railways'. But here a point has to be noted. He did every thing conscientiously and in good faith and transformed the railways. His efforts were well recognized all over the world by academics, business-schools, government bodies and other social institutions. Needless to say that he was quite pragmatic, innovative and forward looking minister of the period 2004-09. His term of five years ended with immense satisfaction and great accomplishment.

In democratic system as of India, elections are held and consequently governments are changed and formed according to majority-votes. The 15th Lok Sabha changed the scenario completely for the railways. There was a great upheaval in administrative set up. The new minister who took the charge had no interest to look into the affairs of the railways as she was preoccupied with the regional politics and had shown preference to West Bengal over the Railways. It was a hidden strategy and the railways had to suffer a great loss due to neglect at the hands of the minister. She wanted to ride both the horses at the same time to have the power and security in political arena. The railways resumed the work on the lines of business-as-usual without any special thrust in policy matter for real change.

The first victim as a concept was 'turnaround'. "What? Why talk about turnaround? It was all humbug - more hyped than real. Leave the concept as it is: where it is. Don't rely on false figures and propaganda. Where is the money or surplus?" These were the main questions put up before the people by the minister who reined the railways for two more years from 2009 to 2011and left abruptly the ministry under the care of a foster father. The railways changed four times their ministers in less than three years. The railways thus became a shuttle cock played in a rough-tough manner only to be smashed and grounded.

The main budget of railways for the year 2009-10 was presented without any consideration of growth and futuristic approach. The day when the budget was submitted, an announcement was made of issuing White Paper simultaneously. About three months – from May 2009 to July 2009 - were spent in creating a whispering campaign against the predecessor just to make a solid background for preparing White Paper. The minister took the initiative of bringing a brochure containing the material more detrimental to the railways past regime of the years 2004 to 2008. Next six months — July to December 2009 - were wasted in drafting and finalizing the White Paper - the only notable 'achievement' of the minister during her first year in office. The issue of White Paper created bad blood and antagonistic situation between two stalwarts — the predecessor and successor — both remained ministers between the years 2003- 04 to 2008-9 and 2009-10 to 2011 respectively. The first main budget (2009-10) of the regime had nothing to do with the railways progress. It aimed at hitting the predecessor and halting the pace of turnaround. The estimates of interim budget were reduced and the pace of progress was slowed down. Thus, budget ultimately added nothing substantial to the 'surplus' or as it was re-named - 'excess'. It was negligible amount of Rs. 0.75 crore of excess (actual) and so this little amount could be appropriated to development fund. The actual figures of 2009-10 had drawn a blank to capital fund and railway safety fund. The actual operative ratio had gone up by 95 percent much higher than estimated - 92.50 percent. The year 2009-10 was wasteful year contributed only liability to the railways balance sheet. No efforts were made to reduce ordinary working expenses (OWE). The gross traffic revenue fell to the level of Rs. 86963.97 crore as against the budget estimate of Rs. 88419.00 crore. This downfall occurred on account of two factors: first, the minister had no will to drive the railways on the lines of the predecessor because she had already scaled down the benchmark earlier set up to improve revenue and second, she was too much occupied with West Bengal affairs as to find no time to think about the railways. She was nick named as an absentee minister and was managing railways through remote control from Kolkata. When the cat is away the mice will play. The railways started deteriorating even more than the previous years from the point view of performance - the years which the minister so vehemently tried to bring under the scanner of White Paper. What would happen if she was judged on the same scale?

Two budgets for the years 2010-11 and 2011-12 were presented to the Parliament on 24th February 2010 and on 25th February 2011 respectively. They did not mean any significant change or improvement. One can judge by the rate of growth in relation to past year in the areas of gross and net revenue achieved, surplus or excess generated and operating ratio attained. Take for example, the year 2007-08 as a base for making comparison - the year as a benchmark of the achievement during 2004-08. In year 2010-11, no money was appropriated to the capital fund. A meagre sum of Rs. 1404.89 crore was generated as excess or surplus as against the stipulated figures of Rs. 3173.09. crore. Why efforts were not made to increase the revenue or decrease the working expenditure? The railway was running on business-as-usual basis — even lower than expected. The working expenses kept on increasing to the tune of Rs. 89474.22 crore as against the budget estimate of Rs. 87100 crore. This increased the operating ratio to the level of 94.6 percent meaning thereby that only 5.4 paise were earned after spending a rupee. During turnaround period the operating ratio was brought down to 75.9 percent. If this was going to be the fate of the railways under the new minister, why the White Paper was issued at all? Why the predecessor's regime was maligned? The situation did not change during the next year too. While the estimates of earnings in the year 2011-12 were increased, proper efforts were not made to achieve the targets. The minister's main target was West Bengal, not the railways. Working expenses went on increasing and the excess was as low as of the previous year. Years passed on one after another, but the financial condition of the railways did not improve. It was this reason that the benchmarks set during the period of turnaround were scaled down in order to have the advantage of the fact that lower targets would not create any trouble and the minister would find more time to fight against the greater forces during West Bengal elections. This hidden politics completely neglected the railways. The operating ratio reached the level of 95 percent and the railway perhaps was heading towards the worst situation to embrace in the coming years.

The Task Ahead

The prestige and glory - nationally and internationally — under the warmth of which the railway is presently basking, are the outcome of their direct link with IIM-A and indirectly with Wharton and Harvard and other prominent schools of the East and the West like HEC School, Paris, and INSEAD, Singapore, etc. Why to lose such good contacts and relationships? The railways staff has the best of the technical and professional skills but for attaining excellence in global marketing, business and trade practices, the modern railways system needs especially trained personnel with detailed knowledge of retailing, sales promotion, generating internal profit system and commercial practices for future investment and growth. The Railway Board lacks most important modern managerial and technical expertise belonging to 'Information Technology' and 'Market Mechanism'. The number of the Railway Board members should be increased from six to eight i.e., two more for the above mentioned streams and areas of specialization to be called as Member IT and Member Marketing. The Railway Board should grow such new members within their specific cadre and not necessarily be injected from outside. But the most important for the railway is to keep itself in touch with the top most institutes of management technology of India and abroad and feel synergetic and dynamic, fully capable of accepting challenges of 21st Century. One may hope that the present incumbent would give up her negative approach and make the Indian Railways world class in every respect.

Intrinsically, the new 'guard' of the railways (joined in May 2009) seems to have developed distaste for intellectual appetite and lives always in agitated mode like an aggressive trade union leader. Be it Nano, Women's Bill or Lalgarh rally, she is famous for creating political tantrums. This only shows her handle-with-care-mindset and lack of intellectual awareness. In the present era of globalization 'togetherness' is the mantra for success. The railways should not only be customer friendly but also focus its interest on individuals of high merits, institutions of national and international repute, the media for critical assessment and propagation, and contacting the public in general to create understanding for generating business. However, this incumbent thinks otherwise: the railways for her are yet another domain of Nandigram or Singur and the predecessor as a rival like TATA. But the whole nation stood up and saw how trickily TATA shifted Nano to Gujarat and branded her as anti-industry, anti-development and an unrelenting defiant leader. Industries do not grow in air: the roads are not built in sky. It requires earth crest - the land surface - to build a factory. Now she speaks for land acquisition, proposes double-line railways project for Singur, attracting farmers to give up land and offering 'willing' farmers services in the railways along with the compensation for the land. She is now unmaking her own deeds, adopting the TATA's ways, and trying to rehabilitate the lost prestige after the exit of Nano from West Bengal. Perhaps it is on account of such schemes of the then incumbent of Rail Bhavan that the opposition tried to nick-name the railways as 'East India Company' because the benefits proposed in her budget speech (2009-10) are East-bound especially towards the State of West Bengal. It is to be noted that out of 301 railway stations to be remodeled as ideal, 109 have gone to the present minister's state. It is the incumbent working in the same way as her predecessor. The stage is said to have set open and wide to fight for the cause of honour and prestige. By issuing White Paper, the great Indian railways controversy on turnaround and dispute over the achievements of the past vs. present incumbent have started engulfing the prestigious name of the railways into an ignoble cesspool of stagnation and the railway department again would stand at the same place where it was in 2000-2001. It was the same incumbent who had during the above mentioned years presided over the destiny of liquidating the empire of the railways!

The predecessor (former railways minister of the period (2004-2009) was not alone in the service of the railways. He performed his activities collectively and without interference to any departmental work. He used to express his views, fixed the targets and waited for the results. His working was transparent and known to everybody — be it financial adjustment based on accounting conventions and rules or engineering process based on tare to pay load ratio. If there was change, it was done on consensus and on government-addressed needs within financial standards as practised from time to time. Some people might not have liked the former minister's use of Officer on Special Duty (OSD) but he was there just to translate boss's earthy ideas into bureaucratic language and majority of the staff worked with OSD as a team. His contribution of "Bankruptcy to Billions" (Kumar, 2008) is a gem of an analytical enquiry created out of otherwise dead statistical material languishing at Rail Bhavan to bring the railways to a lively and dynamic status of international repute with the capability of getting transformed within a short span of time. Those who believe that IIM-A or the team attached with the ex-minister (the predecessor) had not given anything substantial and only repeated the railways own statistics , must read above mentioned book to know how brilliantly the railways progress report was interpreted. They should also go through yet another book *"Indian Railways - A Study in Management"* (Misra, 2009d: 1-305). In pushing the railways forward IIM-A, OSD to the ex-minister, Railway Board members and other middle order officers, and workers at large merge into a team and brought the railways to its pristine glory and grace. One must also give some latitude to the founder-leader of the turnaround movement who initially belonged to the rural hinterland of Bihar and who with great difficulty and determination fought his battle of existence by tearing the constraints of rigid social fabric, and reached the top. It is irony that the person who supported the ruling party to remain in power during its most crucial time, when the Marxists[8] had left it in shambles, is now out of power and accusing fingers are raised on him even from the quarters of the railways which he had served whole heartedly during his stint as a minister (2004 - 2009). It matters little whether the election pact with the ruling party was done or not; if unconditional support to the party is there, the person must be brought with all respect into power fold. Let the reshuffle of portfolios at centre give a chance to the old 'guard' of the railways to serve the society and the nation in his characteristic style of working and, of course, bringing light moments for the people to enjoy inside the Parliament. At least this would save him from the negativities of his successor - new incumbent's impact after getting on to the bandwagon.

Footnotes

1. It was the departure of Lalu Prasad as a minister for railways from Rail Bhavan in May 2009. The general elections for 15th Lok Sabha were held in March/April the same year, but due to the loss of support from UPA (II) government, the ex-minister was not offered any portfolio.
2. Mamata Banerjee joined as minister for railways in May 2009, but was in a different mood and created disharmony by announcing that she would present a White Paper detailing the misdeeds of the preceding regime.
3. This stands for Lalu Prasad, the predecessor of Mamata Banerjee. Both the stalwarts were at daggers drawn in sharing the power game of politics, though they belonged to different states and ideologies and had nothing in common except rivalry, diversity and discord.
4. This refers to a best selling novel by Chetan Bhagat who has tried to show harmony between two culturally diverse states through his personal life story in an imaginative but quite different style.
5. It is a sad commentary on an earlier agreed system of establishing a research wing known as 'The Railway Chair' at IIM-A for better

understanding and interpretation of logistics and transport management as performed by the Indian Railways.

6. Prof. G. Raghuram of IIM-A has produced a Working Paper on Indian Railways presenting a critical appraisal of strategies and processes, which he called 'Turnaround of Indian Railways' in February 2007. It was an outcome of a combined effort put up by the faculty members, research staff and students engaged in fellowship programme. Pages 5 to 20 i.e., 15 in all were related to the findings fully based on railways statistics containing 45 pages. The railways professional cadre and think-tank seemed to be well equipped to produce such studies as facts and figures used in the study were primarily meant for railways own consumption.
7. This refers to Mamata Banerjee who had joined the government as new railway minister in 2009.
8. It is an irony that the person (Lalu Prasad) who brought the railways back on tracks and supported with all his might to save UPA (I) government at the time when CPM had left it in shambles was not included in the ministry though he had four members of Parliament as his own party-men supporting the government. Persons with less strength of their own in Parliament were included in the cabinet.

◆◆◆

2

White Paper: An Attempt to Thwart Turnaround

The turnaround in business terms is a process of change which takes place from the 'performance declined followed by performance improved'.[1] But it is not an iterative activity like that of trade cycle creating ups and downs intermittently with regular intervals. The turnaround normally takes a turn — rather a U- turn, sustains it and marches forward. A vigil is required so that even if the process is slowed down, it may be re-charged with induced vigour to come to a prescribed level or above it, if possible. This concept is basically attached with private sector analysis. The analysis of the public sector like the railways or other such sectors is of recent origin. It was this reason that when Prof. G. Raghurem of IIM — A, used the term 'turnaround' (Raghursam et al, *Vikalp*, Vol. 99, No 2: 87-92) many within and outside the railways were surprised, amused and satisfactorily settled down to know this changing process of the Indian railways as turnaround under a new banner of globalization. But many top bosses within the department of railways who were in the regular service or retired, compared this concept of 'turnaround' to the 'growth model' relating to economic and other environmental factors and criticized the process of such a new interpretation of change or turnaround. Even for those who were not related to the railways, the term turnaround was a surprise because they were the old timers and interpreting institutional economy only in terms of 'rate of growth' and 'environmental factors' responsible for developing the economy and not managerial process and innovative activities. One should keep in mind that 'turnaround' was not a 'growth model' but a given action or a strategy to win over depression or sluggish economy. It had nothing to do with the measures like rate of growth, development or environmental character which pushed up the economy in a normal way.

The concept of 'turnaround' in terms of Indian railways came to be misunderstood, misinterpreted and misconstrued. The organizers of the railways were accustomed to understand the process of development of a linear form or normal incremental value only. But any acrobatic jump, turnaround or a U-turn concept was not in their language of understanding and remained foreign to them. It was this reason that a retired member of Railway Board joined hands with the editor of a reputed magazine to cast doubt about turnaround, questioning 'was it all track II? And added, "Growth is the process of continuation; it cannot be leapfrog" (Aurora, 2007, *Outlook*, Sept, 24: 18-22). His training in old model 'growth theory' did not allow him to accept turnaround model of Indian railways. The system of growth is a consequence of geometric mean calculation having continuity in its process, but a 'turnaround' is certainly a sudden improvement or a jump with the consistency to show a sustained behavior. This difference between 'growth' and 'turnaround' must be made clear to dispel the wrong notion attached to them. Turnaround is a movement but with a motion of turning around just like a knight, changing its position, in the game of chess. It is capable of taking U-turn and sustaining it also.

Perhaps the then incumbent of Rail Bhavan (2009-11), under the influence of the professionals who are trained in planning, growth and public sector economic model of institutional reforms and development with little knowledge of the real import of 'turnaround', has been misled because she lacks the expert understanding of the complicated financial process of the railways and can easily be persuaded to refute turnaround on the grounds suggested by them — rightly or wrongly.

'Turnaround' is not a substitute for growth model or any developmental theory. If one is confused regarding the real import of the concept, he is bound to generate misunderstanding and may be prone to receive the corrupted form of the turnaround as has happened recently with the ministry of the railways. There are two basic ingredients of this concept. First, it moves from bad to good performance and second, it settles down with a sustained performance. Apart from this turnaround has other theoretical approach to its strategies which are normally practised within private sector economy but they do not work well in case of public sector. It was on this ground that Nitish Kumar had to reject the Rakesh Mohan Committee Report although it was he who had initiated it. The ex-minister as the leader of the turnaround too was quite clear in his approach not to privatize, downsize, divest assets of the railways and quit markets or delete unprofitable ventures.

The Strategy

'Turnaround' of the railways is a newly formed concept carrying special meaning to differentiate it from what is generally understood as a growth theory applied to private economies. The Indian railway is a hybrid institution having commercial as well as social obligations to perform and as such the turnaround has been redefined and reinterpreted to suit the public organisation as the railway is (Misra/ Mahapatra, 2008a: 329-337).

In context of turnaround of public-model economy as of the railways, one has to research this process in historical perspective to verify the impact and utility of the railways along with the strategy which it follows to work out the programme of action in achieving the desired results particularly profitability, working efficiency and investment. Judging from the above core factors of turnaround process, we find that basic strategy adopted during the period 2004-2009 was to organise leadership pattern to develop a new 'mindset' of the employees at all the levels with a common agenda to follow. The strategy was also to adopt the organizational culture of the department with a view to generating turnaround situation. It also included changes in sub-strategies like planning, decentralizing and combining human resource management, keeping intact the original structural pattern of the railways. Some of the basic strategies which were harsh in contents and use were avoided such as retrenchment, restructuring and disinvestment. The predecessor succeeded in adopting this process and so he attained the objective of bringing about 'turnaround' of the railways (Misra/Mahapatra, 2008a: 329-337).

The Purpose

The process of turnaround of the railways became strategic and purposeful to follow in the long run. The ex-minister during his regime (2004-09) had made turnaround as an instrument of creativity, innovation and progress. It was supposed to deliver the message of great change to the people who use the railways, workers and employees who run the railways, and the government and the public at large who own the railways. Turnaround was the message to unite and fight for the greater earnings, reducing expenses and cost of production. It was message to increase the value of traffic – goods and passengers - to achieve the target fixed and provide the service at the affordable price. This was also the message to adopt a dynamic pricing policy in order to have the best results to obtain through freight and fare earnings.

The turnaround is to unite people and bring together diverse cultures of the country. It was meant to generate power among the employees and may be called as a rally point for them. It is here to generate revenue by providing better services to the customers — a type of movement finding out ways and means to acquire gainful results out of the programme adopted and action performed. Turnaround is to humanize the railways — giving a human face for attaining higher values of work ethics and life. Turnaround means putting the railways on right track. It has a specific sense of understanding Indian culture and the way of life. No wonder that it is meant to show the spirit of national solidarity, equity and justice (Khare, 2009).

The Assessment

One has to answer the following questions to assess if the leader of the movement succeeded in bringing about the turnaround of the railways. Here the concept, the strategy and the purpose of turnaround have been defined in general terms, and in Indian railways context also, to judge if there has been a turnaround.

1. Has the ex-minister or the leader of turnaround brought changes in the railways from performance declined to performance improved?
2. Has he settled down this change with a sustained performance?
3. Has he accepted the railway with its social obligations?
4. Has he adopted strategies suiting to the railways as a PSU?
5. Were pricing, profit and cost policies attuned with good performance?
6. Was he able to provide leadership to the railways?
7. Whether there was a reversal to this change during his tenure 2004 - 09 as a minister?

The above questions define the basic nature of turnaround and if ninety per cent answers are in affirmative, it leaves no ground to question the ex-minister's achievements as a successful leader who brought changes in the functioning of the railways to attain turnaround in real terms. If one goes through the railways records and statistics, the answer to all above questions are generally 'yes'.

Abortive Attempt

Perhaps the then incumbent of Rail Bhavan and her advisors at Rail Bhavan misunderstood the concept of turnaround, its real intent and usefulness. Thus, it has created mistrust in the whole process and a type of silent movement against its validity has generated among the top bosses of the railways who started refuting turnaround fiercely after the leader of turnaround left the railways. What were those facts and distrustful conditions prevailing behind the move? Was there lack of transparency in ex-minister's ways and methods? Did he not take the work force into confidence? Perhaps one may hope that such queries get response in favour of the predecessor. A type of belligerent atmosphere was created because the professionals inside the Rail Bhavan might have felt insulted or found them side-tracked. Was this the real factor? Even this does not seem to be true because the leader of the turnaround had taken all the employees into confidence. He had always opined that turnaround was the outcome of combined efforts made by all the 14 lakh employees of the railways. What was the real motive behind this tirade against the leader then?

It was an invisible factor, a human weakness that creates clash of personalities - a political rivalry between the two stalwarts which may be described as The War of Roses: Present vs. Past for 'dynastic' rule of the railways (discussed in detail, chapter-5). The ex-minister (2004-2009) had played his share of the innings with the railways. It was the then minister's turn (2009-2011) to start afresh and she desired that the pitch should be cleared without any hangover of the past. According to her, turnaround had unnecessarily hyped the situation and kept the benchmarks quite tough to reach, perhaps unrealistic in estimates. A few of the dominating advisors at Rail Bhavan too had an occasion to add fuel to the fire. They started scripting new CV of the predecessor by dismissing his approach to Turnaround and soaring figures of 'surplus' to please their bosses. It was here that ex-minister's (predecessor's) achievements were decried and the successor tried to abort 'turnaround concept' already conceived, nurtured and sustained by the railways.

Predecessor's Men to Respond

With the White Paper presented to the Parliament by the then incumbent of Rail Bhavan, the predecessor's team seems to have set to counteract it with a fitting reply. The railways turnaround during its leader's regime was neither a scam nor a manipulative practice. It was an innovation, as answer to find out the way to get over the problematic situation created by the Rakesh Mohan Committee Report 2001. It was the worst period of Indian Railways' history and ironically, the period was presided over by the then incumbent during her first stint as the railways minister under saffron banner from 13th October 1999 to 15th March 2001 (presently she has camouflaged under the cover of grassroots effect or more appropriately under 'Trinamool' impact). It was the worst of time: the railways could not pay the dividend to the General Exchequer and was heading towards bankruptcy. The experts had opined that had the railways been a corporation under private system and the new 'guard' of the railways (2009-11) as a CEO, instead of a minister, she would have shown the doors for incompetence and faulty governance,[2] unwept, unhonoured, unsung! But the Indian Railways had peculiar ways and passed through extraordinary historical situations which influenced it most. For example, George Fernandes brought the railways to its knees during the railway-workers strike,[3] led by him, and later on became the railways minister to run or ruin the railways! Likewise, the then incumbent could not find any solution and brought the railways to near bankruptcy in 2000-2001 and as the luck would have it, she remained at the helm of affairs again! No wonder then that there is natural correlation between incompetence and holding power by one and the same person in the railways at different times. A press note to this effect added 'the worst falls came when the old 'guards' of the railways, Nitish and the new incumbent of Rail Bhavan during 1999-2001 were ministers (in their first stint). While Nitish oversaw a fall of 29 per cent, and the present incumbent during her past stint managed to bring it still lower by another 28 per cent (Indian Express, April 2006).

The leader of the turnaround was fortunate to have uninterrupted five-year term (2004-09) as the railways minister and managed to pull out the railways from financial depression and brought it back on the right track. He could create 'turnaround' because he had enough time to experiment, had good advisors, proficient analysts and was a full time minister, not wasting time on others, but working as a true professional with complete devotion, attention and passion and fully stationed at Rail Bhavan. He succeeded because he had a warning signal shown by the Expert Group and the least from him was expected 'not to run the railways on business-as-usual' lines, as done by earlier ministers. There was a non-performer's view adopted by the railways called 'business-as-usual' process which led the railways to decay. The ex-minister

– the leader of turnaround - was alert not to adopt such practices. He never run the railways, sitting at Patna through a remote control or worked as an absentee minister having no control over the railway board officials and the staff and let loose the railways for indulging in regular accidents, derailments, sabotage and explosions.

The railways turnaround created during past regime (2004 - 09) was not a magic but the result of conscientious efforts put up by all the 14 lakh employees of the railways. The leader of turnaround was the binding factor behind the railways work-force. He gave them a national agenda, a mission and a purpose to work for the betterment of the organization. The turnaround brought a new message to the workers, the employees, the middle and higher level officials to perform their duties well and keep themselves away from the cunning designs of pulling down each other which led them to non-profitable results. Turnaround was generating a human face for the railways by reasserting its social purpose and national outlook. The turnaround of the railways was a fitting reply to the protagonists of the Expert Group Recommendations, demanding the railways to turn into a corporate body. It was in true spirit of development, growth and financial rejuvenation that a process of transformation was brought about by the Indian railways.

White Paper as a Confession of Infirmities

What brought the new incumbent of Rail Bhavan to work out for the White Paper? Has she been misinformed by the Rail Bhavan officials that all that glows is not turnaround but manipulation done during all the five years? This seems to be an unbelievable story. What then is the motive behind it? Are the babus at Rail Bhavan having a different story to tell? Or is it just an outcome of human nature which relates to the idea that 'the authority forgets the dying king' and the babus have become loyal to the new master to the extent of creating spicy stories to win the favour of the new boss? Perhaps, this last one seems to be the only plausible cause for the present crisis between two stalwarts, two forces, and two epicenters of the rail-quake generated by the senior babus of Rail Bhavan.

A White Paper is not a thing to rejoice. It is a form of expression of the real-self of the railways - a type of introspection to go into the depth of maladies with which the department is suffering. The White Paper does not repent the past and bring individuals or group to question. It analyses 'self' and find out ways to win over the situation. Realizing this fact, perhaps the then incumbent (2009-11) has pointed out that the White Paper would not carry anybody's 'name' in its analysis. A White Paper is a 'truthful' document - a type of self attested affidavit. It is not meant to malign anybody or any institution. However, in the name of White Paper, if a hidden agenda is being pursued to destroy the image of the predecessor, it loses the sanctity of a White Paper and becomes a mockery - a type of fake charge sheet produced against the person or a type of 'false encounter' done by the police. In real terms, when the White Paper is issued, it seems to be a solemn occasion - a time of actual grief and bereavement over the deteriorating internal situation of the organization or the department. A White Paper is never 'celebrated', nor is it a threatening document to bring the predecessor in the dock as the present incumbent so considers and joyfully brings it out before the Parliament as a substitute to all charges to be framed against her predecessor. The then incumbent of Rail Bhavan - the Trinamool Congress head-was living away from the reality, and forgot that *'Saas Bhi Kabhi Bahoo Thee'* (The mother-in-law was also a newly wed bride some time back) and she must be reminded that her name was associated with the worst years of the railways' history - the period of 2000-2001. The issue of White Paper is just a melancholy duty to be performed by the department itself to assess its weaknesses and threats and compare them with opportunities and strengths. So far there is no evidence to prove that such sincere efforts have been taken by the railways to go for self- introspection and find its own infirmities. Thus, the White Paper seems to go against much maligned and hyped phenomenon of the railways turnaround.

Period Covering the White Paper

The period under the assessment of the White Paper, seems to be intriguing. It includes the period of five years 2004-09 only. Why does it confine to the predecessor's period alone? Why does it not cover a year earlier or a year later than that? Why does it not include the period of present incumbent's earlier regime which brought bankruptcy to the railways to expand the horizon of its analysis? Is it a White Paper or a CBI report?

The period under study of a White Paper is never kept confined to a particular case or event or defined to serve only personal plan or purpose. The process of White Paper adopts a historical analysis, bringing past and present together, frequently crossing the boundaries of such periods to produce an unbiased study as has been done by the Rakesh Mohan Committee Report. It follows the terms of reference and makes them the basis of drafting the report. The present White Paper has not been issued on these lines. It has attacked an individual and a group of people. The truth of White Paper should never be tested on the anvil of falsehood. Why such a White Paper is issued within the 'black' boundaries, evil environments and suspicious situations?

There is a difference of approach between two stalwarts as far as the railways are concerned. The railways and the ex-minister (2004-09) came together by sheer luck during United Progressive Alliance's (UPA's) first term of governance. Actually, he never wished for this portfolio. He had preferences for the Home or the Defense ministries. But equations during that period were so formed that it became difficult for the PM to provide the portfolio of minister's choice. He with folded hands even declined the railways portfolio initially. Perhaps there was no choice for him and he with a heavy heart had to settle down with the railways ministry.

The case of the then incumbent of Rail Bhavan was totally different. She for the first time had enlarged her image and bargained over the office of the railway minister. She was rigid, adamant and unrelenting in dealing with the PM and the portfolio. She put the condition for support to UPA government - 'only when given the railways portfolio': if not, she would withdraw herself from the government. It was a perfect bargain which she could have done with the government. She has no emotional attachment for the UPA government for a rightful purpose to keep it in power. She had an eye over West Bengal and any time can change the political equation. She was one of the most unpredictable entities of all the UPA's components providing just a hair thin majority!

The above case of both the stalwarts, with two different approaches, brings to one's mind a number of questions and also explains the factors which create such differences. The very fact that the predecessor was not initially interested in the railways portfolio reveals one fundamental point that he was to start afresh to write on a clean slate and had no preconditions, notions or attachment to the ministry. It brings into mind a pertinent point that as a minister for the railways he had not to generate any mischievous story behind any of his achievements. Without losing time, he started taking steps, as early as possible, during his taking over charge as railway minister to increase axle load of the wagon - a sure shot for success and he created history within two years by showing U-turn for the railways which ultimately was called as the Turnaround. Just within two years, the railways started bearing fruits. This was the initial start of the turnaround. It was an undeterred case of the railways developing economy. Where was the room, in such a situation, for any suspicion or deficiency for issuing the White Paper?

The Phases of Turnaround

The turnaround of the railways started and developed through several phases. When the leader of turnaround took the decision of enhancing axle load of 4 to 8 tonnes per wagon, it was met with great resistance from the Railway Board. But when the predecessor pointed out, after inspecting physically and finding out on the spot the overloaded wagons and trains running beyond approved limit of the load, uninterruptedly allowed as a corrupt practice and money shared among the railway-staff and the traders - the Board members had no answer to it. What followed it was a much publicized story and on the pretext of 'bulging of the wagons', 'stalling of the engines' or 'wear and tear of rail tracks and rolling stock', no corrupt practice could be allowed to continue. The axle load controversy did not allow generating the cause of a White Paper. The first phase of turnaround started within early months of the ex minister's regime and lasted up to the end of second year i.e., 2005-06.

The second phase of turnaround started with the beginning of 2006-07 by reducing wagon turn round period from 7 to 5 days. The train examination period too was reduced in accordance to the distances covered. Even the length of the trains was revised according to the increase in global trade and India's expanding trade economy. The speed of the trains, especially goods trains was to be increased and the traffic saturation on popular corridors was to be reduced. The number of goods categorized were simplified and reduced from 4000 entries of commodities categorised into 270 to 12 only.

The third phase of the turnaround started in the year 2007-08 and continued beyond the regime (2004-09) of the ex-minister and developed into a sustained growth during the years 2008, 2009 and proposed for 2010 also when the outgoing minister in February 2009 submitted the interim railway budget for 2009-10.

What was Unrealistic about Interim Budget?

While presenting the main railway budget 2009-10, perhaps the then incumbent of Rail Bhavan was ill advised when she said that her predecessor's budget estimates were unrealistic (Banerjee, 2009a: 19). The predecessor (2004-09) had already reduced his robust gross revenue estimates from Rs.100,000 crore to Rs. 95,306.22 crore due to the impact of recession on Indian economy, in general and the railways economy, in particular. When the then incumbent (2009-11) submitted budget, she uncharitably popped up the controversy of White Paper, unrealistic budget estimates of the predecessor and intentionally reduced the gross revenue estimate to Rs 88419 crore. May be, she had a different approach to budget estimates, but calling predecessor's ways of calculations 'unrealistic' is nothing but unethical, non-academic and uncalled for unless a comparative methodology is put forward to prove figures as unrealistic. Wherefrom the then incumbent of Rail Bhavan got her own estimates as Rs. 88419 crore? In fact, it was the outcome of the predecessor's untiring efforts to increase gross revenue from initial Rs. 47370.20 crore (BE) in 2004-05 to Rs. 80901 crore (BE) in 2008-09, that the amount Rs. 88419crore (BE) in 2009-10 has originated. It was The Turnaround Effect that she had coined and arrived at her 'very realistic' estimate. But one can easily predict who may have prompted her to do so. The babus at Rail Bhavan (and babus every where) make a difference and their ways of winning over the bosses are curious. They are able to create a rift between the stalwarts for nothing.

If the total working expenses are increasing and operating ratio is going up, the expediency of the situation demands to put a bit higher level of estimates to bring the situation under control. The credit must go to the leader of the turnaround who in spite of great odds, earned so much as to cover up the sixth pay commission expenses to the tune of about Rs. 14600 crore and still had shown surplus. It was 'pay commission amount' which had earlier created havoc during fifth pay commission report as no planned savings for the needed amount were done. If the railways is presently, enjoying a peaceful environment and almost an easy way to conduct the business, without any resentment from workforce or chances of any strike, it is because of the predecessor who has smoothed railways working, laboured hard to earn surplus during all the five years, created turnaround, reduced the operating ratio and left a wholesome amount as 'inheritance of profits' for his successor to rejoice and enjoy. Just think for a moment: does it make a great difference if gross traffic receipts are Rs. 95000 crore (Predecessor's) or Rs. 88000 crore (present incumbent's) for the budget year 2009-10? The difference of the amount of Rs. 7000 crore is not so much as to be called 'unrealistic' or bring the whole immediate past regime under the scanner of a White Paper? But who ultimately wrote the White Paper? Perhaps those babus who were once behind the ex-minister to generate turnaround. Some might have retired, but others were still there to do a reverse exercise with spicy inputs from the 'consultant'.

When the then incumbent of Rail Bhavan (2009-11) bargained over the railways portfolio to support UPA government, the logic behind it was clear. She had axe to grind for obtaining the railways. But the ex- minister's (the predecessor's) persona was far above in that comparison. He never insisted for the ministry and had humbly declined for the railways in the first instance. This very fact proves that the turnaround was neither a preplanned and sponsored project, nor was it intentionally 'made to order' for a study at IIM-A. Everything moved spontaneously and naturally. The profits and surpluses were strenuously generated first and other things came afterwards in bringing about a turnaround situation. However, the wrong intentions of the then incumbent were clear. She made the railways the 'East India Company' to be operated through remote control from Howrah Head Quarters, working almost as an absentee minister, safe- guarding the interests of the land grab movement, caring more for Nandigram or Singur than Rail Bhavan or the Railways. The railways must be prepared for the massive fall i.e., from boom to bust in the successive years.

Footnotes

1. Turnaround in business terms has been defined in various ways but all definitions converge to a simple point of financial recovery of a company or undertaking that has been performing poorly for an extended time. In order to affect a turnaround, a company must acknowledge and identify its problems, consider changes in management and develop and implement a problem-solving strategy. The possible characteristics of a troubled enterprise in need of a turnaround include revenues that do not cover cost, an inability to pay creditors, layoffs, and salary cuts for officers and non payment of dividends to stock holders. Turnaround is a process of intervention directly by third party or a leader with business in distress and tries to stabilize the situation immediately to achieve sustained profits by reducing cost and increasing production.
2. This refers to a report published in *Indian Express,* April 2006, quoted in 'Turnaround of Indian Railways - A Critical Appraisal of Strategies and Processes' by G. Raghuram, Exhibit 20: Sizing up the Railways Minister, p. 48, WP No 2007-02-03.

3. It was the most notable strike by the workers of the railways under the leadership of George Fernandes (who ironically became the railway minister in 1989-90). In the year 1974 a call was given by the federation of railways workers unions to undergo strike as a protest against the stagnant pay scale operating for the last several years. The working conditions were inhumane, cruel and callous. The loco staff was continuously kept at work till the train ran on its trip often for several days at a stretch especially on goods trains. There were many other causes creating grievances which led workers to go on strike against the establishment. The strike continued for 20 days in which nearly 17 million workers directly or indirectly participated. There were conflicting reports about its success or failure, but one thing was common and positive regarding the strike. There were long term gains and what we see today is the outcome of the past sacrifices done by the workers. (For more see "The Indian Railways Strike 1974: A Study of Power and Organized Labour" by Stephen Sherlock, Rupa and Co, New Delhi, 2001.

◆◆◆

3

White Paper: Subduing the Spirit of Railways

While presenting White Paper on the railways' infirmities to the Parliament on 18th December 2009, the then incumbent of Rail Bhavan found herself in the hyper agitated mode. She got her inner self engrossed in destructive creation of bringing the railways' past achievements to such a demolished state that the White Paper emerged as a part of her own personality to show that she had generated an antithetical view to what her predecessor called a 'turnaround'. But contrary to her thought process, belief and attitude, so maliciously construed, the White Paper neither proved itself true in real terms, nor did it bring a fair assessment of the railways finances to visualize the future course of action. It seemed to be a mischievous bundle of odd conclusions based on misrepresenting the facts to prove the fallacies of the railways.

The then incumbent of Rail Bhavan was such a captive of bureaucratic mesmerised impact of railways administration that she neither found good nor bad in 'creative accounting', but spoke mechanically the way a recorded cassette worked in Delhi Metro indicating stations and instructions. Instead of stations or instructions, she spoke out empty slogans against turnaround and pushed back the railways to a decade or two, even bringing credit to Narsimha Rao a 'forgotten' Congress hero of yester years and C.K. Jaffar Sharief (Ministry of Railways, 2009b: 57) who had long back closed their innings, without any sense of historical compatibility of events and situations. When did the railways fail to pay the dividend? When did the Expert Group report come out? Why such a reverse long jump of so many years, leaving a trail of other ministers of the railways in an oblivious neglect? May be, it is not the present incumbent but persons who prompt her to speak negatively about the predecessor or the turnaround of the railways. They are the real managers of the sordid drama being played at Rail Bhavan.

The new incumbent of Rail Bhavan who joined in May 2009 should be matured enough to understand the intricacies of the railways financial system before embarking upon the fallacies of turnaround and playing with figures of revenue, surplus, expenditure and investment. The Railways have got so many pockets.[1] It is the complexity of their financial system which is very difficult to understand. It can add or subtract the amount from one pocket to another to prove the point in question. The predecessor is not wrong in declaring his estimates. He still insists upon the same. It is the new incumbent who joined after him who is being misguided by the babus at Rail Bhavan and who wants to prove a wrong point right. Why does she succumb to their influence and become a part of their financial controversy? It will require an inquiry through a high-powered finance commission if so needed, to refute or appraise ex-minister's financial achievements including railways turnaround. A White Paper of such a distorted nature with a bundle of oddities and contradiction is not competent enough to pass the judgment. Yes, the new incumbent of Rail Bhavan who joined after the predecessor has a right to discern her own department, its infirmities and its failures, but with a sense of responsibility. It is the same staff which has produced predecessor's facts and figures. The only difference lies in justifying the financial standards, ways and methods adopted for arriving at the estimates. For example, take the case of 'creative accounting'. The incumbent is not going to re-change the 'shift in accounting' process as adopted by her predecessor. Why then so much hue and cry against the creative accounting? Again, she admits that during 2004-2009 the freight earnings have increased, but according to her this has happened because of the better environmental conditions and growth of national economy. It is an oft repeated reply that has lost its validity, meaning and force. It is an old mindset to interpret like that. When the predecessor fails, it is his fault; but when the predecessor wins it is not his victory; it is the environment that favours him to win. What a peculiar logic! The new incumbent, who joined after the leader of turnaround when he left the railways, does not want to give any credit to the former minister; it may be because of her obsessive concern or fear of the predecessor. The railways achievement is not the outcome of just booming economy, but it is due to the clear gains in capital and labour productivity, increase in the market share, profit margin, the quality of service provided and above all the predecessor's political will to bring a change and give a leadership acceptable to the work force. But she has no right to decry the achievement of turnaround of the railways which is a historical fact and has been accepted universally.

The new incumbent of Rail Bhavan, who joined after the predecessor, has many facets to her personality like a diamond. These facets reflect light in darkness. But it seems to be a mysterious black diamond. It is difficult to understand her inner self which prompts her to work, agitate, transform or revolutionize an action, a movement, a thought or a philosophy. She can agitate against Nano, but at the same time wishes to establish a coach factory at Singur and desperately begs for the same land. What a double standard is being adopted! No venture capitalist would go to Singur to invest his money. The railways – a PSU under her control is the ultimate possibility. And the railways have yet to feel her presence at Rail Bhavan. Almost an absentee minister, the railways has gone out of her grip and if she shows her control over the ministry, her agitated mode would not allow her to create anything more than an unstable situation for the railways. Let us hope the railways do not move in doldrums under the present situation.

It is a ritual with the railways to issue White Paper without following it. It is perhaps the seventh time that such a document has been released. The White Paper appears to be a merry-go-round for the new incumbent, who joined after RJD chief left the railways, to while away the time. In this way, the attention of the railways and the people in general would be diverted to discuss endlessly the merits and demerits of the railways' finances and she would find enough time to spend and nurse her constituency with the basic objective to oppose land acquisition for the industries. Who bothers for the railways? She has already wasted a year accusing others, providing nothing for the railways except a White Paper. It is a fact that the old 'guard' of the railways (2004-2009) has lost much ground in Bihar only because he has devoted all his time for the railways creating a turnaround situation. The nation recognizes his services and Bihar too should not remain behind in showing him the gratitude. Serving the government at the centre is a full time job and responsibility and piecemeal efforts will neither benefit the nation nor the ministry.

The first White Paper appeared in 1990 when George Fernandes issued a status paper indicating 'issues and options'. Again, in 1998 Nitish Kumar issued a 'status paper on Indian railways – some issues and options'. A revised version of the same came in 2002. How can the present guard of the railways remain far behind? And she immediately found a cause to issue White Paper. The much hyped turnaround saga of railways was enough for her to refute. On the other hand the predecessor's men were set to give her a fitting reply. A war of words was bound to erupt between the loyalists and the dissidents.

A White Paper is a clear sign of guilt-admission and defeatism on the part of the railways. With the departure of the former minister and the present incumbent being too busy with her West Bengal affairs, especially Nandigram, Singur and her eye on the office of the Chief Minister (which she has now achieved), the fate of the railways seems to be in doldrums. With no body to unite the workforce and provide national agenda for creating fund surplus and fight against the deteriorating situation, as the predecessor did, the railway seems to be dwindling at all the levels of finance, traffic and safety. The White Paper has been issued to nullify the predecessor's contribution. But one can not change the course of history created during the first term of UPA government by the railways. The turnaround is a historical fact and it is here to stay. The railways earnings are strenuous and profits are illusive and one has to pursue actively and grab them strongly. Issuing White Paper is not going to help the railways in any way. The railway needs a dynamic leadership, fully stationed and occupied at Rail Bhavan. The Indian railway is not a toy train to be operated through a remote control from Kolkata!

White Paper Negates Turnaround

White Paper nullifies turnaround. It has been issued inappropriately and indecorously. It seems that a decade of work has been lost and the railway has come to a grinding halt at a place where it was stationed in 2000-2001. Have the efforts of initiating reforms during Nitish Kumar period and creation of turnaround of railways by its leader during 2004-09 been wasted? Actually, issuing White Paper at this juncture is a disturbing factor, an agony created within blissful condition - a type of kill-joy generated within the sphere of happiness. The White Paper was issued as if nothing had happened for the last five years and it was only for the first time that the railways under a new *avatar* - the leadership of the then minister (2009-11) - thought to rejuvenate the finances of the organization which had been so far abandoned even by the UPA government during its first term. This was a totally construed story and a political gimmick showing financial disaster for the railways as an antithetical view of turnaround (Irastimes, 2009, Prashant: 73).

The railways on the other hand, have improved a lot and they have been saved from the impending danger of bankruptcy during 2004-2009 period. The railways developed efficiency, productivity and profitability. The operating ratio came down from 98.3 to 75.9 in 2008. Why was the White Paper issued then? The down trend of the budget estimate showing less profit during 2008-09 (RE) and 2009-10(BE) was a temporary phase popped up due to the impact of the Sixty Pay Commission. After all it was the leader of turnaround who had managed Rs. 4000 crore in advance in 2008-

09 and around Rs. 9000 crore in the budget estimates for 2009-10 for the Sixth Pay Commission. In all, about Rs. 13600 crore extra had been spent and the provision for it was made by the predecessor - a remarkable job done by him in generating profits as well as peaceful environment for the railways' employees. It was a happy occasion to enjoy for everybody linked with the railways, including the present incumbent. Just imagine and compare it with the situation of Fifth Pay Commission period when the railways had reached near bankruptcy due to Pay Commission's impact. The then incumbent of Rail Bhavan who replaced RJD chief at the ministry in May 2009, was also the minister for the railways during 1999-2001. Why did she not issue White Paper then? The railways should be thankful to the predecessor for managing the major part of Sixth Pay Commission expenses in advance.

It seems that White Paper has been issued to undermine the turnaround process achieved by the ex-minister (2004 - 2009). One must remember that turnaround is not an ordinary achievement in the midst of all round failure of the railways prior to the predecessor. Turnaround is a situation mixed with self-introspection for what has gone wrong and for what has to be done to set things right. It automatically includes the self analysis to what a White Paper generally proposes and brings out the remedies for it. A lot of brainstorming and introspection have been done before the turnaround process has been initiated by the railways. A White Paper is not a thing to be issued every now and then. It spoils the dignity of the whole system. Perhaps the then incumbent of Rail Bhavan (2009-11) wanted to re-live her past as a minister for the railways of 1999-2001. But much water has flowed into Ganga since then. The past decade is history now. The railways authorities have developed a new mindset and they are ready to take a plunge into the depth of the problems to prove their efficiency in generating profits. They do not want White Paper: they want a programme of action, an agenda to follow under a dynamic leadership fully devoted to the railways and not a double minded person eager to chew and digest the best of Delhi and the best of Kolkata at one and the same time. This defuses energy and creates problems. White Paper therefore is the product of great confusion, chaos and instability prevailing with the railways.

The then incumbent of Rail Bhavan (2009-11) had developed a paradoxical situation. By issuing White Paper within the saga of turnaround, she seemed to spoil the game of success and aspired to re-write the history of railways' doom (or its recovery?) by her own hands quite anew. If every new incumbent joining Rail Bhavan starts doing this, the railways would never be able to move an inch forward. It would have been better had she started from where her predecessor left the railways without creating much fuss about the White Paper or announcing his 'unrealistic' estimates for the interim budget 2009-10. Who is going to oppose the minister if she increases or reduces the estimates? But she should have done it gracefully.

Perhaps the then incumbent of Rail Bhavan did not believe in the turnaround, surpluses, fund balances and profitability of the railways. She lamented over her predecessor's regime (Ibnlive, 2010: 2), his budget proposals and scheme of work. But the minister must remember that to understand the railways and its complex nature of earnings, costs and profits, one has to understand deeply the working of the organisation, its operating system, its transport economy and its integral aspect of solidarity, unity and service to the nation. A transport system like the railways requires a vigil. It requires confidence in decision making and a great political will to achieve cost reduction, increase in volume of traffic and earning profits. During 2004-09 a mindset for developing railways system and its economy was created (Kumar, 2009a: 10). But now everything is being pushed back. A fear-psychosis is generated indicating that the railway is going again to be a 'lost case' unless the minister rescues it. What are the parameters which determine such a case? Perhaps she has been engrossed in self-defeatism and this has been reflected upon the department which she is managing. In order to have a better understanding of the situation, we must analyze facts and figures, estimates and proposals as put forward in the budgets submitted by both the stalwarts-first as an interim budget and second as the main budget for the year 2009-10.

Budget Analysis - A Comparision

Analysing the interim budget (of the predecessor) as compared to the main budget (of the then incumbent) for the same year, 2009-10, presented in February and July respectively, with a gap of about six months, one may find that the maximum variation of Rs. 4740 crore in gross traffic receipts was shown which the then railway minister (2009-11) described as 'unrealistic' to achieve the estimates so proposed for the interim budget (Banerjee, 2009a: 19). The following figures indicate a comparative study:

Table-1 Budget 2009-10 **(Rs. in crore)**

Sl. No.	*Head of items*	*As Presented in Feb. 2009 by the Predecessor (2009)*	*As Presented in July 2009 by the new incumbent Joined in May 2009*	*Variation*
1.	Gross traffic receipts	Rs. 93159.00	Rs. 88419.00	-4740.00
2.	Miscellaneous receipts	Rs. 2147	Rs. 2207.22	+60.00
3.	Total receipts	Rs. 95306.22	Rs. 90626.22	-4680.00
4.	Total Working Expenditure	Rs. 83590.00	Rs. 81665.00	-1924.92
5.	Total Expenditure	Rs. 84429.74	Rs. 82504.74	-1925.00
6.	Net Revenue	Rs. 10876.48	Rs. 8121.48	-2755.00
7.	Surplus	Rs. 5572.26	Rs. 2642.26	-2930.00
8.	Operating Ratio	Rs. 89.90	Rs. 92.50	+3.40

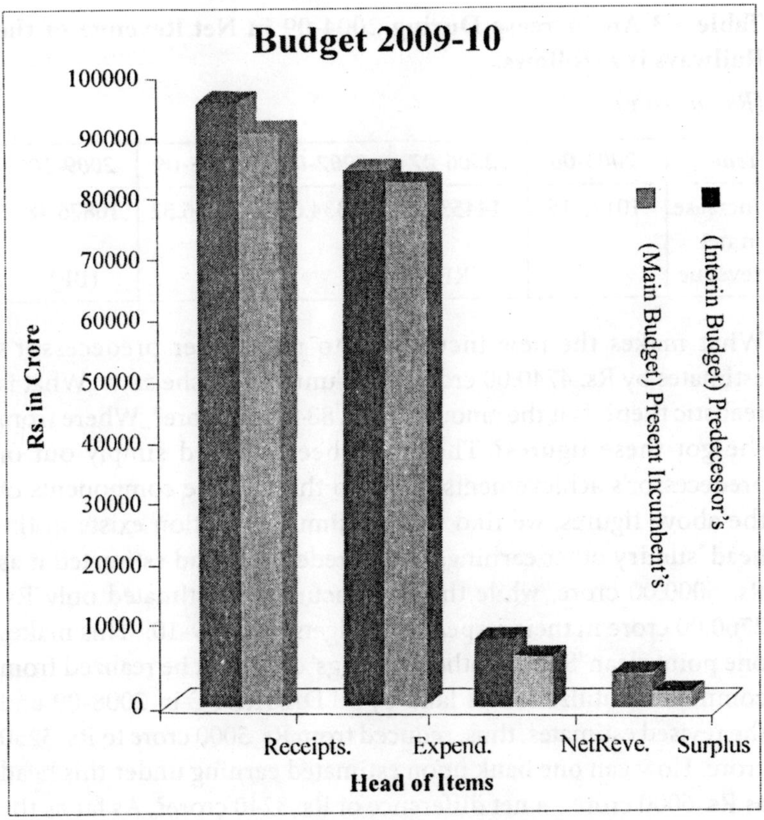

Figure -1 Showing interim and main budget

Table - 2 Total Gross Receipts (GTR) and Total Revenue (TR) During 2004-09 (Including Interim Budget) Are as Follows.

(Rs. in crore)

Year	2004-05	2005-06	2006-07	2007-08	2008-09	2009-10
Gross receipts	47370.21	54491.38	62731.50	71720.06	79862.00	93159.00 (BE)
Total Receipts	48919.24	56752.00	64785.84	73256.57	81659.00	95306.22

Table - 3 An Increase During 2004-09 in Net Revenue of the Railways is as follows.

(Rs. in crore)

Year	*2005-06*	*2006-07*	*2007-08*	*2008-09*	*2009-10*
Increase in net revenue	10143.15	14453.13 (RE)	18334.02	11066.52	10876.48 (BE)

What makes the new incumbent to reduce her predecessor's estimates by Rs. 4740.00 crore? It is 'unrealistic' she says. What is realistic then? Is it the amount of Rs. 88419.00 crore? Where from she got these figures? They have been derived simply out of predecessor's achievements. If we go through the components of the above figures, we find that maximum variation exists in the head 'sundry other earnings'. The predecessor had estimated it as Rs. 6000.00 crore, while the new incumbent estimated only Rs. 2760.00 crore in their respective budgets for 2009-10. This makes one point clear. 'Sundry other earnings' could not be realized from commercial utilization of land by RLDA/IRCTC in 2008-09 and the revised estimates, thus, reduced from Rs. 5000 crore to Rs. 3250 crore. How can one bank upon estimated earning under this head as Rs. 6000 crore - a net difference of Rs. 3240 crore? As far as the left over amount of Rs. 1500 crore is concerned, there has been only slight reduction in all the heads like total passenger earnings (Rs. 691 crore), other coaching earnings (Rs. 250 crore), goods earnings (53crore), and suspense account (Rs. 25 crore) etc. These minor reductions carry no meaning, but the major reduction in 'sundry other earnings' is meaningful as regards to two factors: first, the commercial utilization of railways land and second, the most important perhaps is the 'creative accounting' or the 'shift in accounting system' so adopted. The total earnings through the accounting change for the year 2008 (during predecessor's period) amounts to Rs. 3489 and has been added fully or partially to 'Sundry other earnings.' It is here that the new incumbent wants to hit and make out a case for White Paper. But, why does she stick to Rs. 88419.00 crore (about Rs. 4740 crore less) when normally all budgets presented by her predecessor show an increase of 10 to 15 thousand crore of rupees?

The revised net revenue for 2008-09 and budget estimates of 2009-10 have fallen short of the amount deducted for Sixth Pay Commission which is estimated to be Rs. 4000 crore and Rs. 9600 crore in both the years respectively, making a total expenditure of about Rs. 13600 crore. If we add Rs. 9600 crore to the predecessor's estimates it goes to about Rs 20476.48 crore. In the predecessor's estimate the net revenue, for 2009-10, is Rs. 10876.48 crore and in the present incumbent of the Rail Bhavan, estimate of the net revenue, for 2009-10, is Rs. 8121.48 crore. It is a difference of Rs. 2755.48 crore only. Why so much hue and cry over such an amount and branding it as 'unrealistic'?

The new incumbent's estimated goods earnings are Rs. 58525 crore while her predecessor has estimated it as Rs. 59059 crore. There is no basic difference in passenger earnings too. It is only the difference in 'sundry other earnings' as mentioned above. Apart from this the budgets seem to be on equal footing. There seems to be no logic to call predecessor's estimate as 'unrealistic' and no purpose has been solved by the White Paper except defaming the railways itself.

White Paper: Miniature of the Mohan Committee Report

The White Paper in essence is the miniature of the Rakesh Mohan Committee Report. What the Report could not do at that time, the White Paper has been set to do the same now. The Report wanted to convey in a nutshell the message that no effort whatsoever great would bring the railways on track because of its stagnant character, not showing any inclination to change. The Committee reported, "The Indian Railways have fallen into the vicious cycle of under investment, misallocation of scarce resources ... and deteriorating economy" (The Mohan Committee Report, 2001, Page 61). Almost in the same vein, the White Paper expressed the view that the railways potential was not improved and its growth elasticity was hovering around 0.79 and the share to India's GDP was stagnant at a level of 1.18 (Miinistry of Railways, 2009b, White Paper, p. 40).

The protagonists of the Report 2001 became active to incorporate, in letter and spirit, the old provision of 're-structuring' the railways and keeping the government at arm's length so that it might achieve the aim of 'corporatization' of the railways (White Paper, P. 70, Para 4.6.4). To what extent the re-structuring would be allowed to dismantle the Railways is not very clear, but the process of disintegration has set in silently as the White Paper is an officially accepted document. It has also recommended that the present functional structure of the railways be done away with and replaced by purely business set up. The most important is the re-structuring process of separation of infrastructure from operation. It would naturally lead to disintegration of commercial and operational system of the railways along with manufacturing and engineering activities which were the basis of the railways' establishment in the country. In no less clear terms, the White Paper has shown the audacity of restructuring of the railways' apex body i.e., the Railway Board. This might also lead to the pruning of the authority of the railways at almost all the central, zonal and divisional levels. If White Paper is of any consequence, the concluding remarks foretell the real shape of things to come up sharply.

It has criticized the railways being 'single authority and 'entity' (White Paper p. 69, Para 4.6.1) and opined that this network of ownership must be the part of organizational changes including freight, passenger and suburban services. It has shown its serious concern for cost escalation of different projects. The White Paper goes against the spirit of the railways' employees as far as their service conditions and welfare are concerned. It has specifically shown its resentment over the pension liabilities (White Paper p. 41). "The number of pensioners of Indian Railways is around 11.5 lakh, and the pension bill continues to rise every year". The natural consequence of the increase of the bill has been reflected in pruning out some benefits elsewhere. Perhaps the bonus given to the employees may be the first target. When losses were shown and the 'turnaround' decried, could any authority justify the bonus? "According to an actuarial study conducted in 2005, the actuarial requirement of fund in pension fund was estimated at Rs. 5, 41,948 crore to make it self-sustaining. As this is a very large sum which is not available for appropriation, the railways have not taken any follow up action on this study. However, appropriate provision is being done on an annual basis to meet the yearly liability" (White Paper p. 41).

The other factor which has the same meeting ground as of the Mohan Committee Report is 'cross subsidization' (White Paper P. 65). The White Paper is a lament over the increasing freight rate and reduced level of passenger fares especially second class fares. "As a result, passenger fares in India are low compared to most foreign railways. The high freight rates and low passenger fares make the fare-freight ratio of India's railways one of the lowest in the world" (White Paper Page 65). In India this level was 0.32 but was further reduced during the predecessor's period to 0.26. The fare-freight ratio in case of China is 1:2 and Korea is 1:4. The cross subsidization of one segment by another is the result of India's rural poverty as well as the sizable population living below poverty line. As long as poverty prevails in India, the cross subsidization has to be continued and tolerated. Railway is the only affordable means of transport in India for the rural poor. It has been instrumental in creating mobility of the workforce in the country and perhaps it is in the best interest of the nation and the people that the cross subsidization process be continued. However, the Rakesh Mohan Report and the White Paper — both opined against it.

The White Paper and the Mohan Committee Report in substance justify the same line of action. The White Paper added insults to injuries as the railways were yet not fully recovered from the previous shocks generated by the Mohan Committee Report. Both aim at emphasizing re-structuring the railways which was nothing but downgrading the whole set up. It was destructive, devastating and detrimental to the health of the railways. The very purpose of organizing the institution was defeated and the lifeline of the nation was jeopardized.

The 'White Paper' has damaged the psyche of the workforce of the railways and majority of the people serving at Rail Bhavan. They are astonished by such type of critical assessment about their previous 'guard'. But they are silent because they can do nothing. How long would their silence work? They will ultimately come up to give a fight to such an evil design if it hampers their interest in 'bonus' calculation, promotion or degrading their efficiency. How could they get bonus without surplus? Such doubts have set deep into their minds. The White Paper is silently corroding the fruits of growth, development and the turnaround process, piercing, destroying and devastating the economy from within. In this respect, the White Paper and the Rakesh Mohan Committee report have served the same purpose – *"Killing the Spirit of Railways"*. The White Paper has the startling resemblance to the ideological tautology of World Bank's study, on the one hand and the Rakesh Mohan Committee report, on the other. The working and the impact of both the studies are quite in tune with their aims and purpose and it seems as if the same think tank has been used to produce them. In fact, both the documents — White Paper and 'Mohan Report' have the same genus and technically are produced by hired consultants. Both the reports are the brain work of their respective ministers. The Rakesh Mohan Committee report has based its major financial findings on the expert group of company called M/S Rangaraju and Associate and the present incumbent has hired the services of S.S. Kothari Mehta & Co to create financial bungling and faulty calculation in bringing out White Paper just to malign the previous administration including its leader. Most top ranking bosses at Rail Bhavan of the predecessor's stint have retired and unfortunately, the leader of the turnaround, though served the railways with great devotion and passion, is now out of power. Had he been the minister in any ministry (not necessarily the railways), the White Paper would not have appeared. He would have been the part of the same bandwagon. Even the new bosses at Rail Bhavan would not have dared bringing a faulty financial report, misrepresenting the facts, and miscalculating the figures and damaging the image of the predecessor by presenting White Paper of such a distorted nature.

Footnote

1. The concept was first expressed by K.B. Verma - a scholar and railway professional in his article contributed to 'Indian Railway Finance' titled 'Why so many pockets'? It signifies the complicated mechanism of railway finances and recommends an alternative structure based on standard financial practices

◆◆◆

4

Counteracting White Paper: An Answer to Faulty Findings

It was with a vengeance as if a battle had been fought, for about six months, to work out a document, highly biased and distorted in the history of Indian railways, with the help of a hired consultant, in support of some spicy material and irrelevant financial inputs that a White Paper was presented to the Parliament on 18th December 2009. It was an ever agitated, restless and unstable incumbent of Rail Bhavan, who created a stunning impact of a sudden political thunder by reminding the members of the Parliament that during Budget Session for 2009-10, six months ago, she had assured them that she would place before the House a White Paper indicating the Railways' present organizational, operational and financial status based on its performance in the past 5 years (without naming the person). And she 'proudly' pronounced, "As promised, I am presenting the White Paper to the House" (Banerjee in "Foreword", Ministry of Railways, 2009b). She at last, had a sigh of relief for projecting malignant glare of publicity against her predecessor. On that day, there appeared two papers (first, the White Paper and second - a Utopia of farsightedness - a Vision 2020) prepared within six months! Perhaps a new workaholic culture had infiltrated Rail Bhavan (70 + 62 = 132 pages issued in about 200 days!), not like business as usual, but more than that, a programme of high speed scenario of modern style. It was honorable Ex-President APJ Abdul Kalam, who has 'ignited' the 'vision' approach[1] to the Indian mindset, and since then everybody or the institution has started issuing a Vision - 2010; 2015; 2020… and so on till one reaches the end of this century! Why should the present incumbent or to say the railways, remain far behind? Perhaps this has made her to work out Vision 2020 (Ministry of Railways, 2009b). She feels her dream come true situation quite pleasurably as if the government would last for next ten years and work consecutively (without any break?), so the vision 2020 is a fitting case for the speedy recovery of the railways. It is of course a Utopian plan of accumulated ongoing projects and other schemes requiring lakhs of crores of rupees (Rs.1466304 crore approx.)!

The White Paper, in contrast to the above wishful project - Vision 2020 - is a matter of grave concern as it is perhaps a 'visionless' or more appropriately- a blind or in words of the predecessor a 'black' or a 'blank' paper - and in Shakespearean phraseology, a paper "full of sound and fury signifying nothing". A White Paper is normally not a subject matter of criticism or a matter of producing a counter White Paper. A genuine White Paper is in itself a critical assessment of the situation, facts and programmes. It needs no further analysis or evaluation. A White Paper is a private matter; a type of departmental affair. What have others to do with it? But curiously enough, this White Paper (2009) is unique in approach and an unparalleled phenomenon, in the 'series' of railways' White Papers so far issued, and that it needs a proper mending, a better overhauling with an equally vengeful attitude to which it deserves.

The period of analysis chosen by the White Paper is quite intriguing and the report submitted is retrograde, disastrous and offensive. Why only the period 2004-2009 has been specifically taken into account? Does it not relate to a particular person? It does fall into a graceless situation as it speaks of the malice where naming a person matters little. What matters is the conscious effort of creating an antithetical view of turnaround. It deals with the situation where the work done does not matter, but what is undone, creates a greater challenge not only regarding publicity but for the assessment of the real purpose for which the White Paper is normally issued.

A White Paper is generally known as a creation of self disciplined environment where introspection is followed by better understanding and creativity, innovation and advancement of purpose. It does not intend to malign anybody but brings out the freshness of human values for new initiatives to be taken. In such a situation the real goal, the mission and the motto converge to a point where it develops straight forward attitude for correcting or judging a particular pattern of self analysis. A White Paper thus is a critical assessment of the self and it remains confined to one's own affairs. Critically examined, it works for an institution to develop, for a society to improve and for a nation to establish best of the cultural and social life. It is not a criticism for the sake of criticism, but for the improvement over the past and a forecast for the brighter future.

But, contrary to all established norms and values, the White Paper on Indian railways 2009 emits wrong signals to the persons concerned that consider the railways as a business unit and think in terms of the health of the railways. The parameters of judging the transport growth are wrongly chosen, misrepresented and negatively construed. The White Paper does not help organizers or planners to understand the real maladies afflicting the railways and the oppressive ways that stunt the growth of its finances and the businesses. This White Paper clearly prompts to draw the opaque conclusion against the turnaround process. The White Paper is basically unjust, intuitively weak and detestably irrational and no healthy and decisive step can be taken on its fumbling foundation and distrustful treatment of the subject which it takes into account.

White Paper-A Fallacy

To be judgmental especially about the period 2004-09 only and calling the White Paper as an account of dispassionate reporting is a fallacy. The study seems to have included the information on growth of traffic, infrastructure and financial performance, apart from many other aspects, to make it look like an annual report of statistics and accounts. However, the factors of analysis, included in the frame-work, have not been fully justified and do not give a clear picture of growth when a concluding remark has been made by it that the 'traffic growth performance has been below par for the entire period of the predecessor' (Ministry of Railways, 2009a: 4). Here the single parameter used is the 'growth rate of transport elasticity' in relation to GDP (Gross Domestic Product). This concept is not fundamentally suitable to assess the potential growth of the railway GDP. It has used overrated elasticity for the growth pattern to falsify the earlier achievements, especially in the form of 'turnaround'. The process adopted in calculating the growth potential is also crudely applied. The following concept needs to be noted in this regard:

How can the 'absolute' transport growth elasticity bring a clear picture of a relative term or single mode of transport i.e., the railways? The railway is one of the modes of transport. Other modes are roads, coastal shipping, air, inland water and pipelines etc. How has the White Paper applied the transport elasticity of growth as a measure of a part i.e., railways' elasticity? All the modes of transport have varying degree of growth elasticities. Even if the differences are minute, the methodology applied is weak, crude and unconvincing. The calculation of potential growth of railway GDP is unsatisfactory, unreasonable and incomparable. Hence it needs to be reworked and revised. The conclusion regarding this aspect is:

> Growth elasticity of transport sector as a whole is not the same as growth elasticity of railways alone as in Indian conditions railway has a greater disparity in comparison to Road, Coastal shipping, and Air transport.[2]
>
> Explanatory note: Accepting World Bank's transport model and irrationally applying to a single mode of transport is a technical fallacy. World Bank's reports have not been generous towards Indian transport economy in general and the railways in particular and for the last several years, in one or the other context, has been reiterating the point of de-regularization of railway system

to bring it to the free market forces and ultimately handing over it to private hands. The World Bank's analysis has a typical approach to quantify developing economy in such a way as to bring it down to a 'forced' comparison. The Indian railway is no exception to it. The growth elasticity of railways has to be calculated empirically, given to Indian condition of various modes of transport and their "inter-model sensitivity, elasticity and disparity" (Misra, 2008: 38-43).

White Paper: Faulty Calculations

No absolute transport growth elasticity as multiplied to GDP Growth rate can bring out a clear picture for comparative study i.e., GDP × 1.25 = Potential Growth of railway GDP, as applied by White Paper (p. 4). It is erroneous unless it brings into its fold differential elasticities belonging to other modes of transport and their mutual relationships.

The potential rate of growth of railway GDP should be calculated differently, not on the basis of transport elasticity, but in accordance to demand forecasting and the traffic calculation for the Indian railways should be done separately and not mixed with other modes of transport (as the World Bank has done) , like road, shipping and airways etc. It is because Indian railways has peculiar characteristic regarding demand for traffic. The railways 'loss' in traffic is a 'gain' for road transport and the railways lags behind in competing with the road transport in the present scenario and perhaps the trend may continue in future too. The peculiarity of the Indian railways as linked with its competitor — road transport, brings it to acquire the characteristic of a class of cross elasticity of growth i.e., with the change in growth of road transportation elasticity, the rail transport growth elasticity changes in negative form. All this happens because elasticity of growth of GDP and the transport elasticity are positively related and the railways and road transport are highly competitive in the race of acquiring traffic share.

This race of mouse and cat seems to be everlasting unless transport coordination policy is formulated and practically adopted.

The other factor is intra-sector inequalities of growth of transportation in India. It needs a demand estimate of all the modes of transportation separately including railway transportation – a model that can accurately measure the transport demand for the present and its future estimates. The input-output model of estimating the demand for railways traffic is a better form of projecting growth potential and its measuring technical coefficient than what has been used in White Paper.

It is also important to measure the degree of inequalities of growth of various means of transport in India so that the position of the railways within transport economy may be clearly ascertained. In order to measure the growth of transportation and inequality created within the modes of transport system, one can study time-series data pertaining to different modes of transportation. The other process of understanding of disparity is to study the data and analyze them by calculating coefficient of variation. According to a study (Misra, 2008) in this regard in freight traffic among four major modes of transportation in India, it is the road transportation which has the maximum coefficient of variation, followed by coastal shipping, railways and the airlines in a descending order. This means the spread potential of road transportation is higher than the railways. This ratio of railway to road is 1:1.5. It implies that one unit change in growth of railway traffic is accompanied by 1.5 unit change in growth of road transport traffic as far as the spread potential is concerned. The World Bank too has studied the subject in terms of area elasticity. The conclusion regarding this aspect follows:

1. The railway potential of growth needs to be better estimated using, not 'growth elasticity of transport', but by demand estimate of transportation of the railway separately through rigorous analytical methods.
2. The demand coefficient of transport factor of railway should be calculated within Input-Output framework analysis.

3. Since coefficient of variation for the range of transport services differs in different modes, the single elasticity model cannot be applied to judge the potential growth of railway traffic.

When such are the differences in various modes of transportation regarding their growth spread, demand factor and sensitivity of services, how can it be concluded on the basis of single parameter that 'traffic growth for the entire period was below par'? What was below norm or deficient was the conclusion of White Paper which was fallacious and deserved to be dismissed. Let a detailed analysis be done regarding the GDP and elasticity of growth concept of railways separately before making any swift judgment as has been done by the White Paper. Indian railways is a hybrid institution. One can neither assess its activities purely related to free market forces nor can it be well estimated purely on social obligation performance. It remains between these two limits. This aspect is to be judged on the following facts:

1. Indian railways performs less than cost services to certain commodities and passenger traffic.
2. Some of the projects have negative rate of profits and lines run on losses.
3. Its social obligation outlook is engrossed in its working and goes beyond core transportation activities.

It is because of the above facts that its process of growth potential has to be ascertained in such a way that it includes a controlled system on one hand and the model of free market forces on the other.

Input Output Model for Railways

Transportation process forms the key element of infrastructural framework. It designs the pattern of distribution of economic activities and shapes the system of productivity through its influence and impact. It serves as a life-line, linking market to distributive forces and facilitates exchange and consumption power. It provides productive forces, the opportunity, to come together for enhancing economic development of the areas of local, regional, national and international dimensions. Thus, transportation is a system which creates movement of goods and services with varying degree of speed and spread for generating better productive relationships. Protection, safety, flexibility, comfort and aspiration values are its accompanied factors which determine its utility along with affordability, choice and availability, the factors which make it more useful and competitive.

There has never been only one mode of transportation. Along with progress of civilization there have been developing various modes and ways of transportation - some in use and others being abandoned. It depends upon the capacity which it develops for meeting out its demand for the transportation market. Transportation modes, therefore, are commodity specific, area specific, speed and time specific and there are various other factors which determine their choice. It is a complex affair to determine the demand for transportation service. And in general terms, it is even more difficult to estimate its demand in advance. It also happens that sometimes, the mode of transportation has to create its own demand and in this respect the old law of J.B. Say with a little modification on specific situation, holds good - that the supply has to create its own demand. The other economic characteristic of transportation is that once it is created, it has to be used, specifically within time or else it is destroyed and it adds to destruction of utility. It is this characteristic of destructivity condition which plays the dominant role in making transport policy framework, fixation of price and profit earning by the service a specific mode of transport provides. The Indian Railway is quite befitting an example, in this connection, to show as to how it survived the competition, created turnaround and came to a situation where the policy of reduction in price of the service provided was practised along with the increased volume of traffic.

Theoretical Framework of Transport Demand Model

The demand for transportation is linked with the movement of goods from one area to another. A model of transportation can be created treating transport as an industry where we can establish transportation demand and its input requirements, along with production level of final demand in an input-output framework. A model to measure demand for goods transportation was developed on the basis of Leontief's input - output framework.[3] It may well be re-modeled for the Indian transport demand for general and the railways in particular. Efforts had been made by Prof. P. N. Mathur in framing out the model and Mr. S. R. Hashim had especially worked out for transport system as a whole (Hashim, 1967: 92-108). The model can be expressed in the following way:

When specific quantity of a commodity, say i is moved from an area a to another area b along with the extra flow of the same commodity through production in area b or through import from other areas used up in area b either as inputs for the industries or for the final demand sector, the movement so generated is called transport demand and can be expressed as follows:

$$X_i^{ab} = \sum_{j=1}^{n} X_{ij}^{ab} + X_{if}$$

Here j and f are the consuming sectors (j as Industry and *f* being final demand sector) in region *b*. For transportation purposes inter-sectoral movements are unnecessary and we confine ourselves only with inter-spatial movements (Xi^{ab}).

Each unit of i (commodity) for being transported over a unit distance requires some units of transport services, say ti. If the distance between a and b is d^{ab}, then a unit of *i* to be transported from a to b will require $t_i d^{ab} = t_i^{ab}$ units of transport service and total movement of i from a to b say X_i^{ab} will require $t_i^{ab} Xt_i^{ab}$ units of transport service.

Thus t_i^{ab} i.e. units of transport service required to transport a unit of commodity i from a to b may be called transport coefficient.

The above is just a theoretical model for demand estimation of the commodity. It was used by Mr. Hashim and developed by Late Prof. Mathur, of the University of Wales, U.K.

Application of Input-Output Framework

Adopting the above model, the technical coefficients in input-output framework are obtained empirically on the basis of production demand for one sector by others as a fixed proportion of their outputs. But taking transport as one of the sectors, the same cannot be said about it because it relates to the flow of the commodity over space. Transport need of particular sector depends on where this sector is located. Therefore, demand for transportation becomes a variable depending upon the spatial flow pattern which is not predetermined or fixed.

Hence, the transport demand is to be associated with flow of goods from one region to another (*Xiab,* i.e. flow of commodity *i* from region *a* to region *b*), while other input area associated with the production of the commodity (*Pia*, i.e. production of *i* in region *a*).

Transport, like other sectors, itself requires the products of other sectors as well as that of its own as inputs, and these inputs are also to be transported to where the transport demand is created or located.

Thus, a vector of input going into the transport industry is associated with coefficient *tiab* (*i* excludes the transport sector itself which is related to flow of goods).

Transport Coefficient

Relating to Railways transportation demand for inputs and outputs for goods, we take into account real physical units i.e. Wagon Kilometer (WKm). Thus, the transport coefficient is the wagon kilometer (WKm) requirements of transporting a unit of certain commodity over a given distance. To calculate transport coefficient, one can base the study on Planning Commission's input-output table. The railways should construct its own input-output table, for which it has to establish an input-output cell within RITES in collaboration with The Statistical Institute or The Planning Commission of India.

Indicating Wagon Kilometer (WKm), the loading capacity of a wagon is expressed in terms of different types of commodities transported by the railways according to their broad categories i.e. Food Grains, Other Agriculture, Coal, Iron ore and POL, Heavy Merchandise and Light Merchandise etc. After preparing the input-output table (or deriving Railways' and, other transportation' from already prepared input-output table of the Planning Commission), the process of calculating transport coefficient may be worked out.

Here, the intermediate demand for inputs as well as the vector of final demand for output (goods transportation) may be estimated. It is a tedious study and requires the help of experts from specialized areas. The model as referred to earlier may be used to find out Indian Railways' demand for goods transportation and its input requirements. This study would prove to be true and one must not depend on World Bank's estimates which remained distorted because of unspecified factors involved in the analysis.

Alternatively, in calculating transport coefficient, the input output table prepared by Central Statistical Organization (CSO) may be used (CSO, 2005-06a: 'Statistical Abstract' of various years). These tables are prepared after every five years and The Railways appear in two places as 'rail equipment' and 'railway transport services'. However, it is highly aggregated form of study and minute observation on the railways' flow of goods and services are difficult to be obtained. It is, therefore, suggested that the railways should prepare their own input-output table, detailing intermediate transactions as well as final consumption to come to the estimates of transportation demand and input coefficient.

Supply Factor of Transport

The supply remains seldom inconsistent with the demand for transportation. Normally, it is either in short supply or exceeds the demand ,with the result that it has to adjust with its price mechanism and policy framework. Even there may be fluctuations: in short run it tries to come up with demand with reduction in price and with volume of traffic so created and in long run it has to maintain its demand according to increased capacity so generated.

The various modes of transportation, though competitive in nature, have their own monopolistic tendencies and create specific segmentation of market, unless they coincide with each other, sharing the transportation market in a competitive way. If particular mode of transportation is not well alert, it may lose its share as it has happened in case with Rail – Road competition in India especially in the situation of the Railways freight traffic.

Frieght Elasticity and GDP

The analysis done by the trio of World Bank think tank namely Esra Bennathan, Julie Fraser and Louis S. Thompson, who calculated demand for freight transport, and the study which was extensively used in the White Paper had to be assessed in context of the Indian Railways so as to find out if it was relevant to measure growth model of elasticity on such lines? Was it an accurate measure of growth elasticity as applied to the Indian Railways? Or was there any doubt regarding its efficacy of this process in the present context?

One important fact which came out of the analysis was that the calculation of growth potential of Indian railways as put forward by the White Paper (Ministry of Railways, 2009b: 4, T - 1) did not represent the real potential. It was overrated, misrepresented and doubtfully expressed. It left many grounds untouched, the real doubts unresolved and relevant questions unanswered. Even its very presence in the tabular form seemed abnormal, unrealistic and uncalled for. The subject of the study i.e., 'What determines demand for Freight Transport' does not segregate the railways as a separate identity and the samples taken up are so mixed up that the total Ton- Kilometer of freight ultimately represents the combined mode of transportation. i.e., road freight, railway freight and the freight of the coastal shipping and air transport. Does it make any sense if used for railways alone by the White Paper?

The trio has related the study of freight transport with two variables: (a) AREA and (b) GDP. It means total Ton- Km of a country may be estimated in relation to the Area of the country or/ and GDP. The trio has mainly researched (I) Freight Transport in Ton-Km by road in relation to GDP and (II) Ton -Km by road in relation to Area. It follows that apart from GDP, the AREA of a country has got the greater impact as far as the freight transport of the country is concerned. In calculation of Area relationship to Ton-Km, Russia tops the world. This study has also developed a peculiar way of relationship in its sampling process which has been 'merged' with developing countries and cannot therefore give a real picture. In any case, this study brings out the fact that "the elasticity of demand for road Ton-Km with regard to GDP should be about or above 1.25 for developing countries ..." (here the railways have not been mentioned). However, the study goes on to express:

"Demand for rail freight transport 'appears' to be determined in closely similar ways in both the groups of countries i.e., developed and mixed (developed + developing). "ELASTICITY WITH GDP APPEARS TO BE CLOSE TO UNITY" (Bannathan et al, 1992: 1-29) - here one must mark the capital letters. It is close to unity and not complete unity (1). Even this closeness to unity has got three doubtful conclusions:

(a) The elasticity of freight transport for railways has not been calculated 'separately'.

(b) The elasticity which has been mentioned is less than unity tending to (close to) one but not beyond unity.

(c) The study is mixed or merged with developed countries has been made. Broadly the study does not make any distinction between 'total freight transport' and 'railways' freight transport, which is a fallacy in itself. It also does not make any distinction in the mixed samples of developing countries. How can one arrive at correct conclusion in such a situation? Coming to the characteristic features of Indian railways, particularly of freight transport and comparing them to the study made by

World Bank think tank which has been used in White Paper, one finds a lot of anomalies and can never subscribe to the views and conclusions made by the White Paper especially in the following areas:

(*i*) Calculation of elasticity of transport growth of the railways in relation to GDP;

(*ii*) Total Ton-Km of transport vs. railway Ton-Km of transport.

The Indian railways have the following characteristics in relation to the above facts:

1. There is a great disparity in transport relationships between the road and the Railways. They are not complementary but highly competitive and in relationship to road, a type of 'cross elasticity' has to be studied.
2. That the total transport growth elasticity is not the same thing as railways growth elasticity as has been wrongly accepted by the consultant who provided inputs to the White Paper.
3. That various modes of transport have got varying degree of elasticities.
4. That within railways, the transportation of growth elasticity, varies in degree in relation to different commodities and different traffic markets of the railways.
5. Those within freight transport elasticity there are varying 'seasonal elasticities' for peak and the sleek seasons. The elasticity is not uniform throughout the year.

The peculiarity in relationship of elasticity between road and railways has been well marked and there can be no single rate of calculation for the growth of transport elasticity for two different identities with their peculiarities and style of freight transportation in India. How can World Bank's report on total transport elasticity be justifiable to assess the elaticities of rail transport separately?

The fact is that the White Paper has created a mess of the facts, figures and finances; borrowed the basis of incomparable studies of the World Bank and irrationally brought it in relation to railways conditions to come to desired conclusion. It is therefore necessary to bring these facts to the notice of general people so that they may have the better understanding of the situation and can draw their own conclusions. But conclusions based on unjustifiable relationships can never be accepted.

In World Bank's report, it has been no where emphatically expressed that the railways elasticity of growth in relation to GDP is 1.25 and it is a measure to be applied to project the potential growth in a developing country. The readers must be made clear about this point. The real situation is that 'it appears close to unity' and that is all. It should not be interpreted as '1.25' which has been mentioned in a 'mixed' sample not applicable to developing countries separately and in no circumstances to Indian conditions because of railways peculiar characteristics, status and environment. The White Paper has done great injustice in relating the 'overrated' elasticity to Indian GDP and calculating Indian Railways freight potential ratio.

There are two basic reasons to reject transport elasticity as '1.25' which has been used for calculating the potential growth as has been done in the case of White Paper:

1. That the transport elasticity of '1.25' as mentioned in the study made by the 'trio' of the World Bank, belongs to the combined samples of 'Road, Railways and Coastal Shipping' and not separately for the railways. So it is almost 'total transport elasticity' and not the railways' elasticity.
2. That it is meant for a mixed sample of 'developed plus developing' countries including 17 high and upper middle income countries plus 11 lower middle and low income market countries.

By no stretch of imagination the elasticity expressed as '1.25' is meant for developing countries like India.

The other hidden factor which is missed by the new 'guard'[4] of the railways is that all such studies suggest directly or indirectly to adopt the ways of World Bank to 'de-nationalize the railways or else they would suffer a lot financially and economically. This was the hidden message of the Rakesh Mohan Committee Report too (and was rejected by the work-force of Indian Railways and administration alike) and the White Paper also carries the same hidden agenda. Let the trade unions and the Railway Workers' Federations make a note of it and study deeply the contents of the White Paper. It has degraded the railways' system as a whole. The attack on the predecessor's period is just symbolic — it has greater intention to downsize the organization and liberalize to the extent where it would reach the point of no return and eventually have to privatize itself. In the same way, the findings of the World Bank as used by the White Paper, are extremely meaningful, if one goes to accept the following fact mentioned as the growth 'Mantra' of the transport, in general and the railways, in particular. It states "For developing countries failing drastic changes in transport policy, one may expect rail freight to rise not faster than GDP" (chap. 2, p. 10 of the Report). Indian railways is one of those transport modes which carries greater 'social order factor' to serve than expected by the World Bank. One wonders how the elasticity measure of '1.25' has been applied to the railways freight traffic by the White Paper. It has not been specifically mentioned in the research papers for developing countries by the World Bank. "All that is important to know is that the elasticity remains positive in relation to GDP and it tends close to one, but not actually one" (Bannathan et al,1992).

Calculating the Correct Potential Growth Rate

The actual elasticity of growth of railways transport in India lies somewhere between 0.69 to 0.79 and the optimum situation (according to the study of the World Bank) may be close to one i.e., .9 but does not go beyond one (1). The fact is that Indian railways transport elasticity potential even from World Bank's point of view should be measured according to GDP as follows:

GDP × 0.9 = Potential rate of growth of railways transportation for India

It therefore comes to the following calculation:

Table-4 Correct Potential Growth Rate

Year 2004-05	*GDP Growth Rate*	*Potential GR of Rlys. As Per Hovering Elasticity GDP×.79*	*Potential GR of Rlys. As per Expected Elasticity GDP×.9*	*Percentege of Variation in Potential Growth Rate*	*Actucal Growth Rate of Railways GDP*	*Percentege of Increase as per Expected Elasticity*
2004-05	7.47	5.90	6.72	13.89	7.29	8.48%
2005-06	9.52	7.52	8.57	13.96	8.76	2.22%
2006-07	9.75	7.70	8.78	14.02	9.99	13.78%
2007-08	9.01	7.12	8.10	13.76	9.29	14.69%
2008-09	6.71	5.30	6.03	13.77	-	-

Here the elasticity of potential rate of growth of railways to GDP is greater than the hovering elasticity and much nearer to one which is standard and achievable for developing economies like India. This (.9) elasticity is meaningful, rational and not 'overrated' as is done in the case of White Paper.

White Paper has intentionally used overrated elasticity i.e. 1.25 in order to prove that the growth potential of the railways during predecessor's period did not improve. On the other hand, it declined, showing shortfall, as per expected elasticity to 21.9%, 26.4%, 18.0% and 17.5% in the years 2004-05, 2005-06, 2006-07and 2007-08 respectively (White Paper, 2009, p. 4. Table 1).[5] But these estimates were biased and did not correspond to the correct measure of growth potential.

The researcher has developed a new measure of estimate quite logical and acceptable according to Indian condition of developing economy by multiplying India's GDP with correct elasticity i.e. GDP × .9. On the basis of such calculations, the potential growth of the railways increased as per expected elasticity to 8.48%, 2.21%, 13.78% and 14.69% in the years 2004-05, 2005-06, 2006-07 and 2007-08 respectively (see table 4 col 7).

The conclusion therefore may safely be drawn that the traffic growth performance of Indian Railways had been above par for the entire period (2004 - 09).

The Concept of Elasticity

The concept of elasticity is not a process to be increased or decreased in a whimsical way to project expected demand or growth. It relates to a technical coefficient bounded by variety of factors and can change only in the long run. In White Paper no explanation has been given to the type of elasticity used.[6] Various forms of elasticities have different meanings and impact. Point Elasticity, Arc Elasticity, Cross Elasticity - all have different interpretations, analytical uses and effects. The growth pattern of expected elasticity in developing economy of railway transport of India should be positive, tending to 1, but not exactly one. In the long run the actual growth potential may increase to come to GDP level but not faster than that. Still, this measure of transport growth to GDP is not very realistic or reliable in the long run because it takes a twist and turns with greater growth potential and the relationship changes to a reverse order such that GDP gets affected by transport, infrastructure and other factors and change accordingly.

However, this happens when the economy grows richer or comes closer to the developed group of countries. In that situation, the growth analysis of transport sector does not depend upon elasticity in relation to GDP but GDP becomes the function of infrastructure and other sectors of the economy. Therefore, the best option is not GDP but the actual demand forecast in relationship with transport technical coefficients which belong to a different field of study than elasticity. The railways must develop their own input-output table of Leontief model (as explained earlier in this chapter) to come to certainty of demand estimates. The railways have not touched this model of estimation so far. It is recommended that it must get itself linked with Indian Statistical Institute, Delhi or Kolkata, and the Planning Commission, government of India, for better understanding of the subject.

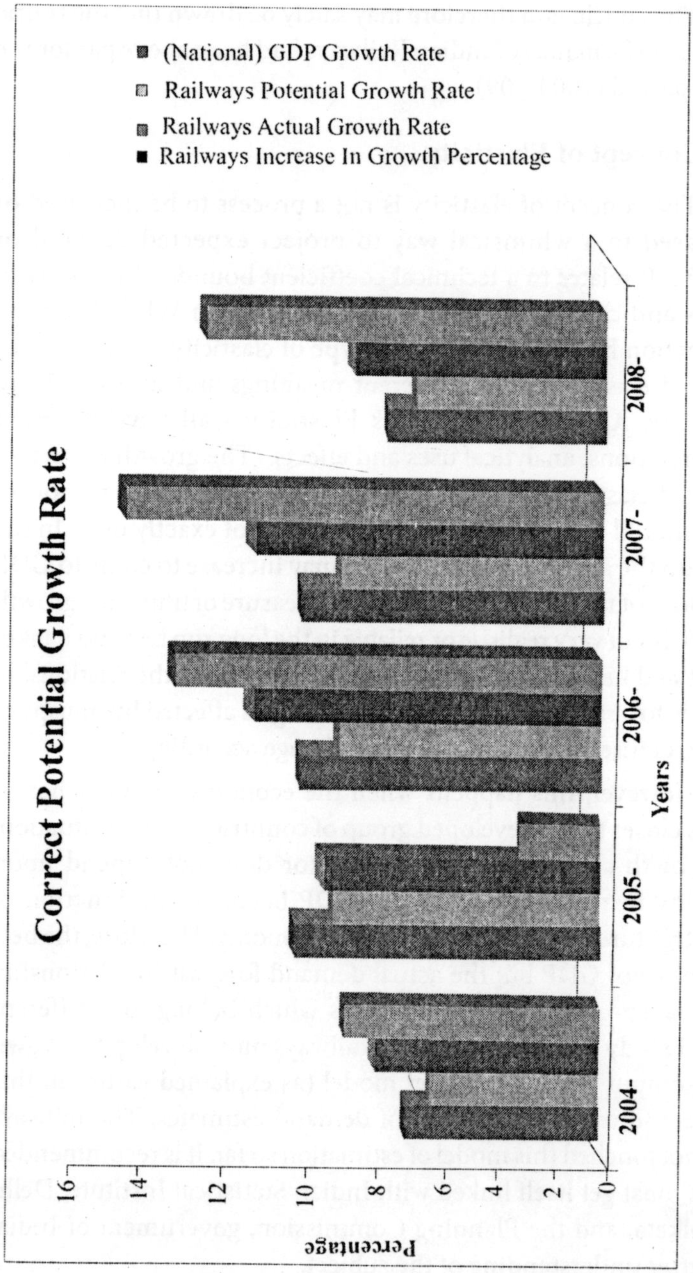

Figure 2 : Correct Potential Growth Rate.

In Indian conditions, there is meaning behind hovering elasticity to the point of 0.79, and the Railway's contribution to GDP remaining stagnant at 1.18. Unless the technical coefficient of production pattern of the Railways changes, one cannot expect any overnight miracle in the growth process of the railways. However, any step taken in this direction, even if it is small, and generates 'some quantum of surpluses', should be appreciated, accepted and followed. The turnaround process was a humble approach towards achieving this programme. Why so much hue and cry over it? Can the new incumbent bring any programme of action without creating change in the present situation? The past achievements should not be neglected, decried or degraded only to prove them as false by comparing them with figures that are 'overrated' and 'mismatched'. The elasticity of demand whether it is consumer goods or relating to transportation or even growth of transportation, directly or indirectly is a psychological concept and has to be dealt with caution. The new incumbent has posed a challenge for herself. Would her achievement for a year in office surpass the predecessor's? It is doubtful. Would she be prepared to be judged on the parameters which she has posed for her predecessor? Perhaps she would not.

Sensitivity Index

Multiplying GDP by overrated elasticity 1.25 is fraught with severe infirmities. The sensitivity index indicates that this may happen only if at least 61percent increase in freight traffic is achieved. Is it possible at one stroke? The Vision 2020 has proposed an increase from 833 million tonnes to a little more than double i.e., 1850 million tonnes or from 538.2 billion NTKMs to 1203 billion NTKMs in ten years. The expectancy of growth projection is more than double and it can only be acquired if freight elasticity increases by 1.75 or 2. Even in this case the assumption is that there is no change in price ratio or there would be no change in competitiveness with road transport or there would be no cross elasticity affecting the increase in freight traffic. It is very difficult to maintain. This projection therefore is not plausible. Coming to the elasticity and sensitivity index analysis as adopted in potential growth of freight traffic on the basis of 1.25 is also not achievable on the same assumptions of prices, competition and cross elasticity. The road transport is so formidable a competitor that the railways have to think twice before taking any step to increase the potential growth of freight transport. The elasticity 1.25 thus is high rated in the above context and it is neither workable nor acceptable (See table 5).

Table-5 Sensitivity Index Showing Freight Elasticity

Year	GDP Rate	GDP × .775	Index	GDP × .800	Index	GDP × .825	Index	GDP × .850	Index	GDP × .875	Index	GDP × .900	Index
2004 -05	7.47	5.79	100	5.98	103.2	6.16	106.4	6.35	109.7	6.54	112.9	6.72	116.1
2005 -6	9.52	7.38	100	7.62	103.2	7.85	106.4	8.09	109.6	8.33	112.9	8.57	116.1
2006 -07	9.75	7.56	100	7.80	103.2	8.04	106.5	8.29	109.7	8.53	112.9	8.78	116.1
2007 -08	9.01	6.98	100	7.21	103.3	7.43	106.5	7.66	109.7	7.88	112.9	8.10	116.2
2008 09	6.70	5.19	100	5.36	103.3	5.53	106.5	5.70	109.7	5.86	113.0	6.03	116.2

Table-5 (concluded)

Year	GDP Rate	GDP × .925	Index	GDP × .950	Index	GDP × .975	Index	GDP × 1.00	Index	GDP × 1.25	Index
2004-05	7.47	6.91	119.3	7.10	122.6	7.28	125.8	7.47	129.0	9.34	161.3
2005-06	9.52	8.81	119.4	9.04	122.5	9.28	125.8	9.52	129.0	11.9	161.9
2006-07	9.75	9.01	119.3	9.26	122.5	9.50	125.7	9.75	129.0	12.2	161.3
2007-08	9.01	8.33	119.4	8.56	122.6	8.78	125.9	9.0	129.1	11.3	161.4
2008-09	6.70	6.20	119.4	6.37	112.6	6.53	125.9	6.7	129.1	8.38	161.4

Source: derived on the basis of multiplying elasticity by .25 with each increasing level of GDP.

The sensitivity Index reveals that with every increase of .25 in railways freight elasticity, the expected potential rate of growth of railways' GDP increases by 3 per cent. Expecting within the range of 3 to 9 or even10 per cent increase in growth potential i.e., multiplying GDP by .25 to .9 keeps the system of expected railways GDP under control. Beyond this limit, it is disturbing and seems to be unattainable. When elasticity reaches unity i.e. 1, even a smaller increase of .25 in elasticity makes a lot of difference. It increases unexpectedly high rate i.e. 25 percent to 56 and to 61 percent and over estimates the potential growth. In developing economies the potential growth rate of railways freight elasticity comes closer to unity (but not exactly unity) because of the infrastructural deficiency and lack of 'free market' interaction in fixing freight rates for goods or other allied services (see table - 4). The potential growth rate should be estimated with a little less than unit elasticity as a maximum potential to be acquired. It is also interesting to note that with increase in GDP, the sensitivity index of elasticity does not move faster i.e. greater GDP does not necessarily need greater elasticity. It also indicates that multiplying GDP with high rated elasticity is not justifiable for calculating potential growth.

Elasticity to GDP—Eleventh Plan Projections: A Realistic Approach.

The Working Group Report[7] on railways eleventh plan projections for freight business has been realistic in adopting elasticity to GDP unlike White Paper which has used overrated elasticity to create intentionally the situation of 'below par for the entire period' of the predecessor's regime (2004-09). As late as 2007 for the eleventh plan (2007-12), the Working Group adopted the transport elasticity as .72 and .87 within the permissible, realistic and unbiased range and projected the potential growth rate of railways freight business. It has developed four scenarios accepting two ranges of GDPs and elasticities. Firstly, GDP growth rate as 8 percent and transport elasticity as .72. Again, GDP growth rate as 10 percent and elasticity as .72. Secondly, it has used 8 percent growth rate of GDP with .87 transport elasticity and also GDP growth rate as 10 percent, along with elasticity as .87. The following Table 6 containing elasticity to GDP ratio as used by Working Group explains the correct and realistic approach (*See Eleventh Five Year Plan: Railways Working Group Report*).

Why did White Paper not create at least two- three scenarios before declaring 'below par' achievements of the predecessor? Why did it stick to 'highrated' elasticity and only one scenario for the assessment of the period 2004 -2009? It is obvious; White Paper has no agenda except downsizing the achievements of the predecessor. The consultant should have gone through various plausible elasticities calculations to GDP (as has been done in assessing sensitivity index in the present study) before using the maximum high rated elasticity which so far has not been used by the railways. Before bringing out White Paper the present incumbent should have consulted railways' own body - the working group - on eleventh plan projections which has used realistic elasticity and worked it out within the range of one to four scenarios.

Table - 6 Example of forecast of Traffic–Different Scenarios with Realistic Elaticity

(Tonnes and NTKMs) Eleventh Plan Projections.

Year	*Scenario M Tonnes*	*1* BTK Ms*	*Scenario M. Tonnes*	*2** BTK Ms*	*Scenario M. tonnes*	*3*** BTK-Ms*	*Scenario M. tonnes*	*4**** BTKMS*
2006-07	688	457	704	472	748	497	765	508
2007-08	737	487	765	511	801	532	832	552
2008-09	789	520	833	554	858	570	906	602
2009-10	845	554	907	600	918	610	986	655
2010-11	905	591	988	651	984	653	1074	713
2011-12	971	631	1079	708	1055	701	1173	779

Source: *Eleventh Five Year Plan, Railways Working Group Report.*

*GDP growth 8 percent, Rail Transport Elasticity .72 ** GDP growth 10 per cent, Rail Transport Elasticity .72 *** GDP 8 per cent, Rail Transport Elasticity .87 ****GDP growth 10 percent, Rail Transport Elasticity. 87.

Here the transport elasticity has been used as .72 and .87 and GDP as 8 and 10 percent by the Working Group of the railways for the Eleventh Plan which is realistic in approach unlike White Paper using highly overrated (1.25) elasticity.

White Paper vs. Cash Surplus

Turnaround has been seen by the new incumbent of Rail Bhavan as a process of halting the sustained campaign of 'privatizing'[8] the railways through piecemeal methods (Ministry of Railways, 2009b: 51, para 2.3.6)). Wherefrom she got this idea? Which theory stipulates turnaround going against liberalization? On the other hand, one should realize that the very concept of turnaround is 'corporate oriented'. In an exceptional way it has been applied by Prof. Raghuram to public sector economy like the railways for the first time. This has been the reason that many of the professionals at Rail Bhavan have not understoond its real import and perhaps due to the lack of knowledge they have brought this wrong idea that 'turnaround is a process of halting privatization'. The new incumbent has accepted that the operational as well as financial performance of the railways in the past five-year period has been satisfactory; doubts have been expressed about the 'quantum' of cash surpluses. Therefore, the issue is not that no progress has been made, but 'abounding' surplus has not been created. The turnaround has fallen short of her expectations. Which is why she cries, "Where are the funds and surpluses"? All that is available is growing expenditure of Pay Commission expenses and insatiate desire of increased pay, pension and appropriation of amount to various funds created by the railways. In anguish, she has started slashing whatever the surpluses have been left by redefining and re-interpreting the terms which add or reduce the cash balances. How can one come to the conclusion unless the concepts are clear? There are hosts of concepts which need to be understood before making calculations.

Table-7 'Understanding Railways' Surplus

Railways' Surplus According to the predecessor and as approved by CAG and Finance Department	*Surplus According to the 'present incumbent's 'Consultant' not approved by Railways' CAG and Finance Department*
Surplus = Gross Traffic Income (+ OLSL + Misc. Receipts) - Expenditure (excluding CCLC). But including OLSL, Appropriation to Pension Fund, Miscellaneous Expenditure, Interest on Fund Balances.	Surplus = Gross Traffic Income (-OLSL) + (- Misc. Receipts) – Expenditure (including CCLC, PCLC, A Appropriation to Pension Fund and Misc. Expenditure.

OLSL (Operating Losses on Strategic Lines). CCLC (capital component of lease charge) PCLC (principal component of lease charges)

The concept of surplus was the peculiarity of railways finance. It originated from the cash generated before dividend and investible surplus and was presented in a new format in the explanatory memorandum of the budget for 2007-08. The concept was the derived performance indicator (DPI) which showed the cash generated by the railways from operations and other activities earned on Fund balances, appropriation to DRF and other railway funds.

Both the concepts – Surplus and Investible Surplus – were meant to serve railways own purpose to justify that like other corporate units, it also generated surpluses reflecting railways' finances in commercial accounting terms and could be presented as Cash Surplus before dividend and investible surplus. The railways as a public sector was least bothered for the payment of dividend because it was a nominal amount and based on the fixed rate (of interest) and easily appropriated. As far as the investible surplus was concerned, it was based on railways own interpretation of various concepts like operating losses on strategic lines, interest on pension fund and the payment of deferred dividend. These items were subtracted from cash surplus to arrive at investible surplus.

But White Paper had adopted an exercise by which the cash surplus was reduced in three stages from Rs. 88669 to Rs. 71663 to

Rs. 62363 and to Rs. 39411, and the investible surplus from Rs. 66804 to Rs. 52520 to Rs.43220 and to Rs. 20268. It was a deliberate attempt to re-process through an iterative system. The total working expenditure increased and surplus decreased in all the three stages.

What was most disparaging was the 'absence' of the page no. 2, table 1(a) in the explanatory memorandum on the railways budget 2010-11which used to be there for the last three years. The page no.2 which was there in explanatory memorandum in 2007-08, 2008-09, and 2009-10 is missing in 2010-11. The concept of cash surplus and investible surplus had been done away with and a new concept of 'Excess' had been introduced signifying something narrow in outlook and approach.

The then incumbent of Rail Bhavan (2009-11) was alleged to be guilty of breach of privilege and her predecessor had every right to make a case in the Parliament before the privilege committee against the 'so called' assessment of the years 2004 -2009 of the railways. But it was another matter that he did not want to do so.

Explanatory note:

There were only two accounting changes introduced between 2005 and 2008: First, modification in accounting with respect to lease charges and second, reimbursement of losses by the public exchequer accruing from the use and maintaining strategic railway lines called OLSL (Operating Losses on Strategic Lines). It was the practice adopted by the railways that all lease charges were recorded in accounts as revenue expenditure. But with revised method the Interest Component of Lease Charges is recorded in operating expenses (Ordinary Working Expenses: OWE), while the Capital Component of Lease is recorded as capital expenditure. Thus, this part is deducted from calculation of the total expenditure. As regards the operating losses on strategic lines, the amount reimbursed on account of this was earlier recorded as reduction in dividend calculation. But now it is included in Sundry earnings or to say that it is calculated as a part of income. Likewise, earlier the interest on Fund Balances was not recorded as earnings but now it is calculated for cash surplus before dividend. All such changes have been approved by the CAG and the Finance Department of the government of India. Any doubts created about these changes are useless except for making false propaganda against the leader of the turnaround.

Table-8 Financial Conflict of Cash Surplus 2004-2009

(Figures as worked out in the White Paper) Rs. in crore

Sl.	*Items*	*Predecessor's approved by CAG*	*Present Incumbents's not approved CAG*	*Variation Impact*
1.	Gross Traffic Receipts	316175	316175	Nil
1a.	Add Operating Losses	882	(Less)-1283	-2165
2.	Misc. Receipts	8908	8907	-1
3.	Total (1+1a+2)	325965	323799	-2166
4.	Ordinary Working Exp.	201234	201234	Nil
4a.	(LESS) Capital Component of Lease Charges	-1678	(ADD) 6778	8456
4b.	(ADD) Operating Losses on Strategic Lilnes	309	309	Nil
5.	Appropriation to Pension Fund	39495	39495	Nil
6.	Misc Expenditure	2074	4320	-2246
7.	Total (4+4a+4b+5+6)	241433	255136	-10702
8.	Interest on Fund Balances	4138	Nil	-4138
9.	Cash Surplus Before Dividend	88669	71663	-17006

Source: Compiled from Explanatory Memorandum of the Budgets (2004 to 2009) and White Paper issued by the Ministry of Railways, 2009).

The table - 8 is a consolidated form of two tables exhibited in the White Paper (pp. 50, 52). It gives a picture how approved and unapproved items have been mixed together to create statistical chaos especially in cash surplus. The predecessor's items and figures are approved by CAG and have no ambiguity. The figures as mentioned by

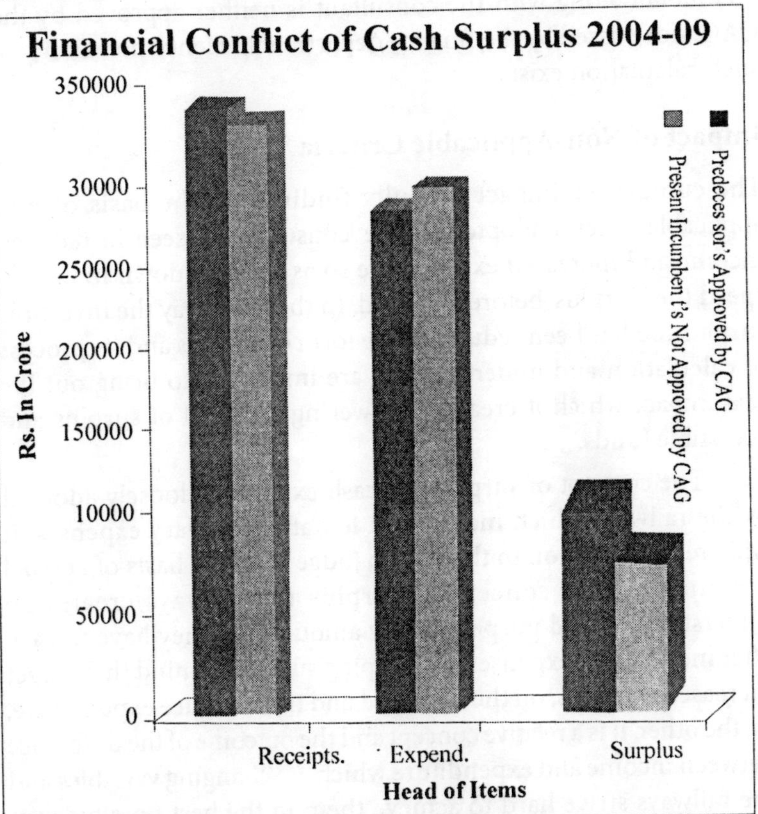

Figure 3 : Financial Conflict of Cash Surplus 2004-2009.

the present incumbent or the consultant are not approved. There is a great variation impact and the cash surplus has been reduced by Rs. 17006 crore. It is easy for a consultant, paid for the job, to do so. He has adopted notional concepts to reduce total receipts by Rs. 2165 crore and increased expenditure by Rs. 10702 crore. Apart from that interest on fund balances to the tune of Rs. 4138 crore have not been included in income or revenue with the result the cash surplus before dividend reduced further to the level of Rs. 71663 crore. The impact of reduction on cash surplus is heavy because it has been affected at both the ends - decreasing revenue and increasing expenditure. The exercise done by the new incumbent along with the consultant is neither approved by the CAG, nor passed by the finance department. Hence no validity of such calculation exists.

Impact of Non-Applicable Criteria

The cumulative impact of faulty findings on the basis of non applicable criteria adopted by the 'consultant' is seen in reduced income and increased expenditure so as to bring down in double speed the 'Surplus' before dividend. In the same way the investible surplus too has been reduced. The form of surplus and its process of calculation and understanding are important to bring out the real impact which it creates in lowering the level of surplus and investible funds.

The concept of surplus is a cash expression loosely adopted by the railways which means cash left after ordinary expenses. It will create confusion to those who judge it on the basis of accrual accounting. The concept of surplus for railways creates an understanding and purpose of the amount that they have to earn after meeting the expenses. By keeping surplus in mind they target increased earnings, on the one hand and try to reduce expenditure, on the other. It is a relative concept and the outcome of the difference between income and expenditure which are changing variables and the railways strive hard to achieve them in the best possible way. They know the amount of dividend to be paid on the fixed basis to the Ex- Chequer. Therefore, they calculate surplus before dividend. The target fixed by the railways is not the payment of dividend but the earnings minus expenditure i.e., surplus.

The then incumbent of Rail Bhavan and her associates targeted predecessor's 'surplus' creating mess of the situation by reducing it at different levels till it reaches minimum (tending to zero) and justifying their point of view of low 'quantum' and halting ways of 'privatizing' railways through 'so called' turnaround. What they expected of the railways during the predecessor's period was not very clear, but by the analysis produced in White Paper it seems she never liked the hyped position of railways as presented by the turnaround. For her turnaround was a myth. Therefore, she started questioning the 'quantum' of the surplus and through the consultant tried to present 'faulty findings'. The methods used were conceptually not clear and the findings were based on non-applicable criteria. Their analysis applied to three basic areas - elasticities, surpluses and ratios. The elasticity concept has already been dealt with. Here, we take the concept of surplus and its faulty calculation done by the consultant. Since its cumulative effect shown in the White Paper is highly detrimental, its process has to be checked, curbed and resisted.

Surplus to railways does not mean 'profits' in the strict sense of the term. The railways have its 'cash based' accounting system and any attempt to compare it with 'accrual' process would create problems. The process of surplus as presented by the new 'guard' of the railways in White Paper is the outcome of the above mismatched concepts. There are two different types of financial approaches. Both the stalwarts are championing their own accounting streams. The predecessor is sticking to his own earnings before interest, taxes, depreciation and amortization in business language. It is called EBITDA accounting system and is mostly used for public sector accounting and the railways finances are based on such procedures. The then incumbent of Rail Bhavan along with consultant brought out the company accounting process - the old concept of profit after tax i.e., PAT accounting system. It means that there are procedural differences in dealing with the finances. As a public sector the railways so far have used the accounting pattern as the government uses it i.e., on 'cash basis' where income and expenses are charged to the books when they actually happen. The glaring example is of 'depreciation reserve fund'. Notionally, it forms the part of surplus until it is appropriated to that account. Moreover, this depreciation fund ultimately becomes the part of investment and planning. The railways have its own way of accounting. There are so many other items which have come to such faulty scanning and the 'surplus' has been downsized or reduced from Rs. 88669 crore to Rs. 71663 crore and continued to be reduced to Rs. 62363 crore to Rs. 39411 and so on. The investible surplus in the same way was reduced from Rs. 66804 crore to Rs. 52520 crore to Rs. 43220 crore to Rs 20268 crore and....

Why such faulty calculations have been done? *How can these be done on accrual basis when order for payment on account of Pay Commission itself has come in 2008 and DRF was never taken as an expenditure on accrual basis.* It has only one intention - to downgrade the achievements of the predecessor. But it does not reflect the real situation. It only confuses and creates conceptual chaos in the minds of the persons who deal with such matters. The railways accounting during the period 2004-09 has been properly approved by the CAG, the Finance Commissioner, and the appropriation accounts under the signature of Railway Board Chairman has been tabled in both the Houses of the Parliament.

A private 'consultant' has no right to overrule the accounting procedure already adopted by the railways and as approved and permitted by CAG and the Finance Commissioner. The White Paper on the other hand lacks vetting by the Union Cabinet or CAG and warranted breach of privilege.

The White Paper has faulty findings, misinterpreting the concepts and mismatching the government and private financing procedures. Liberalization or privatization does not mean changing the pattern whimsically and applying one's own system to downsize the 'approved methods' and the results. The following facts may be noted:

1. The consultant has used double edged sword in slashing down the surpluses. Firstly, by reducing the size of income and secondly, by increasing the size of expenditure so that the balance which is called 'surplus' may get reduced in a double speed. The consultant has adopted his own way of interpreting 'interest on funds' or 'lease rentals', 'operating losses on strategic

lines', adding or subtracting items to calculate ordinary working expenses (OWE), miscellaneous receipts and expenditure etc. This has not only reduced the surplus but created mess of financial management of the railways. Is the present incumbent ready to accept all what has been adopted by the 'consultant' for applying them to future accounting process of the railways? If so why she has not applied the same schemes in her budget presented to the Parliament? It is easy to criticize others on non-applicable criteria, but following the same path for self judgment is very difficult. In such a situation the accounting process adopted during 2004-2009 was correct and the same pattern has to be followed further.

2. The component of lease charges (Rs.-1678 crore), which was to be subtracted from OWE was removed by the consultant intentionally so that it may reduce the operating ratio. On the other hand, principal component of lease charges (Rs. 6778 crore) have been added to expenditure in order to increase the size of expenditure and thus reducing the income, ultimately downsizing the 'surplus'.
3. The operating losses on strategic lines (Rs. 882 crore) which were to be added to Gross Traffic Receipts (GTR) have been cut off and further reduced to the level of Rs. -1293 so as to bring down the GTR and directly and indirectly the reduction of 'surplus' so created.
4. The consultant has made the mess of the miscellaneous expenditure and increased it to Rs. 4320 crore. Thus, creating an extra expenditure of Rs. 2246 crore. The total expenditure has been increased by about Rs. 10702 crore and total income reduced by Rs. 2166 crore creating a great gap in income minus expenditure equal to the level of Rs. 17006 crore and finally reducing the surplus from Rs. 88669 crore to Rs. 71663 crore only on faulty grounds by subtracting income or increasing expenditure, citing concepts like - OLSL, Principal Component of Lease Charges, and totally evaporating the 'interest on fund balances' to the tune of Rs. 4138 crore and bringing down the balance between income and expenditure, thus reducing the surplus.

The railway 'surplus' has been played like a shuttle cock by the present incumbent of Rail Bhavan. At each stroke it was hard hit until smashed and grounded.

The matter did not end here. The present incumbent of the Rail Bhavan further reduced investible surplus from Rs. 66804 crore to Rs. 52520 crore and to Rs 43220 crore till it reached its lowest Rs. 20268 crore. On which ground this had been done? The consultant had an opportunity and the cause of Sixth Central Pay Commission expenditure to cite as an example. But the point which was missed by the present incumbent was that it was her predecessor who enabled her to pay the arrears and pension. Had he not earned surplus, from where she could have settled the matter of Sixth CPC expenses? She knew this fact but directly or indirectly did not want to relate the credit to her predecessor. Perhaps she had forgotten the time of Fifth Pay Commission, when she could not pay even the dividend to the central government. This time her predecessor had managed to pay dividend along with Sixth CPC expenses.

The Indian Railways have yet not introduced accrual accounting but the consultant has recast the accounts of last five years (2004-09) on non-applicable criteria and has tried to underestimate the predecessor's contribution. It must be kept in mind that in railways depreciation contribution is held as a fund and used as an 'investment' for replacement and renewal of assets and which is also treated as an expenditure under planning process. It is therefore an integral part of surplus and cannot be reduced as has been done in White Paper.

The White Paper must come under scanner of the Privilege Committee of the Parliament as well as the Railways Convention Committee for a proper review and check up and should not go unchallenged. It has damaged more than benefitted the railways.

Nothing can be more objectionable than the ratios which the consultant has used to downgrade railways' performance not only of the period 2004-09, but of many ministers and top officials of the past two decades. Even such type of erratic study was not done by highly critical report submitted by the Expert Group during

Nitish Kumar's stint. The sole purpose of the consultant was to bring the leader of the turnaround in the fold, but in doing so the ratios adopted were too harsh and had never been used by the analysts of the railways. The whole study took a long jump, enfolding even the present incumbent's past stint (1999-2001) and others into suspicion. The only question to be asked was: why the new incumbent of Rail Bhavan succumbed to such faulty findings of the consultant? But she had 'celebrated' the outcome of the White Paper - rather rejoiced over it and derived sadistic pleasure. The consultant too, in league with her, was equally responsible for the faulty findings. The ratios which he had used had never been applied in performance analysis of any of the public sector of India. However, on the basis of the ratios which were in vogue in the analytical inquiry of the railways, the predecessor stood the best so far and might be called the highest scorer.

Predecessor: The Highest Scorer

After Independence, covering more than half of a century of the railways financial history indicating gross traffic earnings, it is the leader of turnaround who scores the highest amount of earnings to his credit. No wonder that he is called the Tendulkar of Indian railways' innings. Two basic indicators of profitability, the operating ratio and the return-on-capital, which go in the favour of the predecessor, are 75.9 and 20.7 respectively. The ratio of surplus to the capital-at-charge and investment from capital fund (creating excess or shortfall) is positive and highest at 15.2. These figures belong to the year 2007-08 representing the best of his regime and the best in the railways history. The predecessor not only rescued the railways from being declared as a bankrupt institution, but also brought popularity, prestige and power to the institution which he served for full five years (2004-09) devotedly and worked whole heartedly occupied at Rail Bhavan. Perhaps his devotion to railways was so passionate that his visits to Bihar slowed down with the result that he lost the past quantum of MPs and the seat of railways too. No minister of UPA government of first term suffered so much loss as did the leader of the turnaround. As if it was not enough, our Hon'ble PM who shared a page as a foreword to the book *'Bankruptcy to Billions - How Indian Railways Transformed'* highlighting *UPA (I)*' s achievement of the railways is mum on the subject. Apart from politics, the intellectual propriety demands that the predecessor should not be so marginalized at the hands of UPA (II). At least he must keep the honour of those words which bear the testimony to the turnaround of the railways under his signature; otherwise the history will not forgive him too... The following facts vindicate the predecessor's position:

1. That the predecessor's investment for the tune of Rs. 57000 crore could not have been possible had he not created surplus at all.
2. That all accounting procedures were transparent as they were carried out under the supervision of the finance commissioner and the Comptroller and Auditor General (CAG).
3. That the revised estimates of cumulative cash surplus amount to Rs. 88669 crore to be bracketed with Sixth Finance Commission expenses and re-worked with heads like interest on fund balances amounting to Rs. 4138 crore, principal component of lease charges as Rs. 6778 crore and losses on strategic line valued at Rs. 1280 crore.
4. That the leader of the turnaround had done it without taking any loan, but on the other hand the present incumbent has acquired the loan of Rs.18000 crore from the ministry of finance in the very first year (2009) of her regime to work out her dream projects.
5. That the very fact which has been missed out in the White Paper is the predecessor's initiative to stop the corrupt practice of overloading the wagons and consequently to legalize it (as it was a very old practice). It earned for the railways in the very first year (2004-05) Rs. 5000 crore by this measure only. Along with it , by changing wagon turn round time from 7 to 5 days, reduction in train examination time and other simple measures, the predecessor added another 2500 crore to the earning of the department. Till that period no 'creative accounting' was adopted.

6. The lament over the pressure on rail tracks and their premature replacement was unwarranted for the trains were already running overloaded since long due to the corrupt practices and money shared among the involved persons and the authorities. The increase in axle load by ex-minister (predecessor) was officially adopted in consultation with the railways authorities including the Railway Board and RDSO and also after a rigorous checking and going through the workshop practices of all the concerned zonal railways' experts verifying tracks, bridges and wagons. What was wrong in that measure?
7. The financial factor so involved, as said to have inflated the surpluses, is the outcome of the 'creative accounting' adopted on the lines of financial standards which normally change from time to time in consultation with the convention committee along with finance commissioner and taking ultimately CAG's approval. It was officially recognized and accepted.
8. Between two stalwarts – the war of words had erupted and neither on financial ground nor technical, the then incumbent of Rail Bhavan could make out her case to justify White Paper because it was the outcome of self contradictory process, signifying nothing except breaking down the working of systematic machinery of the railways.

The Prime Minister, Manmohan Singh, in his Foreword to the book *'Bankruptcy to Billions'*, has lauded the success of the Indian Railways during UPA's first term (See 'Foreword' in Kumar/ Mehrotra 2009a: xi-xii). The Railways by using existing resources has exhibited that it is as critical as adopting incremental investment to enhance capacity and productivity. It has been emphasized that the growth of the Railways is not just the outcome of the growing economy of the country, but its own efforts which brought fundamental changes in the way of functioning of the organization. However, the White Paper indicates that the Railways' economy has developed due to high growth of GDP only (White Paper, P. 14, "growth was mainly on account of the boom in the economy").

Table-9 Predecessor's Score Card 2004 to 2009: Cash Surplus *(in crore of rupees)*

Sl.N.	*Head of items*	*2004-05*	*2005-06*	*2006-07*	*2007-08*	*2008-09*
1.	Gross Traffic Receipts (GTR)	47370.00	54491.00	6273.50	71720.06	79862.00
2.	Miscellaneous Receipts	1676.00 291.00	1824.00 282.00	2045.00	1556.51	1797.00
3.	Total Receipts (TR)	49337.00	56597.00	64785.84	73276.57	81659.00
4.	Ordinary Warking Expenses (OWE)	33388.88	35030.00	37432.53	41033.17	54349.00
5.	Appropriation to to Pension Fund	6670.00	6940.00	7416.00	7979.00	10490.00
6.	Other Misce-llaneous Expenditure	-1678.00 +297.00	329.00	417.45	433.59	597.00
7.	Total 4 to 6	38677.88	42299.00	45265.98	49445.76	65436.00
8.	Interest on Fund Balances	392.17	580.00	818.63	1175.38	1172.00
9.	Cash Surplus Before Dividend	11051.29	14878.00	20338.49	25006.19	17395.00

Total: Rs 88668, Rs. 88669 Approx.

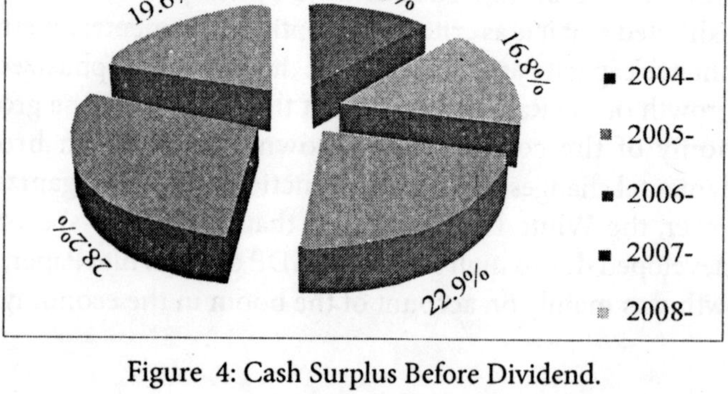

Figure 4: Cash Surplus Before Dividend.

The above Table – 9 indicates the amount of cash surplus created during the period of the predecessor i.e. from 2004 to 2009. It shows Rs. 88669 crore as generated in the past five years. With the change in the regime, the railways could not pick up the pace of earning revenue as was expected for the terminal year 2008-2009. The new incumbent of Rail Bhavan was in a different mood and trying to belittle the achievements of her predecessor. The variation in GTR in the year 2008-2009 was allowed to be minimized intentionally in comparison to previous years. Though the situation was conducive for generating more income, but on an average the earnings were reduced in 2008-2009 by more than Rs. 2000 crore. Moreover, other factors were brought forward to show that the surplus was illusive, unrealistic and generated through financial jugglery. Intentionally, the cash surplus was shown in the descending order to much lower level by indicating expenses on Sixth Pay Commission and enhanced appropriation to Deprecation Reserve Fund, Development Fund and Capital Fund etc.

It is an interesting point to note that in her budget speech for the year 2009-10 on July 3, 2009, the minister spoke at length about the performance for the year 2008-09 which actually belonged to the period of her predecessor. In order to take credit for good performance for that year she said in the Parliament, "Madam, despite the economic slowdown in the last financial year, the railways loaded 833MT of freight cargo which is a 5% growth over the previous year. Traffic receipts grew by 11% to reach Rs. 79862 crore. A saving of Rs. 676 crore was achieved in expenditure through stringent economy measures. Even after having distributed Rs 13600 crore towards implementationof Sixth Pay Commission recomm-endation the railways were successful in generating a cash surplus before dividend of Rs. 17395 crore after fulfilling their full dividend liability of Rs. 4717 crore..." At that point of time she accepted the existence of cash surplus before dividend for the year 2008-09 as approximately Rs. 17400 crore (or actually Rs. 17395 crore). Why then in White Paper earlier cash surpluses were not admitted, accepted and acknowledged which in total amounted to Rs. 88669 crore? The above Table 9, item no. 9 shows its break-up year wise from 2004-05 to 2008-09 giving true and acceptable picture. This happened because the White Paper - a made to order report- was produced by a consultant paid for the job who distorted the facts and misinterpreted the achievements of turnaround.

Footnotes

1. Ex-President, APJ Abdul Kalam started promoting the vision approach through his writings. He wrote *India 2020 A Vision for Millennium* published in 2002. Later, his mission was to infuse the idea of dreaming for India's future among the youths of the country and wrote several books including *'Target 3 Billion'* almost on the same pattern and message.
2. There is greater disparity among the various modes of transport in India and according to coefficient of variation calculated on the basis of CSO statistics relating to railways, roads, shipping and airways, there appears a considerable variation in percentage as 16.18, 23.4, 18.9 and 4.4 respectively.
3. W.W. Leontief who developed input-output model for measuring input coefficients and interdependence of sectors of the economy had also given a framework of transportation measurement. This had been developed and applied in Indian Railways transport services by S.R. Hashim with the help of (Late) Prof. P.N. Mathur of the University of Wales, UK.
4. This stands for Mamata Banerjee who missed to notice the hidden agenda of White Paper. The World Bank lobby tried to infuse the idea of de-nationalizing the railways, on the one hand and Expert Group report tried to restructure the railways, on the other. Both steps were against the national interest and the economy.
5. In White Paper issued by the railways, the figures appearing on page 4, col. 5, Table-1, indicate percentage of shortfall as per expected elasticity. In the present study instead of shortfall an increasing percentage has been shown. This calculation has been done on the basis of realistic elasticity as multiplied by GDP. This brings out a correct potential growth rate of the railways.
6. There are various types of elasticities used in establishing economic relationships. The White Paper has not specifically mentioned about the type of elasticity used. No mention has been made whether it is point elasticity, arc elasticity or cross elasticity. If one accepts the analysis on the basis of price-demand relationship, the other situations are left without any explanations. The elasticity by the White Paper has been used

lopsidedly and many aspects of railways elasticity in relation to substitutes and complementary goods have been left untouched and unanswered.

7. The railways working group formed for projecting freight business was very realistic in approach to elasticity and GDP. Why this model was neglected by White Paper when the study was already made and accepted as a standard form for applying in projecting goods services.
8. This approach is erroneous. There is no such theory which negates turnaround's liberal and progressive views. How the White Paper has come to the conclusion that turnaround is meant for unbundling privatization of the railways?

◆◆◆

5

Railways' Empire: 'The War of Roses'

The Indian railway has a unique position in the life of the nation. It stretches far and wide touching the ocean shores of the Southern states to the high Himalayas of the North and running from the golden sands of Thar of the West to the deep forest of Sunderbans of the East and blue hills and red rivers of the North-Eastern states of India. The Indian railway is so huge and great in size, covering the vast land areas of the country, that it is called a nation within a nation; administered like a 'kingdom' through a set up at Rail Bhavan headed by the minister for the railways wielding no less power than the 'king' of a ruling state. "It is easy to rule the railways than Bihar" admitted the leader of turnaround and added, "at least one has full freedom to work (like a King) with no opposition to pull him down and disturb smooth running of the government" (Misra, 2009d: 226). The new incumbent of Rail Bhavan, joined after the leader of turnaround, in the same vein, was so enamoured of 'The Railways' Empire' that she was adamant to obtain the portfolio as a pre-condition to support UPA (II) regime. On the other hand, the railways had their own problems of operational and administrative nature. They were highly defamed for derailments, collisions and sabotages. It was difficult to complete one's tenure as minister unblemished unless he was truly lucky not to face such calamities. Lal Bahadur Shastri had to resign due to the railway's erratic nature and vagaries of its functioning.

The Former Minister Ruled Over the Railways (2004-09)

Although the past of the predecessor was marred with the shadows of his political ups and downs but his stint as the minister for the railways soared high like a star in fame and achievement who ruled over the 'Empire' like a king, served like a devotee and cared like a loyalist. The railways achieved turnaround from bad performing unit to a good and efficiently performing business entity by increasing productivity, profitability and proficiency. Needless to say, that his passionate, progressive and practical approach brought fruits in the form of enhancing the railways prestige, power and potential. 'He is the monarch of what he surveys' used to be the dictum during his tenure at Rail Bhavan.

The Empire of the Railways became the contention of clashes between the loyalists of the predecessor and maniacs of the new incumbent. Presently, the politics out-manoeuvered the leader of turnaround in such a way that he lost his 'kingdom' as well as 'courtiers' who supported him at Rail Bhavan. On the other hand, the new incumbent's mysterious move of issuing White Paper generated 'the war of words' to fight against the justification of 'turnaround' true or false. There is the semblance of 'dynastic war' between two stalwarts belonging to two states and two parties. Politically motivated, this fight stands for a show down of the rival's strength, power and efficient ways as 'worst' and prove one's own failing regime as the 'best'. Who wins this war? It is difficult to say, but one can imagine the belligerent mood of both the parties that seemingly prevail in the political firmament like that of 'The War of Roses' - not necessarily to defeat or capture the 'Kingdom' but to impose the supremacy of one over the other.

It is symbolic situation like that of 'The War of Roses'[1], not in reality but in thought process and imagination. It seems to be meaningful in essence and purpose. In democracy people do not have despots or despotic wars; there are no kings and no kingdoms 'or dynastic fights over 'The Empire'. But one thing is common between a 'kingdom' and a 'republic'. It is the power game that brings them closer for all the practical purposes. Instead of plots, rebellions and battles, democracies fight for the power through ballots. Interestingly, both the stalwarts are fighting for their 'empires' of the railways in a different style. Whereas the new incumbent has regained it after eight years, the former minister got it and lost within five years. It looks like the process of gaining, losing and regaining just as the historic 'The War of Roses' as if their rise and fall in a continued war so occurred in the British history.

The New Incumbent Gets it Again (May 2009– May 2011)

It was after eight years of desperately longing for the railways that the new incumbent acquired it but not so easily or effortlessly. At the time of disbursement of the portfolios, it was the PM who had prerogative to allot according to his will and the person's ability to hold it, apart from other political factors involved in it. It is political audacity to ask and bargain for a particular ministry. But the new incumbent was adamant to obtain, rather trying to grab the railways. "Only railways" was her conditionality factor for supporting the UPA(II)'s government. Though it was quite embarrassing, she insisted to settle it with the PM and it was she who had to feather her own nest by having the railways - almost a pre-planned strategy. In reality she had axe to grind in clinging to the railways.

The railways run forward as well as backward with the same ease. The present incumbent put it into back gear. The speed was lowered, the estimates declined and the surpluses reduced. All this was done with a purpose. Making realistic in the real sense, her budget was an antithetical to turnaround - a deliberate effort to cut one's own pocket and cry: "where are the surpluses"? A quick survey of the previous year was made to order and she disparaged, "The loading fell short in 2008-2009 to its target by 17 MT i.e., 833 MT instead of 850 MT. The revenue expected from commercial utilization of railways' surplus lands did not materialize".[2] The new incumbent of Rail Bhavan later reviewed her predecessor's estimates for 2009-10 and called them 'unrealistically high targets'. Although she said that the predecessor could not achieve the freight cargo target of 850 MT but it was short only by 2%. Is it such a great fall of percentage to decry? The cargo rate of growth was 5% more than the previous year. The performance in 2008-09 was not so bad to be dismissed as a dismal achievement. The total traffic receipts grew during that period by 11.4% to reach Rs. 79862 crore.

There was saving in expenditure of Rs. 676 crore and a surplus before dividend of Rs. 17400 crore was created, even after having disbursed Rs. 13600 crore towards implementation of Sixth Pay Commission recommendations. The railways were able to maintain internal generation for investment at Rs. 12681 crore and also fulfilled dividend liability of Rs. 4717 crore in 2008-09.

The new incumbent of Rail Bhavan has based all her estimates, even strategies and targets on the past achievements of her predecessor especially on 2008-09 budget performance. While presenting the budget for 2009-10 she unnecessarily targeted her predecessor, decried his achievements by mentioning very clearly 'unrealistic high estimates' of the interim budget submitted in February 2009 and announced to bring out a White Paper, thus generating a controversy. Issuing White Paper, on what? Bringing out on Railways' infirmities or discrediting her predecessor's regime? Or making a case as an anti-thetical view of turnaround? It was difficult for the new incumbent of Rail Bhavan to substantiate charges against the predecessor on flimsy grounds. And when on 18th December, 2009, she presented before the Parliament the White Paper to vitiate the atmosphere of growth and turnaround of the railways, she found no real takers of the story and it ended in a fiasco. The predecessor said that it was neither white nor green paper. It was black or a blank paper and the media expressed doubts over its validity. Since the financial facts, figure, accounts and balance sheets of the former minister were verified through finance ministry and also approved by the CAG, it left no occasion for the new incumbent of Rail Bhavan to take this matter any further. Why did she not make it a point for a full discussion on the White Paper? Lok Sabha neither pondered over it nor did it discuss for even a moment. White Paper was distributed among the members of the Parliament just like other common material is made available to them. It was neither printed for sale nor was it given to general public for the fear of adverse comments. One cannot mislead the nation by empty slogans. It is perhaps the seventh time that such a White Paper has been issued. It has become ritual with the Indian railways to issue a White Paper, revise it and issue again, but with no intention to follow up seriously. This time when she has issued White Paper along with Vision 2020, it carried a great contradiction in itself. You demolish your past and at the same time want to build up an edifice on the same for the future growth, how can you do so? It is like cutting someone's legs and at the same time expecting him to stand. How is it possible? One should be clear in his approach. Either he should say that the predecessor has mismanaged everything and he wants to start afresh or begin with zero bases not accepting any thing achieved by the former minister. But accepting half of the predecessor's working and denying the rest would not be justified. One may decry the years of the predecessor (2004-2009) including the year 2009 because he has a sway over it and then he may find a Vision 2020 accepting the same accounting model. Growth system is not meant for mesmerizing people, programmes or creating magical influence. It has to be brought in as a continuous process. The very fact that the new incumbent of Rail Bhavan has brought about her Vision 2020 indicates that the railways has a potential, that it has taken a turnaround and sustained during the predecessor's regime and that the Vision 2020 is attached to a creative process of growth and development. Railways' Vision 2020 is a branch grafted on the predecessor's trunk or in other words, the branches of the tree are growing with sustenance from the roots created by the predecessor during his stint as the railway minister — 2004-09. The new incumbent has inherited the best of her predecessor's achievements and the best of the railways, otherwise she would have been pushed back to the situation of 1999-2001 when she could not even manage to pay dividend. With the former minister (of UPA's first term), the railways had managed to pay regularly the dividends along with expenses of Sixth Pay Commission. How could she do it had her predecessor not earned the requisite amount?

The new incumbent has reviewed and changed estimates of interim budget in the mid-course. But when she fixed her freight target for 2009-10 as 882 MT or fixed target to earn Rs 58525 crore and Rs 24301 crore from goods and passenger services respectively, what was the strength which supported her? It was nothing but former minister's (predecessor's) sustained growth and strategies. And yet she has to develop a lot of infrastructure, organizational system and control over expenses. A little lack of attention would bring her down the stream. The new incumbent of Rail Bhavan very 'proudly' took the advantage of railways' earning prior to her joining as a minister and said in the Parliament, "Madam, I am proud that despite the combined impact of increase in working expenses due to Sixth Pay Commission and sluggishness in earnings due to economic slowdown in the economy (it is meant for nation's economy, not railways'), railways paid their full dividend liability of Rs. 4717 crore in 2008-09 (it is predecessor's period which she is proud of : see budget speech July 2009-10 p. 21 para 61) and will pay even higher dividend of Rs. 5479 crore in 2009-10 (on whose strength?)". It was clearly on the predecessor's thrust into the railways earnings that the new incumbent was taking advantage of, as half of the financial year was already managed by the former minister before she took over the charge, in the mid way in May, 2009. She should not blow hot and cold in the same breath and must recognize her predecessor's contribution to the railways' earning and surplus.

Two Stalwarts: The War of Words

It seems that between two stalwarts, there is a war of words - a fight of numbers, facts and figures. It is a war of accounting process. It has been erupted and will continue. The former minister or the predecessor is not alone in this battle. The present incumbent has posed a challenge to all the thinking people. They are the people who don't fight for land; they don't support land grabbers and they are not to fight TATA to shift Nano to Gujarat. They are the people who know accounting. They know how to bring turnaround to a firm. They have studied the achievements of the past years (2002-09) and still have capacity to accept the challenge. They are the people best in managerial capabilities in the world gifted with depth of knowledge from Harvard in the West to the Insead in the East. They are here to reassert the historical turnaround of the railways. They have taken every step to analyze, verify and interpret the railways finances during the past regime (2004 - 09). The railways have re-emerged during the present decade. The following facts have to be worked out at the academic and the financial level to provide the answer.

1. Were the railways at the cross roads at the beginning of this century?
2. Was the new incumbent's first stint (1999-2001) as railway minister quite fruitful?
3. How did the Rakesh Mohan Committee Report describe the railways?
4. What immediate steps did Nitish Kumar take to check the impending danger of bankruptcy?
5. What steps did the former minister take during his UPA's first regime to create turnaround?
6. Had the leader of the turnaround changed the railways' functioning from bad performance to good performance?
7. What did hon'ble PM Manmohan Singh write in his foreword to *'Bankruptcy to Billions'* about the railways?
8. What was the hidden agenda behind 'White Paper'?

Even if the answers to the above questions are found satisfactory, the fight is not going to be finished. It has many dimensions of the problem. Presently, it is lull before the storm - tranquility before turbulence. The new incumbent of Rail Bhavan has surprised everybody by her audacity by presenting the White Paper. One can burn one's own house and rejoice over the fire. Well and good. But the person has no right to call up the fire brigade when there is no fire. White Paper presents the scenario of something which has not happened. The steps taken by the predecessor were decried on false ground. Logic behind criticism of turnaround was irrelevant. Actually, there was no occasion for White Paper to be issued. Has the railways been duped by the turnaround? Is the money missing? Was turnaround a scam? Let the new incumbent come out in clear terms - Yes or No? Don't be tricky, mysterious or malicious. Come with a clear heart. Does the railway balance sheet differ from RBI account books?

The historic 'Wars of Roses' were fought and continued between two 'dynasties' for thirty odd years. These wars were fought distinctly in phases. The scale of fighting and extent of disorder were expressed and written by various historians. Similarly, the War between two stalwarts would continue for long. What we see is just a prologue. Should the leader of the turnaround start enacting the first scene? Like 'Wars of Roses', this would also go into the history of railways as a long drawn war between two stalwarts, in the early decade of present century. This has to be fought to protect the honour, prestige and self respect and also to prove that there had happened turnaround during its leader's regime.

The new incumbent is an unstable politician since the days of her youth when she was a member of the Congress Party. She had never shown harmony or peaceful attitude. Pregnant with permanent political displeasure, the new incumbent has never been firm in her approach to political behaviour. She has developed a character which leads her to uncompromising situation (see how inappropriately and unnecessarily she brought out the White Paper; opted knowingly to abstain from Jyoti Basu's funeral showing open disrespect to the leader of her father's stature and defying even legal apparatus to join Lalgarh rally).[3] Disturbing the status quo has been her inner quality and this time her predecessor became a prey of her nature to receive a terrible bolt of her political thunder. Her White Paper is a hired project. She has hired the services of SS Kothari Mehta & Co for the inputs of the White Paper. It is made to order report and lakhs of rupees have been paid to the company for that purpose. The people in general and the employees of the railways in particular must know how public money is wasted and how 'made to order' report is presented to the Parliament only to misguide the innocent countrymen. Had there been the need of the White Paper as such to bring the railways working in order, the exercise would have been simply done by the railways staff without outsourcing the project. The White Paper has so deeply blemished the image of the railways which they had never experienced during the long history of their existence.

Footnotes

1. It had been symbolically used to indicate that the assertiveness of both the stalwarts was nothing less than the war of roses which were fought and continued between two dynasties for several years.
2. This refers to the speech of Mamata Banerjee for Railway Budget 2009-10 submitted to the Parliament on 3rd July 2009.
3. During her campaign against CPI (M) in West Bengal she was in extremely combating mood to dislodge the government. She defied many social norms, even organized the Lalgarh rally defying legal apparatus prevailing during that time.

◆◆◆

6

Indian Railways : Financial and Managerial Syndrome

Impediment to Financial Growth

The main impediment to growth of railways' finances is the lack of an independent authority to control and manage the system which looks after funds availability, functionality, investment and allocation of resources. This may further be attributed to inflexibility in free pursuance of business and decision making.

The railways runs as a government department with full and final control over most of its financial working leaving little scope for free and independent thinking for the managers and bosses at Rail Bhavan. It therefore cannot have the advantage which the corporate sector has in its independent working, implementing programmes and adopting plan of action. Nevertheless, one must not forget that the railways had survived historically a long past as a public sector, dashing out various constraints and critical junctures which came in the way to thwart progress. There was a purpose, need and aim behind this institution which ultimately organized itself as a public sector unit.

The railway transport business needs a great amount of capital to start with. And its gestation period is so long that rarely it is possible for a venture capitalist to dabble into its affair unless he is assured of honourable margin over the investment. This was true during the Raj and holds good even for the present. Much debate has been held about its public sector identity vs. corporatisation, but nothing concrete came out as a result for viable and acceptable system replacing the present status of the railways.

There are various maladies still surrounding the railways and arresting their working and progress.

The political interference i.e. directly by the minister and indirectly by the general ex-chequer is so great that at times the Railway Board feels itself a non-entity, unable to perform its own functions smoothly. Either the chairman or other members of the board have to follow the political decisions or just bypass their time and wait for the retirement. In both the cases, it is the railway which is hurt or in the larger context, the transport economy suffers. But who is to be blamed for this malady?

One can't dismantle the whole system of the railways as the Expert Group or other similar studies have suggested. One can't even go against the constitutional and statutory provisions made for conducting railways' business. The authority of the railway ministry and the minister as the supreme boss has to be honoured. The railway board has to perform its function and somebody should be accountable to the Parliament. To accept all these facts one has to change the mindset of the railways' employees and the Rail Bhavan bosses. They must realize that they are living in a democratic society where nearly thirty percent of the population forms the weaker section. They have to work for inclusive growth and look towards their brethren – the lowliest and the lost. The much acclaimed corporate sector does not understand the language of distributive economy, equality and social justice and work for only competitive advantage and profit even if it has to go for a cut-throat or devastating business activity.

The political interference may be positive as well as negative, but provides ample opportunities and options to deal with. If positive is given name A and negative as B, then the possibilities may be AA, AB, BA, and BB in terms of associative formulation. One can very easily accept a win-win (AA) position and discard BB by providing valid arguments. For the rest of options, the possibility of more positive and less negative scenarios may be chosen. One has to change the mindset in adopting this exercise.

It is believed that the railways suffer from losses due to social obligation factor. But it is not every time and everywhere the same. It has been researched that in most cases it is the wrong policy which is the cause of despair. About eighty per cent of railways' commercial activities are apolitical. Again, the factor of cross-subsidization has been often cited for losses whereas the price policy has found to be the main culpable offender. One has to be reminded of the wrong pricing policy of iron ore and finished steel adopted in this regard by the railways.

It was commonly believed that the dichotomy of the railways' status as a commercial organization, but operating as a public sector has created an impasse in its financial management as a business concern. It was a symptom supposed to generate railway's deteriorating financial condition. Earlier, there used to be equilibrium between railways as a government department and as a commercial undertaking. Both balancing each other — a complete harmony and understanding in financial matters were observed. However, this equilibrium was disturbed by the government in way of withdrawing the budgetary support and investment capital on affordable rate of interest. This compelled the railways to borrow capital on unbearable market rate of interest. The financial stability and strength of railways thus immediately came under great stress and strain.

Those who advocate the canons of financial propriety and smooth running of the railways despite government's withdrawing gradually its support — commonly known as (GBS) Gross Budgetary Support — accept it as a challenge to compete in a global market and bring forward the railways to adopt their own strategies for better financial future and sound economy.

The Indian Railways have changed their total perspective— the ways of looking at problems and learning to adjust with times. The last five years, 2004-09, which came under great debate, discussion and prominence, virtually brought a change in the mindset of the railways' employees, the top bosses and the work-force in general to look towards their organization as a competitive unit. The old concept of monopoly power has vanished. In the present globalized economy, the railways have to interact with the market forces, their rivals and find opportunity to pursue profit, create surplus, and invest to generate further capital on the competitive lines and innovative practices. One cannot forget the words which still re-sound the Parliament, "The whole nation can see to-day that track is the same, railways men are the same but the image of the Indian railways is aglow"[1] (Misra, 2009d: 239-40). This glowing image of Indian railways was brought about by untiring efforts put up by 14 lakh employees, working round the clock, pursuing a national agenda for railways' development, growth and social justice. Those who opposed this objective have brought out a White Paper (2009) out of sheer defeatism and despair.

Railways' Managerial Syndrome

Indian Railway is a statutory body functioning by rules prescribed according to Indian Railways Act 1990. It was earlier working under the provisions laid down in the old Act of 1890. It originated as a government body, worked as a department and enjoyed the same rather exalted status as one of the Navaratnas of the government of India; it ranked only second in financial power and revenue collection (first being ONGC); it occupied first place in order of employment, area covered, the time of its origin, national service, solidarity, and integration. The Indian Railways was one of the oldest institutions which provided first lessons in industrial revolution to the nation. Its status as a life line of the country cannot be undermined. The nation moves with the pace of its movement; when it rejuvenates, the nation feels synergetic and stronger. Needless to say that the railway represents a uniting force of Indian diversified culture, art and the scientific endeavour spread all over the sacred land from high Himalayas to the deep Indian Ocean and from golden sand dunes of Thar to the red rivers and blue hills of North East - the ethereal kingdom - where only clouds rein, not the kings.

This magnificent railway – more than a century and half old – has its own story to tell regarding joys and sorrows; pleasure and plain; hardship and prosperity. What has railway gained and lost during this period? What have been its accomplishments and failures? This has to be judged dispassionately.

The Indian Railway is British in origin. It has been bred, fed and nourished like a Briton. A majestic and royal organization as it is, it has always been a giver not a taker. Initially, it spent more than what it had earned – not to become 'bankrupt' (as Expert Group bluntly and uncharitably tried to expose, and failed), but to establish a tradition to accept that heavy industries and capital oriented institutions need more share and care of government than the corporate entrepreneur. The railway has kept its initial character, working and operating as a government body, quite intact, and sound, and cannot be accused of any malfunctioning of the system on account of its status as a public sector. It is wrong to attribute any such distressing situation to it as a government body. On the other hand, it has gained more than what it has lost as a government department.

There was nothing like ideological audacity in accepting its social obligatory character because the revolutionary movement of 'The Soviet Russia' was born much later than the Indian Railways. The railway as government unit is a British legacy, tested and adjudged to be the best form for the Indian condition. It has brought laurels to India during the Raj as well as Independent India. It worked as a defense measure during war and an ambassador of growth and planned development during peace.

But old institutions do have their saddest thoughts and experiences. They may be regarded as their happiest songs too, as the poet had observed. Nevertheless, the casting shadow of old age on the railway rendered it more rigid, slow and apathetic to the new ways, system and life. It became stagnant, hard and resistant to change. It was this framework of railways' management and organization which was sticky, sick and suffered from various ailments.

Aversion to Change

After the British departure, the railway retained its role as a public sector unit in the planned economy of India. It worked quite gracefully, revamped its style and functioning. It also reorganized and re-grouped into new zonal and divisional railways to chug on as a great national pride, performing the business as a privileged government functionary. It started well and impacted the economy of the nation by its valuable contribution towards growth and social justice.

But as it had happened in case of Indian old feudal values – the same happened in case of professional cadre of the railways – hard to change their attitude – to accept the organization as a 'business unit'. Business demands quick pursuance to profit, alertness to market forces and acceptance of change with times. These are simple matters and do not need any 'openness' and 'global system' to become the part of national economy. These are universal factors and operate everywhere the same way.

With aversion to such simple changes shown by the guardians of Rail Bhavan, the railways started dwindling in their performance in the sphere of finance, economy, administration and management. There was nothing wrong with the system of the railways. But the apathetic attitude of their managers created a type of 'managerial syndrome' which greatly affected the organisation. The time had reached when it was believed that the railways had become anachronistic, obsolete and old fashioned. The new era of road transportation with four to six lanes express ways had dawned which eclipsed the growth of the railways. The four-wheeler revolution of cars, trucks had emerged. Even heavy trucks and tractors cropped up in a challenging way to take away the major share of transport market. At this juncture the professionals of the railways had to perform an important duty. It was to accept the challenge and work out the system quite anew. But they remained complacent; banked upon the 'monopoly character' of the railway and satisfied with the lesser amount of profit. The aversion to change with times on the part of the guardians, managers and the bosses of the railways brought their organization to a highly deteriorating stage.

Departmentalization of Railways

Another symptom of managerial syndrome was railways' departmentalization. The railways as an organization was supposed to be highly integrated but its working reflected a process where each department looked for its own goal, strategy and kept it away from national agenda. It thus created a paradoxical situation. While the railway was an integrated entity, its departments followed separate action, programme and strategy. They had hardly any interaction with each other or know their future plan of action. They remained so separated that they never thought of beyond immediate advantage or tried to include corporate culture to reap the advantage of united action.

Railways' zones and divisions are good for administrative purpose, but in business terms they do not form a complete unit; they just work in parts and show a partial role. Their aims remain separated and they do not adopt unified agenda. It is this reason that a common factor is needed which can keep all units together to achieve a common mission. In this regard one may find that the political leadership is essential to keep all factors together. Here the quality of leadership is very important. The leader should be highly motivated, effective and dominant. His political and social actions should generate impact on the people and his decisions invariably are acceptable to all. He should be the man of high integrity, honesty and social justice.

Why the railway needs such a process of integration and undaunted leadership? The railways have a great potential but due to lack of well organized system and leadership, nothing substantial is possible to be achieved. It is the leader who formulates the national policy. It is the leader who is held responsible and is answerable to the Parliament. The railways speak through its minister and the bosses at Rail Bhavan. They should be given full power to decide the affairs of the railways. The minister occupies a special position. He speaks on behalf of the railways – the service provider. But he also speaks on behalf of the consumers – the service receivers. The supply side remains open directly to the market but the demand remains mute and passive. The leader gives voice to the consumers also. He speaks on their behalf to bridge the gap between the consumer and the producer.

Essentially, the Indian railways have been organized as an integrated system and rarely one may find this aspect in any other railways of the world in such a measure. The Indian railways is said to be unique in this respect. For example, Japanese Railway (JR) is geographically carved on the lines of Indian Railways into regions and sub-regions. But the railway of Japan is disintegrated as far the goods and passenger trains are concerned. Actually, there are two railways in Japan. One is freight railway (run by the freight company) and other is passenger railway (run by the passenger company divided into six zones). Both are working separately in every respect. China is still much traditional in its approach to the railway system. The Chinese Railways (MOR) is under government control. It faces serious challenges on account of its being a part of socialist market economy. The role of government and private sector is extremely confused. Unlike Indian Railways, Chinese Railways (MOR) is highly fragmented, dislocated and generates high cost and extremely poor service. There is no direct line of equation between Indian and Chinese Railways. UK Railway is generally called the mother of all the railways. If any nation is fearless in adopting any change, it is UK, specially its railway enterprise. However, it has so many variations in its style and working that it is difficult to cope with all the aspects of changes adopted by UK Railways. It has a long history and tradition and developed into a private system from its earlier state-owned monolithic organization. Although the new pattern of privatization has been adopted, the British Railways have been changing their tracks and not settled as a system firmly. They have several operating companies, freight companies, maintenance companies along with rolling stock owners; they all are working under a regulatory system and franchise director. It seems like a legendary Pandoras Box ready to be opened at any time. The system is not very smooth and functions under great stress and strain. On the other hand, Indian Railways works smoothly. It is strong enough to face any managerial and financial challenges. It has accepted those challenges and has come out victorious at every stage. The recent turnaround is just a manifestation of its prowess to govern and control.

Lack of Business Acumen

The failure of railways on its financial front to attract profits and larger share of transport market was initially attributed to lack of initiative, financial skill and organizational process. The railways inherently were not well managed to analyze profitability and execute their affairs to improve yield, margins and efficiency. The decline in competitiveness was supposed to be an administrative weakness and suggestions like control and price regulations were meant to create negative impact on the working of the railways. The organizational system was enfolding various administrative and executive maladies and developing 'managerial syndrome' for making the railways sick and sluggish to come to a grinding halt. The symptoms of deterioration and decline were being reflected in the form of failure to pay dividends, decline in market share even of bulk commodities, lack of initiative to face competition with immediate rivals and above all, various operative deficiencies including decades old corruption, unearthed during 2004-05, exposing loss of about Rs. 5000 crore to Rs. 7000 crore every year.

What the Indian Railways lacks presently is the right business perspective and acumen, competitiveness with rivals and a dynamic pricing policy. Within the exiting framework of the organisation, these activities may easily be carried on. However, to acquire these skills, there is urgent need of change in attitude and adopting a new mindset. The regular lessons and executive courses for the above purpose may be provided to the staff with practical on-field-training. It matters little who is the boss. The process of training and accepting new mindset should be continued for smooth running of the railways. The ways, methods and strategies may change from time to time but the fundamental approach to pricing, profits and promotion of sales will remain the same and have to be pursued in the interest of growth and development of the railways.

There are several means and methods to achieve the above goals and the purpose for which the railways stand:

1. There should not be any clash of interests between political mandate and business needs and policies of the railways. A proper blend of purpose and business process be created to acquire the best of both these approaches.
2. A clear cut policy be declared initially by the staff to change and adjust with the situation and the minister should abide by the rule of non-interference and 'hands off' attitude.
3. Trust and confidence are the managerial traits which generate unity, solidarity and cooperative spirit. Accepting this fact efficiency, productivity and dexterity of the workforce can easily be promoted and accelerated.
4. Business acumen, faculty of commercial practice and trading habits are to be inculcated and developed through regular process of field surveys and studies. The theoretical frame work of management aspect can be taught to the middle and higher level managers to develop and understand the inner sense of decision making.
5. Profits rarely come as a windfall. They have to be pursued rather chased rigorously. The transport economy does not follow pure aspect of pricing and profitability. In many ways, it deviates from traditional pattern. This sense of 'profit and profitability' must be kept in mind and followed in field practices.
6. The best way of 'restructuring' is to change the human capital; its mental setup and thinking; its approach to work and service. Once this fact is recognized and strengthened nothing can stop railways from becoming number one in the world. Let the 'Expert Group' remember that merely bulldozing the established steel framework of railways structure will not do. It requires human sense and sensibility to pulsate the heart of the body-business. Behind every institution and machine, it is the human sense that keeps it working in the right direction and order. The human factor therefore cannot be ignored.

7. During very short period, the predecessor of the new incumbent of the railways changed the very basis of its functioning. How did he create such a change? He believed in human capital, the workforce, the employees of the railways and exhibited full faith in them. This brought him nearer to the grassroots workers as well as the top bosses of the railways. They made his agenda as their own and devoted themselves fully to achieve the target.

Business is an art derived through practice and tradition. It is a mindset acquired through dexterity and skill. It is a learning scheme of exchange, pricing, manoeruverability and understanding profit and loss. It is a scientific endeavour to specify action, decision and application of measures in theoretical as well as practical or real life experience. It is a role played by people especially trained for the purpose and for those who try to enter into the arena as amateur to become successful careerist. In all, it is a sense, an action in the world of economics, full of goods and services, ready to perform the process of exchange and marketing on their own terms.

No body is a born business man or a manager but all are born with a mind, a sense or acumen needed to become, with a bit of practice and skilful devotion and faith, either of the two or both. It does not require over hauling of an institution or re-structuring it purposelessly. If you do not have skill or a mindset, even the best possible structured system may collapse like a house of cards. The first and foremost factor, therefore, is belief or confidence – the driving force behind any endeavour. Your faith would work like a miracle in this respect.

Indian Railways since its inception behaved like a 'princely institution' – an heir apparent of the future industrial kingdom of India. No wonder that it started functioning in a royal manner, irrespective of impediments coming in the way of development. "All abide our question, thou art free" – equally applies to the Bard and the Railways. Those who had seen the working of the railways of the Raj must have observed that after the Civil Services, the second choice of Britons had been to serve the Indian Railways.

The railways of the Raj had enjoyed full patronage of the top governance of India. It might be called as the most favoured child of Lord Dalhousie, the Governor General of India during British times (1848–56).

The railways therefore continued to exhibit the royal traits of highest managerial control and authority even after Independence. As inherent character hardly vanishes, the railways showed weakness on the business front. Kings don't rush for business like commoners: they don't access market or bargain on streets like traders. The Railway, therefore, as a royal institution, presented less of business acumen but more of authority, bureaucratic dominance and hierarchical influence even after Independence. This brought the railways down with less of income, resources and productivity. The major concern of the railway today is to change its status from authoritarian entity to an all embracing business concern of a liberal and democratic society. The railway has to shed its old egoistic character of a monopolistic body and turn into a competitive economic unit. The old order must change giving place to the new.

Footnote

1. This refers to the speech of Lalu Prasad who presented the railway budget 2006-07 on February 24, 2006. He formally announced the turnaround of railways and said "the whole nation can see today that the track is the same, railway men are the same but the image of the Indian railways is aglow".

◆◆◆

7

White Paper: A Diagnostic Analysis

It has been observed how financial and managerial systems created a weak front to fight against the forces responsible for railway's deteriorating condition. It is symptomatic of the failing health – a syndrome – generating low esteem, skepticism and timidity which prohibit any kind of improvement for the organisation. It has to be properly diagnosed, examined and identified and effectively treated to eradicate the symptom and the disease.

When the railways failed to pay dividend for two consecutive years; when it got trapped into perpetual indebtedness and fell into vicious cycle of underinvestment, misallocation of funds, poor traffic service and rapidly worsening economy, it was correct to conclude that the doom was nearer and required immediate steps to control further decline. A diagnostic analysis was needed for regular treatment. The trouble was visible towards financial and managerial process and programmes. Although other factors too had their impact like lack of decision making, freedom in taking action and avoidance on the part of the government. Also political compulsions and social obligations were all time accompanied factors de-generating the railway's economy. The increase of wagon-load was the first step taken by the predecessor. It required no finances but courage to implement and fight against the inside forces. Reducing wagon turn round was the second step which increased the frequency of the availability of wagons. The next step was reducing train examination time. It was reasonably lowered to fulfil the present demand for the increase in traffic capacity. These steps were simple but urgent and effective. One has to set one's own house in order without any extra financial help. This brought remarkable change. Within first year of its experiment, the finances increased tremendously and there was no going back on this decision. Turnaround of the railways was generated, accepted and followed as a factor for immediate change.

One wonders how the old formula of tare to pay load ratio continued even in the new millennium which brought many changes and promised better deal but left this aspect untouched. Even the much hyped 'Expert Group' which was supposed to be the custodian of transport and logistics expertise in India had little understanding of the origin and use of this formula and did not mention it anywhere in the 352-page elegy a laborately written on the demise of the Indian railways in 2001.[1] How had the predecessor, in the very first year 2004-05, of his stint, allowed to organizing a workshop to study and change the ratio of payload? It might have been a matter of great surprise to others, but nothing new for the person himself because he was gifted with the deep sense of business and organizational control. The steps which he took were termed as the first principles of turnaround.

On the contrary, the new incumbent of the railways issued a White Paper — a visionless approach to mar the turnaround progress and demoralize the work-force including the staff, for taking any further steps in this direction. Even the budget estimates were revised and the railways were compelled to run on reverse gear.

It is pertinent to make a diagnostic analysis of the White Paper in the light of the turnaround, on the one hand and Vision 2020 on the other. Such a study would bring a clear position of the inherent contradiction prevailing within the approach of the new incumbent regarding the railway system, working and performance.

The White Paper: A Self Contradiction

The White Paper (2009) is self contradictory: speaking two voices, projecting two faces. In dealing with growth of traffic and financial performance, it on the one hand, lauds year over year (YOY) growth for traffic — 8.28 per cent and 6.26 per cent for freight loading and originating passengrs respectively and 7.14 per cent and 9.14 per cent for NTKM and passenger Km respectively (see White Paper table T-2: growth in traffic, p. 6), but on the other hand, keeps an option open for judgment that these improved percentage of YOY in traffic has to be seen against a shortfall of achieving the expected growth based on expected elasticity.[2] Why it has been so restricted? How are the achievements of T-2 of White Paper comparable to 'short fall' of Table 1? It is a contradictory approach. In the Chapter 4 of the present analysis, the wrong notion of elasticity has been explained and instead of shortfall, there is potential increase of growth rate percentage as per expected elasticity (see T-4, col.7 of the present study)[3]

Coming to financial performance during the period 2004-09, freight and passenger earning's YOY growth was 14.11 per cent and 10.52 per cent respectively and total earning's YOY growth was 13.26 per cent. It is a remarkable achievement and given this as benchmark; it will be difficult for the present incumbent to achieve the YOY growth rate in her own period as the declining trends show for the year 2009-10. Why the White Paper laments on the decline in passenger earnings for 2008-09 when it stands 10.52 per cent just equal to compound annual growth rate (CAGR) and for rest of the four years, the earnings remains majestically high per cent? Why this year over year (YOY) growth rate became a mark to insist upon? Still on the basis of YOY /CAGR for freight earning in 2004-09, it stood as high as 14.11 per cent which was a historical achievement. Why did the new incumbent try to misrepresent figures to prove a wrong point? Why wrong elasticity measure was used? Why had White Paper applied non-applicable criteria to prove its own biased view point?

Two Faces of the White Paper

The White Paper projects two faces. It carries a masked face destroying the image of turnaround and another face accepting the changed pattern and achievements of turnaround. The predecessor introduced higher load, a new pattern in freight loading, dynamic price policy for the freight and passenger traffic services – all these fruits of turnaround were accepted with ease but turnaround as an instrument of change was decried. The following are the double-speak expressions of the White Paper (Ministry of Railways, 2009b):

1. "The performance of the Indian railways in the last five years, therefore, has to be seen in the back drop of the high growth of Indian economy" (White Paper, p. 5). Why this condition is imposed? What about the efforts made by the railways to capture the demand? Does it work automatically?
2. "The YOY growth of both freight and passenger traffic has to be seen against the shortfall in achieving the expected growth based on accepted import-export elasticity norms" (White Paper, p. 6). Why this has to be seen like that? What about overrated traffic demand elasticity? Why such wrong conclusions derived?
3. "The last five years have seen marked by high growth in traffic both in freight and passenger (but it was) pushed by the overall economic boom" (White Paper, p. 14).
4. "Increasing the carrying capacity no doubt brought in extra earning capacity but it exposed the track and rolling stock to the risk of premature deterioration" (White Paper, p. 16).
5. "While manpower productivity has increased over the years (2004-09), the challenges of the coming years would necessitate much higher level of productivity" (White Paper, p. 40).When the employees' productivity has increased constantly from. 69,. 75,. 84,. 93 to 1.01 inthe last five years why the clause 'challenges... productivity' has been appended?

In whatever way one may examine and assess the 'turnaround', it is the deliberate clause which starts with 'if or but' that dominates White Paper. Sentence after sentence, paragraph after paragraph, projects a melancholy note of the past five years with little hope of the improvement for the railways.

Swot Analysis: A confused Scenario

It is tated that for the first time an attempt has been made to do a Swot analysis – a tool of corporate world – as applied to the public sector. The study of Swot essentially added to the private economies to find out how much resilience is left to fight with the rival forces and what strategies needed to be followed. The public system is based on targets and the process of planning adopted to achieve them. Therefore, when public economies fail, they produce a White Paper to justify their plan of action and the conditions under which they fail and the steps which they would take to solve the problems of their organization.

Swot analysis is seldom used as a tool of public policy studies. Nevertheless, this study became the part of White Paper to find out where does the weakness lie? The strength of the system have been provided with greater emphasis but only traffic system with operational and commercial strategies along with infrastructure, renewal of replacement and safety measures have been dealt with. The financial status again has found a place with freight and passenger earnings but credit has been given to GDP growth and other sector-wise development of the economy. One fails to understand why due credit has not been given to freight business? Is the freight business a strength or weakness? When GDP has shown 8.8 per cent average growth and other sectors have not moved beyond 8 to 9 per cent, the achievement of railway's freight business with 14.11 per cent is highly commendable is the case of passenger business which has registered the growth of 10.52 per cent. But the areas of 'Retail', 'Commercial publicity' and 'Rail land' utilization are supposed to be the untapped potential factors which require extra attention.

One cannot find any clue where the present analysis will lead to. Working expenses, pension liabilities, railway funds, plan expenditure along with market borrowings and organizational structure have been mixed up in such a way that it is difficult to decipher which way they are lying - towards strength or weakness?

Take for example the pension liability. The White Paper laments on the concept and the organisations which adopt it, accept it, and follow it as the rightful share of the employees after their retirement. Quite in tune with the Expert Group report, the workers are regarded as potential liabilities.[4] The feeling of pension as a 'liability' is derogatory and annoying. Pension is not a charity. It is a rightful share of the earning. Perhaps the White Paper has exposed the railway employees as dead stock to be disposed of after the expiry date like outdated furniture, fixtures, machines and office stationary etc. Those who are instrumental in issuing the White Paper ought to know the fact that employees have very strong unions and are the living force behind their great organization. It is the workforce which has made the railway a great institution and one should not think of rendering them penniless, pension-less and powerless at the age when they needed greater support. Perhaps the modem management is lacking in one of the vital concept of workforce that it requires support from the organisation which it serves for the major duration of his/her life.[5]

Providing pension is not an act of mercy, but it is the rightful claim of the employees. Instead of lamenting over its 'expenses' or 'liability', it should be regarded as a distributive share – a type of 'inclusive growth' for which much is talked about or it would remain merely a slogan. Why harp on gradually reducing the workforce? Why cry over its style of calculation – 'actuarial' or otherwise? It is an 'honour fund' and the minister of the railways and the White Paper must acknowledge it as an indispensible factor.

A caution here to take is necessary. After every ten years the burden of love of the Pay Commission has to be borne with a smile and in the year 2020 when the supposed Vision would be materialized, a new burden of not less than 40,000 crore for Seventh Pay Commission would have to be maintained. As long as Keynesian macroeconomic process dominates our system of monetaray inflation, Pay Commission within the rightful economic growth has to be accepted with pleasure. The new incumbent in her past stint as the railway minister had failed to tackle the situation and she unnecessarily cried over again on Sixth Pay Commission expenses, of which major portion was covered in advance by her predecessor. She must start thinking for Seventh Pay Commission expenses and make provisions in advance, step by step, so that by 2020 it may not a troublesome experience. Writing 'Visions' would not do: one has to act upon and implement them.

Vision 2020: A Great Paradox

Soon after the critical assessment of the railways by the Expert Group indicating that "currently they do not have a vision" (The Indian Railways Report 2001, p. 66), the bosses at Rail Bhavan suddenly changed their attitude and became 'vision minded'. Not only had they strived hard to compose a paragraph as a 'vision statement' appearing on p. 1Vision 2020, they on every step and stage found a workable vision like a burden line of a poem. So the railways now have an accumulated stock of visions suiting every occasion and need like 'Vision Statement' (Vision 2020, p. 1), 'Vision for freight services' (Vision 2020, p. 20), 'Passenger Services Vision', (Vision 2020, p. 22), and 'Five Critical Visions' (Vision 2020, p. 25) etc. These visions seem to be important and are testimony of Indian railway's modified and improved pattern of business and traffic services.

Have you ever tried to laugh open throatily and at the same time ballooning yours cheeks? Perhaps you have not done it. It is a difficult rather impossible exercise unless you happen to be an inmate of a high profile Russian Circus or like Raj Kapoor who used to cry and laugh together in Mera Nam Joker. But the present incumbent of the railways has mesmerized everybody by issuing White Paper and Vision 2020 at the same time; and on the same day. It is like ads-photo appearing for a beauty clinic simultaneously showing two appearances; before and after the treatment like bald headed (before) and newly grown hair (after): or fat body (before) and slim body (after). Likewise, White Paper- presenting railways failing health (before) and Vision 2020 (after) railways gain health. Everybody knows: these ads are only paper jokes; they are never meant to be worked out. When the concept of Vision 2020 was brought before the predecessor and the leader of the turnaround for his comment, he in a hilarious mood opined: *"Na Nau Mun Tel Hoga Na Radha Nachengi"* (neither nine maunds of oil be collected, nor Radha would dance: A Hobson's condition – an Indian proverb). It is a gimmick of modern business management that both the contradictory documents appear at one and the same time. It is up to you, how to take it: cry or rejoice over the situation?

Rail Bhavan keeps many such documents in the pipe line. The moment a new minister arrives, they offer a new document of his/her choice. Believe it or not, the vision document was already there with the railways before the present incumbent took over the charge as-the minister in May 2009. The predecessor had already planned to issue Vision 2025. It was almost drafted and needed a few months more to brush up. Its reference has been given in *"Bankruptcy to Billion"* by Sudhir Kumar and Shagun Mehrotra (appendix 9A p. 95).It is a common understanding that to suit the present incumbent; the Vision 2025 was modified, reduced and compressed into Vision 2020. It makes no difference if a new name is given to an old one. It is old wine in a new bottle.

What is Vision 2025? In order to sustain turnaround for longer period and improving constantly the health of the railways, the predecessor had a plan to issue a document. It was already worked out. But in the mean time, as the luck would have it, the predecessor lost the old majority and in UPA II, a new minister took over the charge of the railways. But the document Vision 2025 remained intact with the railways. The predecessor during his stint as minister has mentioned about this Vision on 26 February 2008. In the budget speech he has expressed, "The financial turnaround of the railways has been achieved by thinking beyond the beaten path, taking innovative decisions in commercial, operational and pricing pol icies and through cross functional cooperation and coordination. For making this magical turnaround durable, we will prepare a 'Railways Vision 2025' document within coming six months which will present new ideas and initiative in a novel manner. This shall outline our preparedness and strategies for the future. The document will set forth the target for the coming seventeen years in the field of operational performance and quality of service. It will also detail an action plan for achieving the stipulated targets and necessary investment thereof. This document will also contain details of customer-centric modem passenger services and various freight schemes to sharpen the competitive edge of railways. This will have a blue print of an organization that encourages transdepartmental decision making to take the railways to unprecedented heights. Route wise planning would be done to reduce traffic bottlenecks, expand the net work and modernize the railways. The passenger services will be governed by two words 'comforts' and 'convenience'. The buzz word in freight business will be 'commitment' and 'connectivity'. All these efforts will lay a solid foundation for the resurgent railways. This document-will inspire the railway management and its employees-to do new experiments and will be like a guiding light for the future generation (Kumar/ Shagun, 2009a: 21-23)".

How much Vision 2020 differs from Vision 2025? Vision 2025 remained only in incubation stage. It was being shaped and reshaped itself but officially did not hatch out. It was very much there in Rail Bhavan. One does not know exactly how such documents are worked out, but certainly they require a team work and cooperation among various internal section-authorities of Rail Bhavan to prepare and finalize them. But it was certain that before the new incumbent joined the railways, Vision 2025 was already drafted and lying at the office of the ministry.

These two visions (2020/2025) differed in several respects. Vision 2025 was pro-turnaround, progressive; growth oriented and did not try to degrade the immediate or remote past. It worked out as a link of the continued chain of developing railways process. It highlighted the achievements and tried to create an atmosphere for durability and sustainability of turnaround. As far as projections any planning were concerned, it had the same mission and purpose.

However, the present Vision 2020 seems to be hurriedly drafted document based on the past experiences and exercises performed. It tried to come up as a great saviour of the railways in the light ofthe White Paper, but both the documents (Vision 2020 and White Paper) seemed to be contradictory in approach and understanding. The White Paper was vituperative while the Vision 2020 was Utopian, brought up as a legendary Pandoras Box including all the development plans based on projections and backlog of the projects — workable or non-workable — without any sense of expenditure required and their utilities including availability of resources and funds. A plethora of projects were mentioned and a heavy amount was estimated for those activities as Rs. 1466304.11 crore. Apparently, the Vision 2020 seems to be never – a – possible plan document. The railways have only three sources of investment capital (a) Internal resources, (b) External resources or borrowings, (c) General budgetary support. Except internal resources, the rest of them have their limitations. The railways cannot afford too many borrowings on the market rate of interest and the general exchequer's support has been dwindling year after year. Internal resources too have constraints. There are many factors to be considered before dealing with internal resources. It must have a constant increasing traffic demand. Transport demand is a derived demand and depends on general economic condition of the country and its GDP. The demand may have some induced factors, but they only work to a limited extent. One has to consider the market share and the rivals which are formidable competitors. Road transport in India is a troublesome factor. The expansion of road traffic grows more in India in comparison to rail at the ratio 1: 1.5 i.e. road moves 1.5 times more than rail system (Misra, 2008: 43). Again, the road has a wider range- and coverage as for as- the networking is concerned and it is highly progressive and provides door to door service. Railways more or less are left to their traditional market. But this too is rapidly decreasing. Given all such constraints, the railways have to adopt a cautious approach. Still, the railways have got a great potential. Being environment friendly it proposes a brighter future and the railways in India have to travel faster, longer and heavier. They must also reflect commitment, connectivity and comfort in passenger and freight business.

Vision 2020 provides an attractive theoretical framework with inspirational philosophy and innovative ideas. It highlights railways special position and role played in Indian economy. It explains its mission, motto and measures needed to be adopted. It tries to discover new areas of application of services to be rendered. It also projects to apply new technology and operative system so as to achieve excellence in production, sales and profits. A document of great hope and potential, the Vision 2020 brings new life and thinking to Indian railways transport system. But how much it is workable and feasible is yet to be seen in the present context of the railway's economy where, on the one hand it issues White Paper for its terrific weakness developed in financial and managerial process and on the other, a robust Vision 2020 for achieving excellence just within a decade? Does it not exhibit contradiction? It is a Utopian plan without viability or feasibility.

Let us examine a few projections and proposals which it carries:

Freight and Fare Projections

If both the documents — White Paper and Vision 2020 — are read jointliy, one may find how two extreme ends are put together, bending to create an impossible situation - paradox - to revitalize a breathless body into a sports-champion. Projections and plans should be scientifically enumerated, estimated and assessed. What are the forecasting models used in projecting Vision 2020? What are the hypothesis and their testing processes used? It has already been revealed that the railways do not use Input-Output analysis for any of their projections. They are weak in pointing out and removal of bottlenecks in growth system. Their regression analysis does not explain the factual situation, relationship and possible projections. A hard core modeling system with rigorous analysis and deep studies are required. The railways, RITES and other research centers have to gear up for better realistic approach to find proper projections and feasible solutions.

How is it possible to change freight loading of 8.38 per cent compound annual growth rate (CAGR) into 259% or ratio of 1:26 within a decade when past five years have shown cumulative growth it: rate only 8 per cent annually? What would be the possible growth rate of Indian economy? Can GDP grow more than 9 to 10 per cent on the basis of CAGR? If not, then how more than two hundred fifty per cent freight loading projection has been arrived at? In a decade with 9-10 per cent CAGR, the railways can acquire only double of its freight loading i.e., moving from 833MT to 1666.62 MT. or approximately 1667 million tonnes and not 2165 million tonnes as expected. Even in this situation one may have an apprehension that the freight loading may be restricted and not cross even 1500 million tonnes by 2020.

There are many such unrealistic projections shown in Vision 2020 like traffic growth of 1407 NTKM (in billion). The following table 10 gives a picture of growth and projections for 2020 in relation to what the actual position was in 2007-08 to 2008-09 as mentioned in the White Paper.

Table 10 : Traffic Growth and Projections: White Paper vs Vision 2020.

Sl.No.	*Items*	*2007-08*	*2008-09*	*CAGR*	*Projections*	*Expected Ratio of Change*	*Remark*
1.	Freight Loading	793.81	833.31	8.38	2165.00	1:2.6	
2.	YOY Chaange	-	4.97%	-	-	260%*	*Growth Expected in 2020
3.	NTKM in (billion)	521.37	538.23	7.14	1407.00	1:2.6	
4.	YOY Change	-	3.23%	-	-	260%*	Do
5.	Passenger (originating in million)	6645.00	7046.91	6.26	15180.00	1:2.2	
6.	YOY Change	-	6.05%	-	-	220%*	Do
7.	Passenger (PKM in Billion)	771.07	839.30	9.14	2360.00	1:2.8	
8.	YOY Change	-	8.25%	-	-	280%*	Do

Source: Compiled from White Paper (2009) Page 6 and Vision 2020 (2009) Pages 16-22.

The table 10 includes passenger services also. It shows that during the past five years (2004-09) there has been an increase in passengers originating to the tune of 6.26 per cent on the basis of CAGR. In the same way the increase in passenger kilometers (PKm) has been 9.14 per cent for the past five year period on the basis of CAGR. The Vision 2020 projected passengers originating from 7046.91 (million) to 15180 (million) in a decade. The expected growth in 2020 over 2008-09 is about 220 % or a ratio of 1:2.2. The passenger kilometer increases from 839 billion to 2360 billion kilometers and the expected growth for the year 2020 is 280% or a ratio of 1:2.8. Is it possible to increase the expected number of originating passengers and passenger kilometers two to three fold by 2020? The past percentage does not promise such a robust future.

Other Goals and Projections

Considering broad goals and projections for Vision 2020, the story again narrates the same unachievable targets. The table 11 provides 'a summary of such projections as contrasted with the past mentioned the White Paper.

Table 11 Other Goals and Projections: White Paper vs Vision 2020.

Sl	*Items*	*2007-08*	*2008-09*	*% Change*	*2010-11-12*	*% Exp-ected*	*2012-13-19*	*% expected change*	*Total Targe*
1.	Doubling + DFC	426	363+DFC	-85.2	1000 km	275	11000 km	109	12000 km
2.	Gauge Conve-rsion	1549	563	-36.3	2500 km	440	9500 km	126	12000 km
3.	New Lines	156	357	228	1000 km	280	24000 km	104	25000 km
4.	Electr ification	502	797	158.8	2000 km	251	12000 km	117	14000 km
5.	Procu-rement of Wagons	22753	24115	106	33909	141	255227	113	289136
6.	Locom-otive Diesel	222	257	115.8	690	168	4664	115	5334
7.	Loco-motive Electric	200	220	1.02	555	252	3726	115	4281
8.	Coaches	3101	3139	102.9	6912	216	43968	116	50880
9.	Stations	-	-	-	12	-	38	-	50
10.	High Speed Corridor	-	-	-	-	-	2000 km	-	2000 km

Source: Compiled from White Paper (2009) pp. 6-7 and Vision 2020 p. 25

Note: Item no 1 – 4 are in km; 5 – 9 are in units.

The steps taken with reference to works and projections like Doubling, Gauge conversion, New lines and Rolling stock procurement have been mentioned in Table 11.The moderate growth rate in the past years (2002-09) does not justify to project extremely high targets for 2020. For example, the White Paper mentions that the addition of new lines has averaged 220 Km only per year in the past five years (White Paper, p.7). How can one expect to leapfrog 1000 Km per year from the next year to achieve a target of 1200 Km of new lines by 2019-2020? Even if DFC new lines are included, this is not going to make much difference because DFC adds about 105 Km of new lines annually. The same case applied to most of the other goals and projections (See table 11). The worst case happens to be of gauge conversion where it requires more than 440 % increase to reach the target. It is an impossible proposition almost a Utopia to achieve. The situation relating to backlog of ongoing projects is very precarious. A long list of ongoing railway projects has been appended as Annexure I (Vision 2020, pages 34 - 43). If capacity enhancement and modernization works (Vision 2020) are added to it as given in Annexure II, a complete picture emerges for the stupendous task to be finished, taking into account the projected as well as unfinished work. It needs about Rs. 1466304.11 crore for this combined activity. Whether the railways are prepared to take such a risk is doubtful. Moreover, getting completed the backlog of ongoing project does not come under the priority list of the present incumbent.

Thus, the railways are in a great dilemma. Should they get new projects completed or old projects worked out? It requires funds in lakhs of crores to take up both of them as estimated by Vision 2020. The cost of ongoing projects would continue to increase year after year. The railways have to come out of this vicious cycle. Bringing out White Paper and Vision 2020 together is a sign of this great confusion and chaos. The railways have to choose direct path – a reasonable action plan – a mix of past and a vision of future with a clear understanding to work and win and not decry the past or the achievements of the predecessor.

Footnotes

1. This refers to the Expert Group report titled "The Indian Railways Report - 2001: Policy Imperatives for Reinvention and Growth". There has been no reference to the need of any change in 'tare to pay load ratio' which has followed the old formula of axle loading. At one point on page 295, Vol II, Part II, a passing reference to the average tare load of wagons has been given in comparison to South Africa. In fact, the Expert Group has no idea that the tare to pay load ratio can be improved within existing conditions as Lalu Prasad has done and turnaround of Indian Railways is possible through home made remedies.

2. During the predecessor's (Lalu Prasad's) period the YOY growth rate of freight as well as YOY growth rate of originating passengers have followed an increasing trend but the White Paper accepts this phenomenon of improved YOY as against a shortfall of achieving the expected growth based on expected elasticity. It means that in spite of increased YOY growth rate, the White Paper is reluctant to accept the improved scenario.

3. An Analysis has been done with the reasonably growing elasticity for achieving the expected growth rate. This has found that on the basis of elasticity as 0.9, the expected growth rate of railways GDP has increased during the years 2004-2008 (see Table 4, Col 7).

4. In almost all the studies of railways finances, the concept of pension has been treated as a burden and harmful phenomenon. But it should not be dealt with like this. Pension is the part of that payment of labour which the worker puts extra in relation to his paid labour. It is a natural phenomenon of labour force to produce surplus for which no payment is made. It is labour's efficiency, work culture, devotion and loyalty towards the enterprise for which he is paid in the form of pension after he retires from the job. It should not be treated as liability but a rightful share of the worker.

5. The modern management system lacks the characteristic of a distributive economy. It is not based on equity and justice. It thrives on more of exploitation and less on personal risk. It uses other's money, material and labour. They have developed the principle of living on others resources and managing them for their own benefit. The concept of bonus, pension and payment for excellence and efficiency do not form the essential part of their programme of action.

◆◆◆

8

White Paper: The Past and Present Scenarios

What laurels have the Indian railways earned by maligning their own past? Which way are they heading ? Why has the turnaround been so brutally treated? Who initiated and maneuvered the White Paper? Perhaps you would not find any satisfactory answer or logical explanation to such queries.

The Past Experience

The past of the railways was filled with many a problem, but it gave sound ground and proper viewpoint to explain the situation for taking action with a firm hand. They stood like a rock even during their failing moments. They never felt as weak as we find them today. It is the inner strength which is required for the survival of an institution. The Indian railways need it more at present because they have lost their confidence, zeal and zest in dealing with the problem. It was not so in the past. The railways were bold, strong and courageous in the bygone era. When, for instance, during British Raj, the situation was so precarious that the companies were earning profits at the expense of recurring loss to the railways; they did not issue White Paper, but boldly fought the unprecedented situation, pondered deeply over the problem and took a decisive action to stop the 'guarantee system' which was troubling the railways, Lord Lawrence, the Viceroy, in his minutes had recorded that the experiment of guarantee failed due to the fact that 'the whole profit used to go to the companies and the whole loss to the government'.[1] But no individual or any regime was blamed for the failure of the guarantee system.

It was felt that the government under the circumstances must control the railways - their administration and finances - to prevent the exploitative tendency of private companies. It took the decision to abolish guarantee system in a phased programme. During this process of development two important facts surfaced - one, the emergence of the idea of total state management of the railways and two, the formation of the Acworth Committee. The railways were in a fix to decide their future course of action. They thought to bring out a new system so as to organize them according to the local (Indian) conditions and aspirations of the people of the country. It was difficult to decide in that manner. Had there been a minister like the new incumbent, the railways would have issued White Paper as early as 1920. They would not have formed the Acworth Committee or thought to make railway's management and finances 'Indian oriented'. The railways during the British Raj were more abstemious, dependable and cohesive than what we find them today. It was this reason that they survived, worked confidently and developed into a strong organization.

Many far reaching changes took place in Indian railways during 1920s and 30s or before the World War II when the funds deteriorated, especially the reserve fund. In this process the whole material of more than 26 branch lines were dismantled and diverted to the war including locomotives, coaches, wagons and track material. This was most depressed period of railway's history, but they maintained their cool in the hope that after the war things would be set right. They showed no grudge to anybody or any institution. One fails to understand why the new incumbent of Rail Bhavan created such a problematic situation by issuing White Paper and paid lakhs of rupees to the consultant for providing spicy material to degrade the predecessor's achievements.

The present experience of the railways has once again proved that they never took the refuge in White Paper during the British period. Not that the colonial governments don't issue the status paper: they do make such studies but only once in a blue moon. It was rarity for them since they were not vituperative or damaging for their past regimes. Even failures of the predecessors were handled properly. Indian railways had inherited a rich tradition from the British regarding managerial and financial system , but in the wake of their present political advantage, propaganda and rivalry, the ministers do not even spare their own department to decry, they adopt it as the strategy for their success. The partition of India reduced the coverage of the railways, their assets and earnings to the level of two thirds and the railways worked as a lame department until the new process of reorganization and strengthening the system was planned. The regrouping of the railways was done on the basis of geographical division initially into six zonal systems created by the Railway Board. Later on, three more zones were added and by the end of 1966, India had nine railway zones to administer. All such development took place without any fanfare, propaganda or issuing White Paper. Presently, the Indian railways have been divided into 16 zones (excluding Kolkata Metro and Konkan Railways), controlling 67 divisions at the lower level and headed by the Railway Board at the top consisting six members and a chairman.

The present White Paper issued on 18th December, 2009 is still a mystery for the majority of the employees and top bosses of the railways including Board members. Some say that even the PMO and the Cabinet Secretary were unaware of the issue of such a White Paper on the railways. It is the brain-work of a few persons who guided (or misguided?) the new incumbent and hired the services of a consultant whose name has been officially kept a 'secret'. On the basis of a report of RTI, it was found that both the ministers took the services of the same consultant – the former for changing the financial process and shift in accounting and latter – for finding piquant material to be incorporated in the White Paper to cry down the achievements of the predecessor. It is difficult to ascertain who is right? But the present incumbent who wields power, and who has presented the White Paper "on behalf of the few" seems to be more sinned than the sinner. Appointing committees, writing term paper and presenting status paper or White Paper have become pastime for the railway's under-worked staff. They need something to do during their spare time when they come to attend Rail Bhavan.

The facts and statistics are already collected by the junior staff. They have to formulate new theory either 'decrying' or 'appraising' a particular action in accordance to the accepted policy framework. The present White Paper is thus, a systematically programmed activity worked out to 'malign' the immediate past (2004 - 2009) through statistical analysis made to order.

The railways have become habitual of issuing White Paper. Some say that the White Paper issued by the new incumbent is the fourth of its kind in the series within a decade or so. But, actually it is seventh in regular order considering the departmental status report submitted separately, to highlight the problem within the railways own administrative circle. A.V. Poulose was the only railway officer (retired) who took notice of the present White Paper (2009) and instantly reacted to its analysis of 'overrated' elasticity. Much earlier to it[2], he had opined that there was surfeit of White Papers and the railways must stop this practice of exposing problems every now and then. Instead, the railways should carry on the follow up activities as suggested by internal analysis and research performed by their professionals and experts. The railways should not outsource their studies and expose their infirmities. They should try to find out solutions instead of writing about them without any follow up action. They should learn the lesson from their past – the railways of the Raj - which raised the problems, tried to solve them without any exposure or propaganda.[3]

George Fernandes: First to Issue White Paper

It was George Fernandes who for the first time after Independence issued the status paper in 1990. It was entitled 'status paper on Indian railways: options and issues' (Fernandes, 1990). It happened for the first time that an official analysis of the departmental needs, introspection, aspirations, failures and success and proposals for development was made and future plans and estimates were projected. It was an elaborate statistical process and progamme of study which tried to establish railways transport economy as an important, indispensible and integral part of national system.

It pointed out financial and managerial needs and action plan through which the railways organizational system could be benefited. The first and foremost was financial scarcity which was hampering the growth and progress of the railways economy. The mobilization of resources was one of the major issues of the railway transport business. It was realized that the revenue was declining and the railways traditional monopoly authority was losing its power, pressure and promotional value. The market share of the railways was sharply reducing and a great competition with road transport had set in. Even price policy was not in sync with the system and fare and freight were irrationally adopted. It was suggested that a reasonably fair pricing system be adopted so that revenue may be increased. The rationalization of freight and fare system should be adopted for better prospects of the railways. The position of the railways was exalted in the eyes of the people and gracefully attractive status as lifeline of the national economy was established. It had to serve the people, on the one hand and protect the honour of the nation, on the other by recognizing it as a unifying force of the country's social, cultural and political setup. No other institution or organisation can boast of such a solidarity syndrome associated with it to provide internal unity, integration and security.

The business aspect of the railways needed to be improved and the market forces should be so organized as to benefit our transport economy especially railway which was the only mode providing goods and passenger services at affordable freights and rates.

The status paper issued in 1990 had explained the truth behind the railways affairs and its functioning. It was natural for the people to have great expectations from the railways to get better services as a public sector on attractive terms. They had high aspirations and the organization was supposed to fulfil them relating to investment, efficiency, planning productivity and pricing which formed the basis of the status paper. The financial condition of the railway had to be improved and extra budgetary resources found in the wake of sharp reduction of support from general exchequer. Examining the situation the status paper added, "It is an effort to tell the truth. It also raises many questions confronting the railways on how to fulfil people's expectations and aspirations and ask everyone to participate in an exercise to final answer because every Indian has a stake in them"[4] (Fernandes, 1990:1).

The status paper maintained that people should show a participatory process in solving the problems because the railways belonged to the whole nation and would remain always in the service of the nation. However, a type of self introspection needed and the role of the railways and the government at the centre should be redefined to come to a common platform. The railways had provided less than cost service to many of the items especially food grains to keep the prices under control and adopt other social obligations. In this light, the government of India should also help to provide resources like electricity and diesel on reasonable rates so as to reduce the energy cost. The railway gets electricity three times costlier than actual cost from state electricity boards and NTPC.

The important facts which came to the limelight to rejuvenate the railway's economy were to mobilize the internal resources because market borrowings had their own limitations. According to business rules 1961, it is the prerogative of the ministry of finance to handle borrowings and floatation of market loans by states and central governments. It is because of this restriction that an indirect method of market borrowings was arranged through the IRFC. Up to the end of 1991-92 IRFC had raised bonds amounting to Rs. 5230 crore for providing rolling stock. The other fact was to reorganize investment policy. In this regard depreciation policy has also to be changed. Again, the creation of capital fund has resulted in diversion of railways surplus to less remunerative projects while at the same time outlay on replacement (DRF) were cut back. The problem of cross subsidization was hampering the growth of traffic of freight and reducing its speed because of excessive demand for passenger traffic. A rebalancing process had to be adopted.

The main thrust of the status paper 1991 was on internal resource generation. The pricing policy was also to be adopted in such a way as to generate sizable revenue for investment. It was also accepted to reduce the costs and increase productivity by better utilization of assets; by better operating and scheduling practices which could result in substantial cost savings.

Nitish Kumar's White Paper

The second most important White Paper was issued during Nitish Kumar's stint as railway minister. It was a status paper issued in 1998 under the title 'Status Paper on Indian Railways: Issues and Options' (Kumar, 1998a). A revised version of the same came in 2002 (Kumar, 2002) which was updated to financial needs, estimates and schemes covered. The paper maintained the real character of self introspection and each point was taken up after much deliberation, discussion and debate. It paid special attention to the funding of sanctioned projects. In this context the present White Paper (2009) seems to be an amalgamation of past status papers with added vengeance to bring the predecessor and the regime (2004-2009) to the dock and disparage the saga of turnaround. So it lost its dignity as a genuine status paper which normally remains neutral towards persons, institutions and the period or regime.

Nitish Kumar's status paper revealed that out of a total of about Rs. 59000 crore worth of ongoing projects, a major component was financially unviable. The railways had a large number of shelf projects such as New Lines, Gauge Conversion, Railway Electrification and MTP plan heads which required about Rs. 38000 crore for completion. In the beginning of 2002-03, a revision of the status paper covering various issues, and options was published , depicting crisis, causes and trying to find solutions by putting several questions to answer in a self introspective manner. The paper covered many problems concerning the railways like financial health, freight business and cost escalations, pension problems of the employees and much discussed problem of cross subsidization and the balancing issue. Almost all the problematic areas were covered and 'no occasion' was left for issuing further a White Paper as was done by the new incumbent of Rail Bhavan.

It was said that until 1998-99, the railways had been generating profits 'as usual', but due to the implementation of the Fifth Finance Commission, their finances deteriorated sharply. The 'wage' and 'pension' liability had doubled to the tune of Rs. 19000 crore in 1996-97. Outstanding electricity bills amounted to Rs. 1865 crore. Even lease payment to IRFC had doubled to Rs. 3041 crore in 1995-96 and due to cumulative effect of all such liability, the railways had to defer payment of dividend partially during the year 2000-2001 and 2001-2002 amounting to Rs.1823 and Rs. 1000 crore respectively. The operating ratio also worsened to all time high i.e., 98.3 in 2000-2001. As a public sector it was expected that the railways would discharge their social obligations to meet their working expenses and generate sufficient funds for investment. Losses which the organization has been receiving on account of its social service burden amounted to about Rs. 43282 crore in 2000- 2001.

Regarding freight business, it was brought to notice that Indian railways should either cut down the cost of transportation or face the risk of the loss of traffic. The issue was whether the country could afford stifling economic growth because of high rail freight rates or should freight rates be decreased? The case of passenger traffic presents a different scenario. Passenger traffic constitutes 60 per cent of the transport cost but only 32 per cent of revenue. The worst year was 2000-2001 when losses on account of passenger services and other coaching services amounted to Rs. 4875 crore. The railways had further assessed the input cost on account of staff cost, pension outgo, and energy cost. Staff cost amounted to almost 50 per cent of traffic receipts. Apart from this, there has been an increasing tendency of subsidizing passenger services by the freight earnings of the Indian railways. The major steps to be taken were to control the expenses on social obligations, support market borrowing for investment, reduce losses on passenger traffic, restrict fresh intake to work force, adopt a comprehensive policy of energy consumption and stopping cross subsidization by creating rebalancing between freight and passenger earnings ratio. The major points included in the status paper presented by Nitish Kumar in Lok Sabha on May 27 were as follows:

1. Need for a phased increase in passenger fare to ease freight rates, massive cross-subsidization to passenger fares by freight services was causing a loss of freight traffic to trucking. Annual cross-subsidization was Rs. 2800 crore during 1997-98.
2. The railways had to increase more than double their investment from the level of Rs. 33000 crore in the Eighth Plan to Rs. 85000 crore in the Ninth plan to retain the present share in transport.
3. The paper proposed to seek power for electric traction on low tariffs, currently being supplied at three times the generation cost.
4. It also demanded that facilities like inland container depots (ICDs), set up Concor, be treated at par with ports and given benefits under the Income Tax Act.
5. The paper also sought government approval for commercial exploitation of railway land and air space to upgrade passenger and freight terminals and also a supplementary source of funding for railway development.
6. The paper suggested the creation of a development fund for rail over- and road under- bridges through one per cent and ad valorem levy on purchase price of road vehicles.
7. It sought compensation for public obligations, like running un-remunerative passenger and commuter services and carrying essential commodities at subsidized rates, currently costing Rs. 1800 crore for commercially unviable but socially relevant projects, the paper suggested funding through outright grants without dividend liability for execution and operation of such projects.

It was so comprehensive and practical with real analysis done the status paper prepared during Nitish Kumar's stint that no justification warranted to bring out any further White Paper unless a dubious objective discrediting a person or a period was involved. The present White Paper (2009) thus seems to be a malicious, attempt to downgrade the predecessor's achievements and the saga of turnaround.

A Glut of White Papers

Producing White Papers with options and issues, status papers along with revised versions, special issues with suggestions and observations, occasional papers with problems and perspective have become a normal process of Indian railways. Nitish Kumar issued White Paper thrice: first, the original one, on May 27, 1998; second, on July 8, 1998 and third the revised version of the same in 2002. These papers provided instantly a dubious popularity, an inopportune occasion to recapitulate follies without any corrective measures. Earlier White Papers used to be a genuine case of self introspection and a basis to generate debate and discussion. But now it is used as a weapon to fight against one's predecessor or the past regime. The railways is in the habit of issuing them in volumes without any intension to take follow up action.

The railways have done a lot of studies and published several reports, issued recommendations of various committees, submitted their suggestions, followed advice or opinions. The railways believe in operation - good or bad – but have never entertained debates, discussions or expert views. The glaring example is the 'Expert Group Study - The Indian Railways Report 2001 - Policy Imperative for Reinvention and Growth'.[5] It has not generated even simple debate over its recommendations except that the polished corridors of Rail Bhavan have decided quite honourably to put it deep in the archives of the railways, not to see the light of the day again.

The first 'Status Paper on Indian Railways: Some Issues and Opinions' was issued on March 1, 1990 by George Fernandes, the then railway minister. Another study followed was entitled 'Bombay Suburban Railway System – Suggestion and observation'. Nitish Kumar issued Status Paper on May 27, 1998 during his first stint as the railway minister. It was reissued on July 28, 1998 titled 'White Paper on Railway Projects' for encouraging debate over railways affairs and forming it as a base for encouraging setting the tone for renaissance of the Indian railways as they march towards the new millennium. The confidence of Nitish Kumar increased and during his second stint as the railway minister a revised and updated version of his earlier White Paper was issued in 2002. At the time of issuing it he added, "I am confident that the Status Paper - 2002 will generate wide ranging debate in the country and some useful conclusion will emerge and the scrutiny and new options thrown up in the deliberations will surely guide us finding the right path for Indian Railways".[6] Then, there is a study regarding Railways' electricity; use and safety and in July 2007 a paper was added entitled 'Electricity Safety – Perspective in Rail Transport'. A new study was added as a 'Position Paper – PPP in Railways' in October 2009. One cannot miss to mention here that an elaborate description of the Railways Status was given in the form of an Expert Group Study on 'Indian Railways Report – 2001'. It was the final nail in the coffin of the Indian railways popularly known as The Rakesh Mohan Committee Report. This study was "a pathetic elegy elaborately written on the tombstone of Indian Railways. Sentence after sentence, paragraph after paragraph, reads like an obituary. The colourful exhibits and boxes are like wreaths on the gravestone, paying homage to a fatally wounded, financially dead organization."[7] (Misra, 2009d: 73).

The present White Paper on Indian Railways (2009) is perhaps the seventh of its kind issued like a bulletin from an ICU (Intensive Care Unit) of some specialty hospital explaining railways vital financial and managerial organs performing 'below normal' and the earlier 'dose of turnaround' to revive the body-railways was much 'hyped' and ineffective to meet the requirement. The railways are still being treated at ICU and it will take more than a decade (according to Vision 2020) to bring them to normal condition if resource mobilization to the extent of Rs. 14 lakh crore is kept intact for the treatment. There appeared so many White Papers but no debate or discussion took place. Even at the Parliament the White Paper 2009 was presented on the last day of the Winter Session and no time was sought for discussion: it came, it saw, it vanished was the fate of the White Paper 2009.

Arranging seminars, conferences, discussions and debates is a healthy sign of a lively and liberal democratic society. Accepting the outcome of discussions and opinions of others which are sound and constructive is a good tradition to follow. But quietly deciding alone and sticking rigidly to one's own viewpoint is not always safe. There should be room to accommodate outside air and windows must be kept open for light to filter in. The world of railways is mostly rough and tough. This results in its mechanical approach to functioning. One may not find any occasion to interact with academics, participate in open debates and seminars or attend conferences - national or international - if traditionally linked with the railways attitude. Indian railway organisation works in a closed circuit, neither allows nor appreciates the outside intervention. The turnaround tale and OSD's scripting the 'Railways Transformation' has met with negative impact in the form of White Paper (2009). The presiding deities in Rail Bhavan even can't tolerate any wisdom coming from outside, more so from superannuated railway officers. The sitting bosses and sub-bosses are creators, destroyers and saviors of their own railways.

The railway needs profound thinkers, policy makers and practical persons who can rebuild and deliver well to the organization; who have capacity to formulate policies and implement plans under their own care. It is like a war-operation, a little deviation and slackness would prove fatal for the railways.

The issues concerning the railways are innumerable. They have choices with them but under constraints. The bosses at Rail Bhavan have become immune to think about innovative ways and action. In such a situation how much open discussions can be benefitted? Bringing all the White Papers together and sorting out the major issues seems to be logical alternative. They may be enumerated as follows:

1. A National Railways Commission should be set up to declare policy on rail transportation and also to suggest ways to implement it urgently.
2. The role of the railways and the government at centre should be clearly defined.
3. Rail-road co-ordination policy should also be announced to check cut-throat competition as a future precautionary measure.

4. The backlog of railway projects should be clearly categorized as viable, non-viable and those unworkable should be listed and removed.
5. The national fuel policy should be re-worked in the light of railway's demanding new approach to solve this problem.
6. The transport market should be competitively shared on sound principles of transport economy, growth and development.
7. The old issues like costing, pricing, cross subsidization are realistically handled including railways social service aspect without any ideological or dogmatic approach attached to them.
8. Private Public Participation (PPP) blue print should be brought out and implemented without delay.
9. Freight and rates should be rationalized and goods services should properly be time-tabled in the interest of the consignors.
10. Multi-modal logistics parks and container services be enhanced and remodeled.
11. Tare to pay load ratio should be increased and a new wagon policy be adopted for all the rail routes of the country.
12. Laying new rails, replacement of old rails; doubling and gauge conversion are continuous activities and should be done under the control of a 'central authority'.
13. Speed and capacity of trains should be enhanced according to new benchmarks.
14. Suburban and non-suburban railway services should be separately organized.
15. Status of Indian railways should be re-emphasized as life-line of the nation, no less important than Atomic Energy or Defence.
16. Railway Board should have two more members for better control and efficiency i.e., Member Marketing Management (MM) and Member Information Technology (IT). They should look after new managerial and innovative practices and market orientation of the railways. They should also maintain tele-communication technology and computerized information

system and must have their say in decision making. They should initially be recruited and promoted 'to the highest level from railway's own cadre and should not be injected from outside corporate sector to maintain cohesion and homogeneity. Indian railway service (class I) should develop one more category as IRMS (Indian Railway Management Services) and graduates from management, information technology, B. Tech and B.Sc. computer science should be selected for this service.

Present Scenaro: Railways in Reverse Gear

The railways present a peculiar scenario of running in the back gear. After achieving a great landmark of success during last five years (2004-09), its operative mechanism suddenly turned into the reverse process.

When the new incumbent of the railways joined UPA II as the minister, her immediate aim was to demolish the image of her predecessor and declare the turnaround fake and interim budget estimates unrealistic. It was a tricky decision and scheming pronouncement. The benchmark already fixed by the predecessor seemed hard to achieve and there was no short cut to realize the targets. It was the reversal of goals and strategies. The railways adopted to move backward in the hope to change the track for better opportunities.

Boom to Bust: The Budgetary Process

The years 2008–09 and 2009–10 were decisive as far as the role of the new incumbent was concerned. The first confrontation was in the interim budget vs. main budget estimates and second was the sluggish market impact on transport business which prevailed during the last few months of the predecessor's stint. Had the predecessor continued, there was no question of his being unrealistic in estimates for the interim budget because he would have strived hard to achieve the targets as he did for the past four years. But the new incumbent of Rail Bhavan was not interested to keep the railway on the same track or rigorously to work for getting the turnaround process sustained. One must know that nothing moves in transport market unless hard and instant efforts are put up to capture the market. The profits too are illusive and need to be aggressively chased. But no appropriate steps were taken up by the present guard of the railways.[8]

The railway budget for 2010-11 had confirmed that the railways had gone haywire. This was obvious from the fact that the operating ratio (the ratio of total working expenses to the earning - a higher ratio implies degeneration), which was 90.5 per cent in 2008 - 09 had sharply risen to 94.7 per cent in 2009-10. This showed that the incumbent did not manage to invest according to her own announced plans for the last year (2009-10) budget. In fact, she had very meager funds to invest signifying dwindling state of the railway's economy since no sincere efforts were made to improve the finances, though the business environment was favourable.

The gross traffic receipts in 2009-10 (RE) at Rs. 88,356 crore were a little lower by 0.1 per cent compared to the budget estimates (BE). On the other hand, the total working expenses increased to Rs. 83440 crore mainly due to higher ordinary working expenses by 4.1 per cent to Rs. 65500 crore. Consequently, the net revenue and the surplus (excess) of the railways declined substantially to Rs. 6480 crore and Rs. 951 crore in the revised estimates (RE) from Rs. 8121 crore and Rs. 2642 crore in the (BE). As a result net return on capital investment declined to 5.3 percent from 6.6 per cent in BE. Thus, the financial performance of the railways deteriorated in the revised estimates of 2009-10.

The revised estimates of 2008 - 09 had placed the total working expense at Rs. 72490 crore which was higher by 8.9 per cent than the budget estimates (BE) of Rs. 66590 crore. The increase in gross traffic receipts, higher than the BE in 2008-09 was offset by the above increase in the working expenses with the result, the operating ratio in 2008-09 deteriorated to 88.3 per cent from the budgeted level of 81.4 per cent. The surplus of the railways declined to Rs. 6355 crore in the RE of 2008-09 from Rs. 11787 crore projected in BE. As a result, appropriation of capital fund declined by Rs. 4965 crore from Rs. 10840 crore in BE. The net return on capital investment went down to 10.6% in RE from 15.8% in the BE. It may be indicated that the deceleration in financial ratios was on account of the provisions made for implementing Sixth Pay Commission award which in the RE turned out to be much larger than BE.

The percentage of increase in all the components of the budget for 2009–10 was far less than the percentage increase in the previous year 2008–09. This showed the declining trend of the percentage of increase. For example, the gross receipts would increase in 2009-10 by 7.3 per cent while in 2008-09 it had increased by 14.9% a year ago. The freight earning would grow in 2009-10 by 7.8 per cent while in 2008-09 it was 14.5% in the previous year. This was also the case for passenger earnings. It would increase to 8.9 per cent over the RE whereas in 2008-09 it was 12.5% a year ago. It meant that in comparison to 2008-09, the percentage increase in different components of the budget 2009-10 was much slower, sluggish and very low a year ago and presented an economy running in a reverse order without any initiative on the part of the railways to improve.

Lost the Track: The Role Reversal

The epicenter of the railways' destructibility, passion and change shifted from New Delhi to Kolkata – the original capital of India's subjugation under British rule and the new incumbent's home city. It seemed to be symbolic for ultimate doom as the city hosted almost daily the top railway bosses of the Rail Bhavan commuting by rail or airways to consult the minister to run or ruin the railways. This may be called 'unity not in diversity but in distance' – a new concept mixed up with old characteristic feature – which the country so proudly exhibits and the railways at present is the glaring example of this phenomenon.

It is said that the railway has lost the track, missed the aim and forgot the role – the basic tenets of the organized set up – which keep it alive, united and synergetic. The railway as government department re-introduced the old 'expenditure model' of working without caring to mobilize finances, resources and investment capital. The new incumbent of the railways has introduced a plethora of schemes and programmes for which she herself is not sure where from the resources would be arranged. A shift has been shown in favour of private-public-participation (PPP) in many such areas where it was supposed to be difficult to get proper response and support. The dependence on this process has been accepted to such an extent as to render it completely unworkable. Private capital never arrives to help the public undertaking unless there is assured and guaranteed profit made available i.e., 'private benefit on public cost'.[9] The railway had a bitter experience of the same in the past.[10] Still, it is allowing this for the sake of liberalisation and free economy forgetting the lessons of the past.

A committee under Amit Mitra has been formed to bring out and assess the proper role of private participation in areas like railway's land use and other unorthodox ways to increase the resources, but nothing concrete has come out so far. The new schemes and proposals with heavy expenditure have been envisaged but no plan of action has been drawn to bring them to reality. The work process seems to have been reversed; the agenda is missing and the force has no clear mandate to follow. There have been tall promises but no genuine efforts made to fulfil them. The railways add on new schemes every year, but without any indication of the old schemes being completed. In year 2009-10, nearly fifty stations were promised to be modernized out of 309 identified as 'Adarsh' stations (Banerjee, 2009a: 4). Where have those schemes gone? How many medical colleges and nursing colleges started as promised? What has happened to lay down 1000 km. of new rail tracks every year? It is surprising how the railway would lay down 1000 km. of new lines when its previous record on this front has been very dismal? On an average it adds less than 100 km. of route length; 150 km. of running tracks length and 300 km. of total track length including tracks in yards, sidings and crossings at stations etc. Is it not an unrealistic approach or a real exercise in deception? Nothing has been done as promised relating to the following:

1. Flagging off inter-city double decker trains.
2. Provision of toilet facilities on EMU/DMU trains.
3. Construction of special coaches for physically challenged people.
4. Establishing 1000 MW power plant in Adra.
5. Allowing tickets to be sold at post offices.
6. Taking over of Basumati Press in Kolkata and modernization of railway printing press.
7. On board infotainment services.
8. Taking over the control of Burn Standard and Braithwaite & co. and Braithwaite & co.

It seems the railway has entered an era of empty promises, non-workable plans and unserviceable programmes. How long such a process would continue?

The Safety Front: Disastrous Railways

Discipline, work-culture and sincerity are the traits needed to be revived for the organizational promotion. However, this must start from the top to be percolated to the lower level. Devotion to work, constant vigil and alertness to follow action are so important to the railway staff – running or stationed – that no proper development can take place without them. Training, refresher courses and regular reminders and circulars are required to make them vigilant and dutiful. The railways have to organize their operative system and other functions on a war footing which are essential to transform them to be more spirited, powerful and competitive. Any slackness on their part would be fatal for the future progress and growth.

Presently the railways have proved to be weakest rather disastrous on safety front. Accidents, derailments and collisions have become parts of daily life. It is doubtful if one can feel secure and safe after boarding the train. Even traditional and simple measures of safety are flouted and collisions take place on many minor and flimsy grounds which do not behove well with such an old, experienced and famed railway. How drivers sleep on duty ignoring signal? Or how outer or inner signals fail immediately before arrival of the train? How station to station communications are allowed to go standstill in this era of electronically managed system and their alternative ways? The new incumbent of railways blames it to 'human error'. It seems the only human error is no other than the incumbent herself – a press note added. Her involvement in West Bengal affairs has left little time to look after the railways. She rides two horses at the same time unable to balance them. The railways have gone out of her grip and the country is suffering on account of such differing ways, callousness and irresponsible behavior. No wonder that she has been treated as holding the portfolio not of railways but of 'Derailways and Collisions'.

Over 200 accidents in about a year is not a record any government should feel proud of, more so the UPA II which had shown significantly high evidence of railways' achievement during its previous regime. What has gone wrong since then? Is it the system failure brought about due to irresponsible governance at the top? It is a well known fact that the present incumbent of the railways tops the list of absentee ministers and she is so illusive that the Rail Bhavan has yet to recognize her. Reputed national dailies have fashioned the story of accidents, collisions and derailments by putting up the facts that about eighteen major railway collisions have taken place during July, 2009 to September, 2010. The toll figures are shocking since train accidents are rare in most advanced countries where they refuse to compromise on safety grounds. The rail accident at Sainthia (West Bengal) is a glaring example of how irresponsible and mismanaged our railway system is? About 67 people are instantly killed and hundreds of others seriously injured. Within the period of little more than a year, about 300 people lost their lives and thousands others were seriously injured in 18 major collisions. If all minor accidents are also taken into account, there have been more than 200 accidents, collisions and derailments since May 09 in which 428 people died.

This state of affairs of the railways' management and working is alarming and not only on financial front but on safety grounds, the railway has shown very disappointing performance. If the railway does not improve its internal functioning and control over its wanton cruelties, we can't hope of anything better but disaster, devastation and destruction.

Footnotes

1. During British Raj in India when the railways started, they were running on the Guarantee system i.e., the investors were assured of a regular income whatever be the situation of traffic earnings. Lord Lawrence, the Viceroy in his minute dated 9 January 1869 strongly recommended state construction and ownership of railways because "the whole profits go to the company and the whole loss to the government..."
2. A.V.Poulose had opined in his article "Indian Railways: A Surfeit of Status Papers" published in the *Financial Express*, Nov. 11, 2002 that they should try to find out a solution instead of writing about them without any follow up action.
3. The Railways of the Raj tried to solve their problems without issuing Status Paper. Action was important for them. They knew merely stating problems would not work.
4. George Fernandes in his introduction to the status paper has opined that for the first time an effort is being made to tell the truth about the railways. It is important for the nation to know because the people have great expectations and also because they have greater stake in the railways as a public sector
5. This committee was formed on December 31, 1998, with terms and reference to estimate financing requirement, identify the sources of funding and study models of structure and ownership and to recommend suitable regulatory arrangement for expansion and development of Indian Railways.
6. Nitish Kumar in 2002 issued a status paper as a guideline to find right path for Indian Railways.
7. See 'Restructuring the Railways – A critique' in Indian Railways Turnaround, p.73.
8. After 2009 no proper efforts were made to chase aggressively the profits which might have stabilized the railways economy. The Railways Budget

2009-10, and 2010-11 added no significant investment with the result the pace of railways slowed down almost like a snail.

9. This refers to Lord Lawrence's statement mentioned as note number 1 above.
10. The private investors demand assured income in whatever form they invest. PPP system is no less fraught with evils than the old guarantee period.

◆◆◆

9

Turnaround and White Paper: Face to Face

By putting turnaround and White Paper face to face, one may judge the sincerity of purpose and promptness of action of one incumbent as against the tricky scheme and faulty intention of the other. Turnaround was brought about as a natural process of the railway's recovery from financial illness; whereas White Paper was issued as a damaging programme to degrade the past achievements. Turnaround was innovative and creative in action while White Paper aimed at image- destruction and demolition. They stood just opposed to each other.

Indian railways were already in shambles but the Status paper made the real revelation of their deteriorating condition in clear terms. The most important common concern was the backlog of the railway projects-the more they were delayed, the greater was the cost escalation of the projects. Ultimately, during Nitish Kumar's period they were classified as viable and non-viable so as to avoid latter projects. The Mohan Committee had damaged the prospects of railway as a unified body by its suggestion of dismantling the organisation. When in 2004 the new minister joined the railways, the situation was precarious and fund balances had already touched the minimum.[1] Under the circumstances, a formula of 'profits through volume generation and cost diminution' was adopted. The holes were pegged through which the revenue used to flow out. The decade's old corrupt practice of overloading wagons which had official 'patronage' was checked and loads were re-channelized to create more revenues to the railways. Wagon turnround time was reduced and train examination period was reasonably lowered.

These were measures which did not require any rocket science to understand and apply. The period 2004-09 brought a remarkable change and a new life was infused into the railways. The whole process was termed as turnaround — the profit making system - which worked and transformed the railways' financial position. (Raghuram/Shukla, 2007: 87).

The railway managerial system has its peculiar characteristics which keep it away from human touch and normal working relationship. Perhaps the concept of human behavior in organizational system of railway is in some way lacking. It reflects two major deficiencies. One, the railway does not accept opinions, views and sound suggestions provided by others - insiders or outsiders. They have their own expertise and decision to follow. Second, the moment the 'insider' retires or becomes 'outsider'; they do not care for him or his contribution to the railway. It creates the problem of social, psychological and human relationships. Here we are putting things in a broader perspective. The workers and staff have their own groups and association, but they are good at micro level only. The railway has never thought over as to why even after being most studied subject, it lacked the major breakthrough of a growing system and developing economy. The reason seems to be simple. It has its own circumscribed way of thinking and operational process, never tried to move out of rambling tracks.

The practical aspect which followed this situation was that it discarded the 'turnaround' immediately after its leader left the railway and issued White Paper just after the 'turnaround' concept was widely accepted as one of the winning points of the railway's financial events. The railway is the same; the workers and the staff are the same; but the key persons in power and positions have been changed. They behave differently because their senior colleagues and bosses have retired and the predecessor is not in a position to come back. It is the same staff which had generated 'turnaround' but now damaging the cause of progress. It happens because there is the shift in power game.

It was irony of an irony that the same staff scripted the White Paper. It was like loving and killing together. The railway has this peculiar characteristic of showing love and hatred at the same time. It will boomerang the new incumbent of the railways the moment she leaves the portfolio or the power attached to it.

The White Paper (2009) is the outcome of this deficiency of human behavior which does not care to establish relationship that grows along with the growth of the system. The White Paper calls the predecessor's achievement as 'so called turnaround'- a derogatory and degenerated form of expression to degrade the image of the leader of the turnaround (Ministry of Railways, 2009b: 51). The White Paper brings about a plethora of deficient programmes and levied unfounded charges of financial, accounting and administrative nature against the predecessor. The White Paper came out as a colourfully designed brochure containing 70 pages spread over four chapters. Drafted in vituperative made-to-order style, the document's third dot (point) of the Chapter I page 1 reads, "The 'main' finding is that if the generally accepted growth elasticity for transport is applied, the traffic growth performance has been below par for the entire five year period". Here three clauses are important to be noted: "main finding", "below par" and "entire five year period" (Ministry of Railways, 2009b: 4). Perhaps the new incumbent of the railways does not want anything more to say. It is enough to crush the turnaround straight in one stroke. 'Other' findings are subsidiaries. The main shot has been fired and is enough to bring the person down to earth.

The other chapters worked like fuel to the fire. The Chapter II of White Paper reviewed the performance areas of the predecessor. The White Paper accepted the growth of the freight revenue of the railways but not on account of predecessor's efforts but gave credit to the boom in the country's economy. Again, increase in carrying capacity (CC) was accepted but doubts were raised about the efficient operational value due to more of wear and tear of track and rolling stock. How peculiar was the analysis? Growth of freight system and increase in CC were accepted but with doubts and a pinch of salt. Things were improved but not to the level of 'full satisfaction'. It has criticized price policy and expressed that though in common parlance and understanding freight and rate remained unchanged but in practice they were increased under dynamic price policy and there was 44% compounded increase in freight of food grains and 35% in fertilizers. Even in passenger earnings there was a compounded growth of 1.27 percent despite no formal fare increase announcement.

What an occasional White Paper means for public sector or a government department, a SWOT analysis means for a corporate sector. Both perform the same purpose but in a different style and functioning. SWOT analysis is a managerial form of study, a process adopted in the field of business, to see and judge its working, performance and adoption of the future planning on that basis. It is a strategic intrinsic system of a corporate world to follow. It never suits a public sector which is unable to follow or decide its own course of action on the basis of SWOT analysis. The White Paper 2009 along with SWOT framework seems to be a mismatched phenomenon. When the railway is unable to follow its basic pattern, what is the use of doing such an exercise?

Moreover, the reviews presented in the form of SWOT analysis of the past performance for the period (2004 - 09) have been done 'to gain insight into railways working and throw light on various issues which the railways are facing to-day'. But while making such analysis the White Paper fails to clarify and distinguish the real strengths and opportunities from inherent weaknesses and threats. In White Paper, 2009, using Swot analysis (Chapter II), almost the same items have been posed as sources of strength as well as weakness. The opportunities and threats could not be sharply categorized and classified. For example, railway freight traffic has been shown as a potential strength but at the same time also shown as a declining factor – a source of weakness due to economic slowdown when the target of 850 MT was missed by 17 MT – a short fall of less than 1 percent only. White Paper has shown freight traffic revenue as a dependent variable of economic growth rather than an induced factor to push up railways revenue. When you accept your strength as weakness causing declining revenue and ultimate defeat, what more can be expected of growth and development? Such type of confusion prevails through the whole SWOT analysis as adopted in White Paper.

It was a direct hit on the predecessor's accounting changes that Chapter III in White Paper was added. It is interesting that while predecessor's accounting process was approved by the finance ministry and the CAG, the analysis presented by White Paper was out sourced and a consultant was hired to present and manipulate the whole financial process in order to pull down the predecessor's viewpoint, achievement and success. It is approved vs. unapproved financial battle fought between the predecessor's and consultant's analysis. It has generated great controversy and as the statistics are regarded as the greatest form of lies so should the financial system and approach also be regarded as the greatest manipulative device to prove and change anything – truth into falsehood or light into darkness. They have different ratios and financial equations to prove and establish a particular view point. It is financial jugglery and manipulation. Since the very beginning, the White Paper adopted a 'high rated' elasticity to prove that everything was 'below par' during the predecessor's period. Later, in Chapter III of the White Paper modification of accounting was done in such a manner that not only surplus before dividend which was the best part of the achievement of the predecessor, was reduced almost by one third but the figures relating to 'investible surplus' were so reduced as to render 'non-existent' and the Railway Board had to put aside this controversial financial aspect out of their accounting books. One may be at a loss to find out that Table 1a showing investible surplus from Explanatory Memorandum on the Railway Budget has been removed.[2] It only proves a point earlier discussed that railway is not an organisation one should patronize to provide any suggestion for improvement or changes. It has a habit of tracking in the darkness and feels happy the same way.

Coming to 'issues and options' as analyzed by White Paper, nothing new was added as a positive measure to reform the railways. All the issues and options were earlier dealt with in better form by Nitish Kumar's White Papers and also the same problem was analyzed earlier by The Rakesh Mohan Committee Report. Even George Fernandes' Status Paper had in fact expressed in much more clear ways the issues and options, tracking the 'truth' of Indian railways than the present White Paper. Yes, in one sense it excels others – defaming the predecessor, bringing a bad name to the railways and reviving the forces to de-nationalize the railways. One can go at any length to find such references in the brochure of the present White Paper.

The present White Paper is a pathetic elegy, an obituary on immediate past (2004-09) and a *'Syapa'* (lament) on seemingly dead railways. What hope has been left to revive the railways now? What are the ways to be adopted and how?

It is difficult but not impossible. One has to change the mindset as it was done by the predecessor. The environment has to be kept clean. The malicious propaganda against a regime of the past or the predecessor is not going to help the railways in any way. By decrying the past regime and not mentioning the name of the person is a debased political game. One must muster enough courage to come openly and declare the name of the person behind that regime. But people are intelligent enough to understand the ignoble move behind the tirade against a regime or a person. Not naming the person, but indicating the regime, does not mean that one is free from malafide intentions. It has happened for the first time in the history of the railways in India that a successor has brought out a White Paper against the preceding regime only to malign it. It is not a good sign of creating a healthy atmosphere for the work culture of any organization One must come with a clean heart to generate harmony and healthy atmosphere. Turnaround was neither a scam nor embezzlement. It was not generated out of any corrupt practice. Why then such a hue and cry over the past regime? It has blemished both the administration and the department of the railways. Let a congenial atmosphere be created so that the railways may bring back the past glory. It is possible if all the problems of freight and passenger business along with the problems of infrastructure, efficiency and productivity of the workers, problem of cross subsidization, capacity expansion, toning down cost escalation and organizational changes are handled properly. It is only then the railways may dream of a good future. They had enjoyed bright past and one must bless them with a brighter future.

The Turnaround Conquest

It was turnaround conquest of the bankrupt railway and its declining economy that a battle against deteriorating system of finances was fought. The forces of freights and rates were strengthened. A sense of fighting against the rivals was infused and the railway was armored with competitive business to acquire the lost territory of traffic market. A type of fierce battle was fought against threatening forces to establish control over the competitors.

The Battle of Change

This may be called the battle of change and transformation. The old mindset did not encourage changing its outlook. Although there was need and urge to get a new system, but the process was not so simple to be adopted. It required a leader with great confidence and vision to bring a change. The urgent necessity was to remove financial constraints, operative rigidity and managerial deficiencies.

The railway system required a novel approach and re-invigorating work culture. The managers and top bosses needed new understanding and mindset to work in the environment of free economic set up and liberal market conditions. The workforce has to develop an attitude which may transform into an efficient, productive and responsible force. The change starts with the change in view point, mental makeup and understanding of work process and performance. The change starts with changing conditions, circumstances and environment The railway demands change in system, pattern and behaviour. It also necessitates change in productive relationship, creativity and innovative practices. It was to bring a systematic transformation and turnaround providing first lessons in the art of business practice and competitive field-fighting with the rivals.

The System and Control

The turnaround conquest captured the mal-functioning of the system and acquired control over the failing railways finances. It brought to limelight the factors responsible for de-generating the process of expanding railways revenue, productivity and competitive spirit. The turnaround toned up the system and introduced a new programme of action, creativity and inventiveness.

The railways were to adopt a new policy with changed attitude and mindset. The functioning of the system was well thought out. An agenda of work and improvement for the railways was urgently needed. Thus, an immediate action plan of reform and revenue enhancement was chalked out. The increase in the volume of traffic as the basic principle was accepted to be worked out. This was accompanied by reduction in cost, increase in productivity and flexibility in price control. Thus, a system was established known as volume-price-relationship. It meant increase in traffic and reduction in freight and fare leading to profit. In acquiring this scenario, a sense of market mechanism was needed and the prevalent transport behaviour regarding the movement of goods and services was to be understood. The relative elasticity of demand for traffic had to be ascertained and causes relating to its rise and fall were to be figured out. The turnaround had established a system by winning over the following constraints which hampered the railways' business:

1. The loss making railways could be converted into profit generating force by accepting the fact that the quality of transport service had to be improved.
2. The freights and fares had to be affordable, reasonable and dynamic in their functioning.
3. The productivity and carrying capacity had to be increased, first within the initial framework by intensive transport activities and later by extending the rolling stock and traction power.

4. The new process of rail laying technology and maintenance of old rails; sleepers and bridges had to be adopted.

To start with, wagon load was increased, the old formula of tare to pay load ratio was changed, the wagon turn round time was reduced and train examination process was rationalized for better use of rolling stock. The turnaround not only gave new thought but demonstrated that improvement could be done and profits achieved by accepting change and adopting new order and system of transport activities, provision and control.

Consequence and Legacy

Turnaround established a victorious scenario of railways' growing economy with the benefits accruing to the areas of pricing, costing, loading and revenue generation. Turnaround re-modeled the railways system and provided new concept of change. The turnaround created the spirit of confidence and belief and power to seek new ways for developing railways business bringing it to logical consequences of profitability, sustainability and competitiveness.

With turnaround, the railways learnt and experienced how monopolies fail to attract business. It was a changing process from monopoly to monopolistic competition and to perfect competitive system. The railways' share of market was falling and profits were dwindling without any relief from the rival modes like roads, pipelines, airlines and shipping lines etc. The railways thus changed the view point and accepted the truth behind the business as transporter that they had to live in the market place where there was competition, rivalry and fight to acquire market share. Sitting idle won't help the railways.

The profits were related to proper organizational system, technological innovation and market conditions. One should be aware of these facts and strive hard to pursue them. Those who criticized 'profitlessness' of the railways forgot that the concept of profit was never out of sight, only they were trying to work out the business activities and allowing profits to follow. Modern economy believes in volume of production, cost reduction and sales promotion. Profits follow as a natural consequence. The increasing rate of surplus generated year after year within 2004 to 2008 demonstrated how Indian railways focused on productivity, market share and margins as their business strategies. All these achievements were the natural outcome of turnaround.

Turnaround has left its legacy in the form of changed ratio of wagon to pay load. It was turnaround which brought a new load system and the railways adopted CC +8 +2T in BOXN wagons on specific iron ore route and normally allowed 22.9 MT pay load. The new incumbent of Rail Bhavan too had accepted it as a part of improvement and legacy of predecessor's contribution. It was effortless advantage which the new incumbent had received.

As a part of legacy of turnaround, the new incumbent of Rail Bhavan or the successor enjoyed the benefit of reduced wagon turn round days as well as train examination time. Increased pay load and reduced turn round wagon days from 7 to 5 became normal for railways. Both steps added Rs. 5000 crore to Rs. 7000 crore annually to the railways' finances.

The railways received transformed economy and healthy financial and managerial set up as a legacy of turnaround which not only sustained itself but created self confidence, indubitable faith and competitive spirit to fight against the forces vitiating the transport business environment. Railways started showing increased income and profitability on the basis of reduction in cost, stepping up productivity, rationally adopting price policy, promoting sales and expanding the market. It broke with its traditional past and brought a new era of growth and prosperity. The new path was developed through the process of turnaround which established its victory over failing railways and bringing it back on the track. It was turnaround conquest that saved railways from falling into debt trap and bankruptcy.

Facets of Turnaround

The predecessor of the new incumbent of Rail Bhavan - the leader of the turnaround – was the first man in the history of Indian railways who changed the axle load.[3] The subject was dormant since 1968 and an old formula of tare to pay load ratio was being practiced. The very essence of the change was the increase of axle load of about 4 to 8 tonnes per wagon, in general and the iron - ore route, in particular. Two main factors were involved in such a change: first, the tare to pay load ratio and second, the corrupt practice of over loading wagons beyond permitted limit.

Tare to Pay Load Ratio

The above facts were the starting points of the turnaround of Indian railways. The predecessor took the initiative to change more than half a century old formula of tare to pay load ratio which was used in the twentieth century and probably the formula might have been originated during British Raj in nineteenth century. Practising such an old formula and adopting outdated tare to pay load ratio had kept the carrying capacity (CC) of Indian railways stagnant, perhaps the lowest in the world. Normally, key wagons in India carry 20.32 tonnes per wagon as the fixed load except on selected section which was 22.9 tonnes. According to International standards and comparing this to Australia, Brazil, USA, South Africa and China, it was very low. Australia had permitted axle load of 37.5 tonnes.

The predecessor adopted 4 to 8 tonnes more load per wagon and it developed a new system permitting CC+8+2T in BOXN wagons on specific iron-ore routes, first as accepted by the pilot project and later allowed on regular basis by RDSO and Railway Board.

Those who criticize the axle load pattern specially the authors of White Paper (2009) commenting about the pressure on 'rail tracks', must follow the opinion as expressed by RDSO and the persons involved in the pilot project[4] and their deliberations at the workshop organized by the railways at Rail Bhavan in (2004-05). An experiment was performed as part of a pilot project to understand the effects of extra loading over tracks, bridges, body of wagons and the speed of the trains. About six zonal railways took part in such exercise. There were no adverse effects found except in few minor cases which were supposed to be handled with improved skill and engine-man-ship of the drivers and their associates.

It was concluded by the workshop that the challenge to run CC+8+2T freight trains be accepted. One very important and satisfactory idea came to be noticed that 'all negative effects did not happen together'. This was an encouraging, rather positive point, which could be used in giving green signal to the extra load as proposed. It was an economic and technological necessity for the railways to change and adopt new ways of loading. The railways had been properly changing the rails and improving the tracks regularly according to the latest mechanical changes used to carry heavy loads worldwide. The rail tracks were fully prepared to bear the burden of extra load and RDSO had granted permission up to 25 tonnes of wagon load. It was a pity, rather disgusting, that no mention of this fact or the exercise performed during the period 2004-05 was made in the White Paper produced by the present incumbent. This proved the biased attitude shown towards the predecessor and his regime.

The Corrupt Practice

The second factors relating to corrupt practice of overloading wagons illegally is a corollary of the first factor. When the wagons are already being overloaded through the corrupt ways, where does the question of pressure on tracks and bridges arise? Where does the logic of tare to payload ratio come into picture? The tracks are being already used heavily: the pressure on rails is being already pushed up and no adverse effects are yet seen, where does the problem of overloading come in? The fact is that the problem has two dimensions. First, the corrupt system must stop and second, the resilience of the tracks, bridges, wagons must be periodically checked and improved.

The predecessor during his stint as railway minister in the very first year (2004-05) unearthed a corrupt practice prevailing in the railways and fought individually to stop it by allowing wagons to be loaded 4 to 8 tonnes officially. This was less than the loads that were already being loaded through corrupt practice. The Railway Board had no answer to the predecessor's logic and approach of legalizing load per wagon because it was already being done for the last several years.

It is strange, rather disgraceful, to find that no mention of the railways' corrupt practice of overloading the wagon was made in the White Paper issued by the present incumbent of Rail Bhavan. It was predecessor's first step to stop the corruption and the starting point of turnaround. In the same way no credit was given to the predecessor who was instrumental in legalizing the increased load per wagon and generating profits to the railways to the tune of Rs. 5000 crore from this single item. It proves that the White Paper hides more than it reveals.

White Paper Camouflages Appearance

It seemed from the very first day when the new incumbent of the Rail Bhavan joined her office that she was up to create some type of malicious move against the predecessor. This became quite evident from the tenor of her budget 2009-2010 speech when she declared that a White Paper would be issued to prove that the last five years (2004-09) of the predecessor were lost only in projecting a 'make-believe world of turnaround' for the railways. When after six months the White Paper appeared it was camouflaging appearance, hiding more than revealing. The turnaround alluded to three factors: a booming economy, changes in accounting norms and hyped up propaganda by the media and B-Schools. It was an unrealistic approach to understand Indian railways. Turnaround was termed as 'so-called' as she could not find any surplus worth mentioning for investment or appropriation to development and capital funds. The main budget (2009-10) therefore altered the predecessor's estimates of interim budget (2009-10).

It takes normally two financial years to reach the actual amount received or spent on different items and finalize the estimates of amount spent for budgeted year (BE). There remains a large margin to play with business activities in order to meet the estimates, keeping them at higher, lower or balanced level. A little slackness would reduce the earnings. On the other hand, conscientious efforts and provisions made for improvement may allow the targets to be reached or even surpass them. When in interim budget presented by the predecessor, the revised estimates had shown increased level, how suddenly a year back they were reduced unexpectedly? Though meltdown of the economy may be a plausible answer, but retrogression through effortlessness and downsizing the achievement of the predecessor may be the real answer in this case. Meltdown had its own impact but that was fully considered and original budget estimates were reduced accordingly from Rs. 100,000 crore to 93,159 crore. And in revised budget (GTR) was estimated Rs. 88,355 crore. Had the predecessor been in office, neither the actual Rs.88,669 crore nor the revised estimates Rs. 88,355.91 crore would have fallen to such a level. Given all due consideration to slowdown, the railways would have earned GTR between Rs. 90,000 crore to Rs. 93,000 crore. It was due to non-commitment of the present incumbent that the gross traffic earnings of the railways were reduced. Her absenteeism, lack of responsibility and devotion for the cause of railways proved fatal for the economy as well as lives of the people because of the increasing rate of collisions and accidents.

The present White Paper, unlike the past status papers is deceptive in appearance. Earlier papers were issued with a marked difference compared to the present. They were objective in approach and analysis and issues and options were evaluated dispassionately and put up before the railway for perspective planning and helped the government to improve trouble free rail service for the country. The present White Paper has no such aim. The purpose of the paper got defeated the moment it took a circumscribed period-based study of the immediate past. It tried to create a debate over 'financial turnaround' and presented a passionate and subjective study degrading her predecessor's achievements. She could not succeed in her mission because the White Paper was submitted to the Parliament on the last day of the winter session (2009) and no time was left for its discussion. Outside the Parliament, there were no takers of it and in academic field nobody bothered about what was happening to the railways.

At the face of it the White Paper appeared to be colourful, glossy and looked like a corporate sector's dazzling document for sales promotion and publicity. But it had camouflaging appearance. It was neither telling the inside stories of the railways nor showing any real self introspection and deficiency which may be regarded as a true Status Paper. It was just a five - year (2004–09) vituperative progress report signifying that all was good before it and would be better after it. It was the intervening period that was supposed to be bad. The tragedy of the White Paper was that it projected a bright future based on the darkness of the past five years. Never the present incumbent thought that she was getting her own point defeated by decrying the predecessor's period. You can't rejuvenate a dead body. You have to cremate or bury it only. With turnaround almost declared 'false', the body of the railway fell down the track support-less, powerless and motionless. It was turnaround which had saved the railways from becoming bankrupt and getting into the death trap of financial indebtedness. How can one expect a bright future grounded immediately on a bleak past?

Like a Greek tragedy, the White Paper first laments over its melancholy duty of issuing it, falsely describing it as 'dispassionate'. Then a short summary of 'trial and execution' was covered within first three pages. The first chapter starts with background and reviews of traffic infrastructure and organizational set up. Chapter II was supposed to be a SWOT analysis, but it got mixed up with the traffic analysis, operational and commercial strategies and earnings and working expenses giving a confused picture of its own analysis. Chapter III provided with tragic episode and an execution scene was drawn giving a live effect of how the railway was brought to the gallows. Pages 50 to 52 of the White Paper indicated that a perfect rope was brought round the neck and the railway fell down like a ghost after tightening of the rope – the process described further when the body-blood (surplus) was slimming down step by step bringing it almost to a negligible amount. When there was no surplus, no investible surplus, it seemed almost a lifeless institution. Chapter IV of White Paper was added just like an obituary – written in the form of issues and options, perfectly in tune with lamentation of a Greek tragedy - 'an oxodus' - a ritual performed at the end.

The Budget 2006 – 07

It was the historical occasion when the predecessor was going to announce unheard of achievement – the turnaround – of Indian railways. It was the historical budget (2006-07) being presented to the Parliament which announced the fund balances grown to the level of Rs. 12140.41 crore and the internal generation, before the dividend, estimated to a level of Rs. 12966 crore and the operating ratio has been favourably reduced to 83.2 percent in the year 2005-06. The year 2005-06 was declared the starting year of turnaround. The freight loading that year increased by 11 per cent and the growth in revenue reached more than 18 per cent. On the basis of the previous trend the target of goods loading was increased from 602 MT to 668 MT in 2005-06 to 726 MT in 2006-07 and freight revenue was targeted at Rs. 36490 crore. The freight loading thus increased to 123 MT in two years.

As far as the ordinary working expenses[5] (OWE) were concerned, it increased by Rs. 1795 crore in comparison to the previous year due to the increase in fuel prices. It was here that the shift in creative accounting was done to bring more transparency, reflecting changes in accounting. These changes brought a favourable situation affecting a reduction of Rs. 1616 crore in operating expenses. Over all revised expenses had been kept at Rs. 35184 crore (2005-06) which was Rs. 416 crore less than the budget estimates. As a result of these changes, the accounting system reflected an improvement in operating ratio i.e., the same was reduced to 83.2 per cent in comparison to 90.8 percent in 2004 -05. The turnaround process was explained as increasing profits in freight segment by adopting the 'increase volume and reduce unit cost' strategy. In the case of passenger segment the strategy was to increase number of coaches and occupancy of trains, reducing travel time and reducing losses in catering and parcel segments.

The budget was historical in the sense that for the first time 'the turnaround' achievement was announced. It also adopted many new steps as a policy change. For example, dynamic pricing policy was adopted for passenger as well as freight services during peak and non-peak seasons i.e., premium and non-premium services along busy and not-so-busy routes respectively. A new transport policy of private-public-participation (PPP) was adopted for significant improvements in rail services.

A Great Historical Event

Railways' turnaround has occurred during the predecessor's regime and sustained till the last year (2008-09) of his stay in the office. It has been regarded as an event of great historical importance – a conquest – of better managerial system over railways' deteriorating economy and dwindling finances as depicted in various studies and researches conducted by professional groups, expert committees and official reports. It is historical in the sense that it has come to be known as a turning point, recognized by academics from Harvard in the west to Insead in the east, accepted by print and electronic media together and declared as a rallying point and solidarity factor generating stability, integrity and unity within national political scenario and social set up. The turnaround has established its mark as a great achiever, a successful entity and profound performer as super institutional power impacting its role to transform railway's financial system.

It has found a permanent place in the financial history of Indian railways. A great catalyst as it is, the turnaround has moved the railways from its failing situation of suffering losses to an organization of making profits within a short period of about two and a half years. How has this dramatic situation come about? What strategies have been adopted? The success story of the railways quick march to the glory is a fascinating study and one must try to find out how this has happened. The coming of predecessor to Delhi and holding the charge of the ministry of the railways was just a coincidence, a chance or luck during UPA's first term of governance. It is a great trial and the predecessor has to prove his mettle worth attaining success as a minister, a founder of turnaround and an achiever of change to stagnant and financially depressed railways. The predecessor put forward the theory by analyzing the facts relating to railways style of working for generating revenue. Three immediate factors seem to be responsible for creating change and bringing success.

The first factor is elasticity of transport demand which plays an important part in determining revenue. The railways are the best example of this phenomenon. With the fall of freight rate, the volume of business goes up. The second factor is the railway being an asset-rich organisation. Most of its capital is the 'block capital' or the fixed capital and productive use of wagons, tracks and locomotives has to be ensured. The decision taken in this regard is, never impulsive, but based on reasons to bring the advantage of any change resulting only in a slow manner. The diversification of such an asset is not possible or easy and one has to work out the possibility of any action within given constraints. The competitiveness with other mode of transportation poses greater problem and has to be tackled within a rigid framework. However, one factor in this regard is encouraging. The Indian railway had the best financial cadre and can work extremely well in designing budgeting process or financial system which does not require any re-structuring as the expert group has emphasized. The railways, therefore, is safe in their hands provided a meaningful political leadership is attached with it. The predecessor, during his regime (2004–09) had given a national agenda to the railways and with his creative leadership the turnaround process could be generated.

The third characteristic feature of the railways' organisation is its departmentalized form which keeps it separated from each other. They do not think beyond immediate goals and seldom make synchronized efforts to have the advantage of a corporate culture. This creates a negative effect on the railways. It is here, the role of minister as a leader begins. He has to bring together different departments to work for a common national goal. Those who think that the railways should be kept at arm's length from political influence and financial impact and control of the central government are wrong in their approach. There are two reasons for this kind of thinking: one, there ought to be someone to integrate the railways, bringing them to a common platform and two, a political leadership is compulsory as per constitutional provisions because the railways are accountable to the Parliament. It requires a political leadership to perform this role. This brings the centre power nearer to the railways and the railways becoming the powerful link between the public and the Parliament; central government and the department of the railways. This dual role cannot be played by the Railway Board or the member finance as they do not represent the public or are accountable to the Parliament.

The above factors provide a meaningful role to the minister for the railways. He has to frame the policy as well as give leadership to the organisation. The role played by the predecessor during his stint as the minister (2004-09) was quite powerful, effective and advantageous for bringing change and creating turnaround which proved to be a historical event. Whenever the history of the Indian railways would be written specially the first decade of the present millennium, the role of the predecessor would be recognized as the creator of the great event of turnaround who successfully transformed the railways from doom to boom during his regime 2004-09.

The Global Impact

The success story of Indian railways achieved during the period 2004-09 could not be confined within the country. It reached beyond its borders towards the west and the east impacting international service and business worldwide. The governments of various countries also started judging the Indian railways for its great potential and many business collaborations began to work concerning areas of mutual benefits. The Indian railways were recognized all over the world for their achievement of turnaround, increasing revenue and favourably acquiring operating ratio as 75.9 percent- the best in the world- during 2007- 08. The total revenue receipts for that year were Rs. 73256.57 crore and increase in net revenue amounted to Rs. 18334.02 crore.

The CEO of General Electric – Jeffrey Immelt – felt interested in Indian railways and met the predecessor - the minister for the period – to congratulate him on the achievement of turnaround and said, "It is music to my ears. It seems strange– rather unbelievable - to know that a person from the rural hinterland of India has brought about this spectacular change within a short period and making great profits". He further added," I am certainly amused and happy to hear that politico from rural Bihar is talking about unit cost, volumes and profitability".[6]

Ms Karine Le Joly, Director of Academic coordination, International programmes HEC School of Management (Paris) called on the minister for railways in New Delhi on August I, 2006. She came to Delhi to study the great achievement of turnaround. She was highly impressed by the success story of the railways and showed keen interest in learning about the steps taken by the predecessor to achieve turnaround in such a short time. Ms Joly said that HEC School of Management was conducting training programme for Divisional Railway Managers (DRMs) of the railways at the institute. She also said that the significant success of Indian railways in such a short time had compelled her to make a case study of it.

US Professor of Economics, National Defense University, Washington, called on the predecessor - the minister during 2004 - 09 along with a study group on May 1, 2007. The delegation was interested in studying in detail about the turnaround process of Indian railways. They were given all requisite information and told that it had been possible because of strong determination and vision for the development of the railways, increase in occupancy of trains, more coaches for the passengers etc. With the increase of axle load, rationalisation and flexibility in tariff policy, the desired results were achieved. The delegation was informed about the railways' plan of Dedicated Freight Corridors, modernisation of tracks and signals, manufacturing of light -weight wagons and provision for e-ticketing and online enquiries through the countries.

Japan's minister of transport visited the Indian railways and a delegation led by Mr Tet Suzo Fuyushibe called on the (ex) minister of the state R. Velu, Ramesh Chandra, (ex) member (electrical) and senior officials to discuss the matter of mutual interest. The Japanese minister was highly impressed by the turnaround and extended cooperation for the Dedicated Freight Corridor flagship project. A feasibility report was conducted for the project and compiled by October 2007.

It was almost the fag end of the predecessor's regime and new elections were to be held in March/April 2009. He made a hurried trip to Japan, Singapore and Malaysia. While addressing the students and the faculty at INSEAD, Singapore on May 5, 2008, he explained how Indian railways turned over a new leaf. India has shown the world that the Bengal Tigers along with their brethren of south eastern sub-continent have come out on the prowl and ready to take their economic share of the new kill in the areas of production, distribution and transportation. The predecessor had also visited Malaysia along with his team of experts including (ex) chairman, Jena and (ex) OSD Sudhir Kumar to finalize some important deals in favour of the Indian railways.

White Paper Foils Sustained Growth

When turnaround started showing its appearance after 2005–06, in the budget speech 2006-07, the predecessor made it clear by announcing that the turnaround had taken place and financially the railway had come on the right track. The rest of the years were spent in keeping the turnaround situation intact and sustained. It required great efforts in achieving the targets fixed specially for goods and passenger traffic.

The railway economy grew during past five years at the compounded annual growth rate (CAGR) for freight loading at 8.4 per cent and for passenger kilometers at 9.14 per cent. The total traffic earnings grew at the rate of 13.26% while separately freight and passenger earnings grew at 14.11% and 10.52% respectively. Contrary to this situation during the year 2009-10, under the control of the present incumbent, the achievement shown by revised estimates in comparison to the budgeted estimates of the year 2009-10 is dismal. There has been a diminishing trend in GTR and passenger earnings. There has been no marked improvement in total receipts as well. The total working expenses have shown an increasing trend with the result net revenue fell down considerably and operating ratio ultimately gone up. The following decreasing trend has set in the economy after the sustained growth of turnaround was foiled by the present incumbent.

Table. 12 Final Trend During the Present Incumbent of Rail Bhavan

Sl No.	*Item*	*2009-10 BE*	*2009-10 RE*	*Shortfall/ Increase*
1.	Gross Traffic Receipts	88419	88356	-
2.	Total Working Expenses	81665	83440	+
3.	Net Revenue	8121	6490	-
4.	Surplus	2692	951	-
5.	Appropriation to			
(a)	Development Fund	2000	951	-
(b)	Capital Fund	00	00	00
6.	Operating Ratio	92.5	94.5	+
7.	Ratio of Net Revenue to Capital at charge and investment	6.6	5.3	-

Source: RBI Analysis of railways statistics.

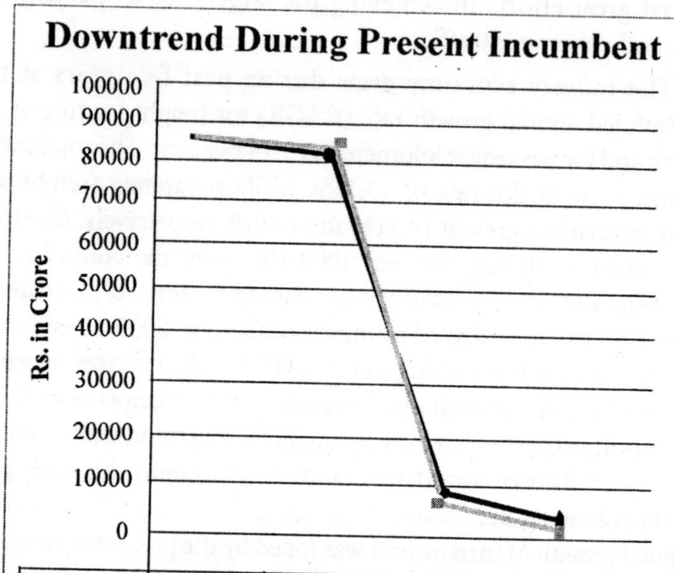

	Receipts	Expenses	Net Reve.	Dev. Fund
◆ 2009-10BE	88419	81665	8121	2000
■ 2009-RE	88365	83440	6490	951

Figure. 5 Showing down trend

If one analyses the situation, he finds that the trend set in is not encouraging. The estimates of the budget 2010 - 11 are not going to be achieved and the actual financial position of the year 2009 - 10 would be discouraging. This is the effect of not taking steps to sustain the developing trend achieved by the turnaround. With coming of the present incumbent , the whole system got deteriorated because of neglecting the economy, not accepting the fruits of turnaround and sending wrong message to the workers and the staff by publishing and issuing the White Paper. This White Paper mars the progress of the railways and creates a dent in the psyche of work-force. The table-12 shows the real position of the railways and bleak future which it promises to project.

Footnotes

1. This refers to the period 2000-01 when fund balances were at an all time low. The opening balance for the said period was Rs. 48.37 crore and the closing balance was Rs. 358.75 crore and the railways were unable to pay the dividends to the Ex-Chequer.
2. In Explanatory Memorandum on Railways Budget for 2010-11, the page (2) on 'statement' of cash and investible surplus' is missing. They have actually removed the 'statement' without giving any explanation for the same.
3. The axle load or tare to pay load concept was for the first time to be discussed in 2004 after the old formula introduced in 1964 found to be redundant. It was a daring step and required a strong leader to implement a new and changed system of wagon loading.
4. It was not a hurried step to change the axle load. A well thought out plan of pilot project was launched to study the pros and cons of the system and a workshop was organized to discuss the matters relating to axle load to arrive at an agreed pattern.
5. Ordinary Working Expenses (OWE) denote the expenses incurred for operation of the railways system including general governance and services, repairs and maintenance of permanent way and works, motive power and rolling stock, plants and equipments, traffic expenses, fuel, staff and other such expenses.
6. This refers to the CEO of General Electric, Jeffrey Immelt who spoke to the media about his impression of the progress achieved by the Indian Railways and the leader of the turnaround after meeting him at Rail Bhavan.

◆◆◆

10

Reform, Not White Paper: Bring Back the Glory

Brooding on infirmities and events of the past is obnoxious for positive thinking and real change. It does not add to innovative thoughts or dream process to be recapped. It downgrades self esteem and inner force to chalk out a workable plan. About a decade back the railway was already sapped up and was declared a bankrupt institution.[1] Whatever was done to revitalise it by the predecessor, the White Paper got it depressed again. It was a journey from bad to worse. White Paper induced the downfall of the railways intentionally and effectively. It stood at the junction that almost lost its points, links and signals.[2]

White Paper took a partitioned view of the problem. The study was neither holistic nor impassionate. It was limited in scope, analysis and became a part of self mortifying factor of diminished power to grow and bring changes. Almost all the chapters contained diminutive style of working and provided unhealthy situation for the progressive ways to be adopted. The railways were stagnant, below normal and hovering around less than expected traffic demand and low performance.[3] Its tracks and rolling stocks were over burdened;[4] its operational efficiency did not match global benchmarks[5] and losses increased year over year. It camouflaged its earning and surplus and got deteriorated much after changes in accounting norms. The primary concern therefore was the falling market share, inappropriate pricing policy, cross subsidization and a backlog of ongoing projects. It was weak financially and managerially and required a bold step for its transformation.

'Restructuring' is no answer to the railways' woes. It has been several times suggested but there seems to be no scope for its acceptance. It is a buzz word of modern management. The railways have nothing to gain from it. The railways are 'too old' to take the lessons in 'new' managerial programmes and actions. Actually, the management system has little to offer to the railways. The railways established their own system of management and organizational set up much earlier to the birth of the science of management. The management science was almost in incubation when the first railway chugged on its way in U.K. The development of transport through shipping in early seventeenth century led to establish industrial revolution in the European continent which brought railways early in nineteenth century a sense to create their own style of functioning, management and organizational process. They had also been changing tracks for betterment and for them the buzz word like 'restructuring', 'reinventing' and 'policy imperatives' seemed shallow in context of railways own tenets and ideology of progressive change and reform. The railways had their own in-depth, practical aspect of work experience and learning which proved to be more sound and useful. They have their own stalwarts, luminaries and founding fathers - their own Druckers and Porters (or Foyals, Taylors and Webers). Why should railways go for borrowed system of management re-structuring? Has anybody tried to bother about to know the fore fathers of world railways or precursors who established them in India? The pioneers of the railways had developed their operative principles and philosophy behind rail-line construction and management. The railways are indebted to them and follow their principles and advice for 'rejuvenation'. The railways have to look after the affairs of management, organization, finances and businesses. They have developed their own time tested principles which they have adopted and practised.

George Stephenson is regarded as the father of railways who for the first time developed economically usable steam locomotive. William James a few years earlier to him had suggested developing and using steam engine into national network of railways but he became bankrupt and could not do it further. Stephenson along with others, however, got an open opportunity as he was already working on the same commercially viable system. Many historians believed that Stephenson was the originator of the railways. The success of Stockton and Darlington railway added new chapter in the history of world railways. New projects like linking Manchester and port of Liverpool got the first modern railways established in U.K. Railways quickly became essential to the swift movement of goods and work force that were needed for industrialization by 1850; many steam powered railways had reached the fringes to build up London.

James Watt, William James and George Stephenson were the pioneers of the world railways who contributed at different stages various innovative systems to make the railways modern and usable. Later, many joined hands to develop them and the railways became the precious possession of both sides of the Atlantic Ocean - Eurasia in the East and North America in the West. The persistent efforts made by the leaders of the railways from 19th to 20th centuries had contributed a lot of practical as well as theoretical knowledge and understanding of the working of the railways and improved their useful-ness for industrialization.

These pioneers along with several other leaders of railway brought forward new theories for operational and managerial system. A few of them may be mentioned below:

Basic Principles of Railways' Operation and Control

1. Railways operate on the basic engineering principle of linear movement on wheels in relation to distance and time accompanied by a fuel system which need to propel it. It sets the operative principle of the railways.
2. 'Land' and 'rail tracks' are their basic fields of possession and operation which in general are actively associated with national authority. It is risky to base or transfer them into individual hands. It governs the principle of ownership of railways.
3. Since railways join land and the people together, their service to the people is the basic factor of operation and railways are meant to serve them. In turn, the railways win the loyalty and

goodwill of the people whom they serve. This mutual faith generates the principle and purpose of their existence. The much hyped idea of 'lack of purpose of Indian Railways as expressed by the Expert Group was erroneous and faulty. The Expert Group needs to know the relationship of 'land' and 'rail tracks' with the working of railways which stated the 'purpose of their existence'.[6] It was not in a good spirit for Expert Group to have dictated a 'purpose statement' for the Indian Railways (See exhibit 1.21: purpose statement of the Indian railways, Expert Group Report, P. 32).

4. There is always a scope for improvement in operative system and bringing changes for the betterment relating to the growing pattern of the railways. It belongs to the principle of efficiency and productivity.
5. Railways are an integrated force. As such they have no 'spinning off' activities. It governs the principles of holistic approach with non- core activities similar to core activities.
6. The principles of reform and change are the parts of railways operational system, ownership and authority, and loyalty towards organisation and service to the people. It is with this sense that the reforms are emphasized for the betterment of the railways. The railways do not need any 'restructuring', 'reinventing' or issuing White Papers. It needs reform, for better services, operation and earning revenues.

Reform, Not White Paper

The railways under the stewardship of the new incumbent of Rail Bhavan have refuted the claims of the predecessor in White Paper as well as Vision 2020 issued on 18th December 2009. The minister has shown in Vision document how Indian railways can be made into a vibrant and modern railways system by 2020. Such attempts have been made earlier also but they have been floundered because Indian railway has shown unwillingness to change its structure. The latest example of such an endeavour has been of the Expert Committee Report (2001) which has made extensive recommendation for 'restructuring' and 'total transformation of the railways'[7] organisation but has failed. Establishing committees, bringing out reports and issuing White Papers will not do any good to the railways unless an action plan for definite reforms is taken up. The words like 'restructuring' and 'reinventing' belong to modern managerial jargons and seem to be indispensible passwords used for any access to the information system of change or transformation. But these are heavy and confused words and mean many things to many people. Restructuring includes the progammes from simple change to the total transformation – from changing railway time-table to change the set up of Railway Board. And yet the concept of restructuring does not get a final picture. It may propose to change the whole structure of the railways, the ministry and the government as has been recommended by The Rakesh Mohan Committee Report. Owing to its multi-faceted appearance and impact, the concept of restructuring has never appealed to the railways.

Issuing White Papers now and then without any intense need and purpose to follow up makes mockery of the 'Paper' as well as the 'organisation'. White Papers work like rituals with railways. You issue it for the sake of issuing. It is issued with great pomp and show but ultimately stands meaningless.

Reforming the railways is the only way out. Reform them with a purpose, aim and mission. One must develop a broader outlook and a sense of deep understanding and devotion to the institution. The railways are down to earth organization and need greater patience, courage and confidence to change it. 'Reform' is a soft word carrying a sense of submissiveness, sobriety and purpose. It does not need any hurried action. Reform is a process which has a definite beginning, middle and end. It does not require earlier structure to be demolished for getting new structure erected. It does not dismantle the old to be replaced by the new. Reform is a peaceful and friendly process which suits the railways well.

Bringing Railways on the Fast Track

In order to emphasize the restructuring of the railways as a precondition for change, the Expert Group Report (2001) used two words — 'Repairers' and 'Re-inventors'[8] – signifying two different approaches, but preferring 'Re-inventors' for getting the railways transformed. The Group attached different connotations for these words going into the details of their make-believe linguistic interpretations without any clear cut understanding of the word, information process and their usage (Expert Group Report, p. 290). What does 'Reinventing' mean? How does it differ from 'Repairing'? The Group has dealt with the meaning of the words almost confusing their connotations. Why and how repairers are conservatives? What is the intent of Restructuring? Why is it needed in the governance arrangement between management and Parliament? Actually, all these words like - Repair, Restore, Renovate, Re-build, Reform, Reinventing, Revamp and revolutionise, Reorient, Remodeling etc. belong to the same group of 'change' varying in relative intensity and approach but bringing the same development and transformation needed for particular work and purpose. No word should be discarded or differentiated in relation to other as the Expert Group had done between 'Repairers' and 'Re-inventors'. Take for example, minarets of 'Taj Mahal' had been repaired to bring to their normal sheen after they got withered. But they were not 'reinvented'or're-engineered'. Reinventing is a heavy word. You cannot reinvent 'Taj Mahal': it is neither feasible nor desirable. But bringing extinct dinosaur on the planet again would be an act of 'reinventing' the monster. You can re- invent the extinct species if you have such a highly developed scientific system and research studies in DNA reconstruction. But what does 'Reinventing' of the railway mean? The Expert Group has added a separate chapter in the report (See Expert Group Report, Vol. 2 Part II, pp. 287-336). What specific purpose does it serve?

The best way is to use the word 'Reform'. It includes the best of 'repairs' and the best of 'reinvention'. It denotes real change for betterment; for growing and developing system of the railways and for organizational and administrative changes. Our motto should be to reform the railways. Restructuring and reinventing the railways will mean that it has to be reshaped and re-incarnated - to be reborn! How is it possible? Perhaps the Expert Group is trying to invoke the spirits of Stephenson and Dalhousie to re-invent the railway in India! Reforming the system of railways is easy to be grasped and understood. It can be applied to the whole system or to the part of it. It can work in separation as well as jointly. It requires common understanding and ability to change the pattern, strong will and courage to alter it and conscientious effort to transform the organisation.

It was an accepted truth that the railways were faltering for the past several years specially since the early years of the first decade of this century. Needless to mention that it passed through a crisis in the years 2000-01 and 2001-02 when Indian railways could not pay dividend to the government of India and deferred the same by Rs.1823 crore and Rs.1000 crore for the above years respectively. The fund balances depleted to Rs. 359 crore after withdrawal of Rs. 2400 crore from old balance of DRF. The net revenue before dividend deduced to Rs. 1071 crore. The operating ratio, which indicates the health of Indian railway, stood at 98 percent. In real terms, it could be much more than 100% had Indian railways not deferred the dividend and withdrew its fund balances.

Immediate and Long Term Reforms

Turnaround adopted during 2004-09 was immediate step to save the railways. If the new incumbent of Rail Bhavan thought that it was all fake, or much hyped a phenomenon, what immediate action she took to protect the railways from imminent collapse? She on the other hand, added more expensive schemes to create deficit and arrest the forward march of the railways which was generated by the turnaround efforts of the predecessor. If a minister has political mandate and a populist view to project and propagate, he must also realize that he has national responsibility of a ministry to run, not ruin it. Instead of attending the patient on the death bed, the doctor changed priorities and allowed the failing patient (railways) languishing to his fate. This was how the new incumbent of Rail Bhavan treated the railways. On the other hand, she was enjoying merry-go-round joy trips of Kolkata-Delhi-Kolkata looking after state politics more than railway affairs and after six months in abeyance brought the White Paper to dazzle the people falsifying that the patient who was supposed to have improved during 2004-09 was actually lying in a state of 'coma'. The only question arises here: What immediate steps she took to save the patient?

Yes, she did take those steps. She announced populist measures generating nothing to the railways' revenue. These unplanned schemes were to create more deficit as no new avenues to accrue profits were opened. The budget 2009-10 was expenditure-based and no exercise to find out exact resources was made. Even proposed paper-work on such revenue aspects was not completed. It was almost a downward journey with nothing to offer substantially.

Turnaround as Immediate Remedy

The predecessor did not allow his stint to go waste. His contribution came to the limelight because it was immediate, unorthodox and his own creation. No member of Railway Board suggested the predecessor to increase the axle load. They were rather opposed to the idea. A corrupt practice of over loading wagons was being adopted since last decade and there was no one to check it. The idea flashed the predecessor to convert it into profit making. Thus, the story of turnaround started. It earned the railways Rs. 5000 crore annually. And it did not end here. Many such simple measures were adopted with determination and confidence and a growth line of action was drawn. The railways were made to suffer by earlier stalwarts because they did not apply their own sense to promote railways. Why a corrupt officer would reveal his own corrupt practices?

The immediate measures of reform worked wonders for the railways. The years 2004-09 were termed as golden years of the railways. It was the period of turnaround. It was the period of initiating reforms. It was the period of changing mindset of the employees, workers and the top bosses. It was the period to generate profit without changes in fares or freights. It was the period of the test of the leadership where the predecessor or the founder of turnaround was declared as the best minister by *'India Today'* in 2006. It was the period when surplus before dividend grew maximum. What elses is the sign of a golden period of the railways supposed to be?

It was out of animosity that the White Paper was issued and the best period on non-operative criteria was adjudged to be of Jaffer Sharief's[9] who hit the highest rail accidents including one of the greatest tragedies the railways had near Tundla - Allahabad section. Why the consultant did not include this collision as operative principal of judgment while declaring Jaffer Sharief's period as the best? The new incumbent of Rail Bhavan and of 'Sainthia-fame'[10] too had topped the list of accidents and she had no remorse of all such because within 48 hours of the accident at Sainthia, she attended Lalgarh rally with usual joy and fun-fair as if nothing had happened, even when the victims of the accident could not be properly placed and admitted to the hospitals. After all, one must keep in view that there is a simple logic behind it – 'people have forgotten past accidents: they will forget the present (Sainthia) one too'.

An Approach to Long Run Reforms

After Independence the railways were re-organized and some improvements in technological aspects were also achieved. But during this time a peculiar situation cropped up. The railways started using mixed rolling stocks - old and new together. The old stock consisted of less efficient technology. The traction force were steam powered with old system of vacuum based brake and most of the wagons were four-wheelers with plain bearing and low carrying capacity. This resulted in difficult train formation for longer and heavier transportation. During this period eight-wheeled BOXN and BCN wagons were also introduced with better quality coupling and carrying capacity. However with a mixed wagon stock, forming a train was still difficult, but the system continued with less operational efficiency. There were other problems which the railways were facing like frequent en route marshalling and examination of trains. For this purpose several marshalling and goods yards were maintained and a new set of wagons forming a train required frequent inspection causing delays along with engines – requiring repeated halts for operational needs like collecting coal and water refills and change of running staff. Though technological change and better operative system were adopted, yet the movement of traffic became less efficient because of bottlenecks created due to wagons which required frequent separating, transferring and re-arranging to form new trains. The system of train operation was getting more and more sick, weak and ineffective.

The Gujral Stint (17th November 1980 to 6th February 1983)

The chairman of Railway Board, M.S. Gujral during his stint in 1980s, with great determination and confidence, brought spectacular changes and reforms to the sick system of rolling stocks. It was a revolutionary change and transformation created by him through adopting several strategies and technological manipulations. Firstly, he tried to re-group wagons according to wheels, couplings and bearings. The traction power was assigned long and short distances for operation according to the capacity and the power used by them like steam or diesel. En route examination system of trains was replaced by end-to-end examination process. Secondly, the retail freight load practice was terminated and new system of 'block and point to point train' was introduced. Railways supposed to be meant for heavier and longer train system and retailing was corroding the efficiency of the traffic movement of the railways. Thirdly, he adopted improved technology of brake, bearing and coupling system. Fourthly, improved wagon capacity was accepted as the basic formula for freight system and new form of BOXN and BCN wagons were initiated and high capacity diesel engines were used. Finally, he ordered the steam engines to be phased out and new era of highly improved traction power was established.

The Gujral Effect on railways was sustained for two more decades and rolling stock along with the traction power improved a lot which provided greater opportunity to develop the railways' transportation efficiency. But within the process of growth some unfavourable factors cropped up after 1990 or with the emergence of liberalization policy and new economic reforms that started hampering the smooth running of the railways. It ultimately reached the stage of no return and in 2001 it was declared at the verge of bankruptcy. Why such ups and downs took place when many new programmes favourable to railways growing system were already adopted? Railways as the department had several wings and forms of activities. They were interrelated to each other rather interdependent. If operative system seemed to be working well, the managerial or personnel department did not cooperate as it was supposed to be. Even if everything within railways thought out to be working well - the central government or the Ex-chequer on its own behalf got cut or reduced the support to the railways. The success which Gujral achieved was due to the fact that he worked before the period of new economic reforms and his influence during mid 1980s or early 1990s worked quite all right. But liberalization started picking up commercial and economic threads; the central support started dwindling for the railways. The railways were still workable provided 'a new Gujral' or a reformist comes out to revamp the railways' system. But it was not to be and the operative, managerial, financial and commercial systems of the railways came to a grinding halt in 2000-2001.

India's foreign exchange crisis during Chandra Shekhar's stint as PM was the immediate cause which ultimately shifted Nehruvian Model of mixed economy to a forced process of liberalization. There were other remote factors - national and international - responsible for such abrupt change, but this brought a great U-turn in the policy framework. Though the railways survived as a public sector, but slowly the budgetary support of the central government declined on policy grounds. The railways were not prepared for it; its professional bureaucrats were not ready to carry on such a burden and their work-as-usual attitude became harmful for the railways. They had a different mindset, though professionally well equipped; they could not stop the railways going off the track before their own eyes.

Competitiveness of the Railways

The other factor equally dominant was the competitiveness brought within business firms due to global effect and liberalization. They came face to face with the railways. The railway which hitherto was enjoying traditional advantage of enjoying monopoly power and as a heavy weight 'champion' of the transport system was specially challenged by the road transportation and year after year it was swallowing up the railway's market share. There was method to fight against such competitive force but the managerial slackness of the railways did not allow countering the challenge.

Until the pre-economic reform era, the railways were enjoying the privilege of being a pampered Navratna under the scheme of 'freight equalization', bulk products like steel, fertilizers transport cost was neutralized by the subsidy paid by the Public exchequer. In the same way 'oil pool account' system played the same role for oil products as did the fertilizer scheme. All such indirect benefits were gradually cut off and the policy of liberalization started demolishing the advantageous arrangement so far enjoyed by the railways. This was the decade of 1990s or to be precise the period between 1992-z2002 (VIII and IX plan period). However, this period had witnessed an improvement relating to quality of tracks. They were being replaced by much stronger and more durable and heavier tracks and nearly an amount of Rs. 30000 crore was spent on track renewal . This was done in order to accommodate the racing horses of the railways, imported as well as indigenously produced, to run on these rail tracks. Those who malign the predecessor that heavy wagons would damage the rail tracks have no idea how much improvement of rail tracks, sleepers and bridges has been done. The turnaround as well as heavy load were possible because of the earlier reforms in replacing tracks were achieved. This provided opportunity to the leader of the turnaround to go ahead with his schemes of increasing axle load with greater confidence and courage. It is a pity that Rail Bhavan bosses have come out with an obsolete logic of 'wear' and 'tear' of track and rolling stock in the White Paper on Indian railways, 2009 (chapter II, p. 14).

The present situation of the railways demands reforms - immediate and long run – to be incorporated to bring the system on the fast track and make the organization fully capable of generating sufficient surplus for investment and proper growth.

A Blue Print of Reforms

One can derive a blue print of reforms from the debates and discussions carried on by various committees, groups and reports. In doing so one must keep in mind that extreme views never pay in the long run. A logical and conscientious approach has to be accepted. The concepts which ramble round should be avoided and the acts which generate a vicious cycle have no scope for inclusion in the list of reforms. Most of the topics which have been covered by long and detailed discussions only conclusive part of them may be retained and added to reform activities. One has to generate the possibilities of such reforms and find space for their acceptance. It is the craftsmanship of the leader, a logical understanding of an organizer and a principled approach of an achiever which may bring the real change and reform. Railways are no exception to such ways. Only a will to change with determined action is required. The outline of such reforms is as follows:

(*i*) Reforms should occur within the existing framework of public sector status of the railways.

(*ii*) Realization of the fact that liberalized economy has come to stay should be made to the railways - their workers - the staff and the bosses.

(*iii*) The work-force along with managers and top officials should adopt a compatible 'mindset' to work as if they are running an enterprise which is technologically, managerially and commercially oriented.

(*iv*) Indian Railways work within a political and democratic setup of the country, as such at every level rights and duties to go together and the authority is accompanied by transparency and responsibility of work and action.

(*v*) The minister is the voice of the people. As such he has a mandate to fulfil or speak on behalf of consumers who utilizes the services of the railways. Pricing a commodity or service in the market needs both the forces of supply and demand. In transport market of the railways, there is no body to speak on behalf of the consumers (demand) and the price is fixed by the dominant effect of one side i.e., supply only. Here the minister comes for consumer's rescue. The minister on the other hand is also responsible for the efficient working of the department. This double and crucial role of the minister makes his work complicated and challenging. He has to inspire workers like a leader, coordinate activities like a friend and serve the organization like a helper and a common man. He has to pay due regard to the professionals of the railways to earn respect and regard for himself. It is a mutual feeling which has to be maintained every day, hour and minute.

(*vi*) The "professional bureaucrats' of the Railways have to change their attitude the same way as almost the whole Indian Administrative Service cadre has changed. Not for toeing the line of the boss or the minister but for the sake of democratic values which demand that both the minister and the bureaucrats should converge to a point where the aspirations and hopes of the common man reside. If any one of the two deviates from this process – the guilt must lie on the side which does not converge. The railways have lost much of their social and commercial values because of the lack of such approach.

(*vii*) The basic principle of 'ownership and management' should be maintained and must remain in one hand and at one place. It is the offshoot of Acworth Committee recommendation which consolidates ownership and operation of railways in one hand. It makes the functioning smooth and easy if operation, control and ownership belong to a single authority.

(*viii*) Railways is an integrated force and it does not produce 'spinning off' functions commonly known as non-core activities. Actually the concept of core vs. non-core is unjust. The very idea of non-core function is a misnomer. It is a catch phrase from the world of management and creates confusion.

Japan railways earn 70 percent of their income from those functions which are not directly related to rail operation like rail – land use, advertisement, leasing railway buildings, running railway establishment, use of cable work etc. They run on non-core functions and maintain a sound financial health.

(*ix*) Indian railways must learn to live on their own resources. It is futile to harp on the same tune that central budgetary support is dwindling. They must try to develop their own earning process so as to generate more surplus, investment, production and thus increase profits and revenue; the railways should take it easily as a policy change. The budgetary support for the railways declined three fold from 75 per cent during 1975-80 to 25 per cent during 1997-2002 and it maintained almost the same declining trend. But crying over this fact would not help the railways. They must explore all other avenues i.e., Internal resources, external assistance and outside borrowings and develop into a self reliant enterprise.

(*x*) Cross subsidization should be treated as a social phenomenon. It is a type of activity based on distributive economy. As long as India's 30 per cent people live below the poverty line, the cross subsidization has to be accepted as 'reform within reform' - a type of solution to reduce poverty rather than considering it as a problem. One has to change the attitude to accept it as a positive action than a negative factor showing fare to freight ratio as the lowest in the world. But our people below poverty line are living at the lowest rung of the ladder. They too need an affordable transport system to use.

(*xi*) The railway runs through its work force. It's an indispensable part of this system. The first-rate service of the railway can be provided only by the help of railways' employees - the staff and the workers. The policy so adopted by reducing its strength to 'right size' i.e., to the level of 1.18 or 1.2 million is correct but no retrenchment process be adopted. Only a slow process of reduction in strength is maintained.

(*xii*) The policy of corporatisation and divestment is neither desirable nor feasible in the present context of the railways. Those who propagate the theory of privatization eventually think that it is the panacea for all economic ills. One must keep in view that no ideology-driven concept of corporatization be put forward. The railway is too mature to borrow the idea either of ownership or corporatization from any outside source. The nationalization of railways was done not on any ideological ground but on the expediency of need and demand and took 19 years to get the process completed. There was no ideological haste in taking such a step. The railways' nationalization was adopted as a natural course of action. It was an activity basically needed for the smooth functioning of the railways. It must also be accepted that privatization of Indian railway was not an easy task as there were very few takers of this idea because of special characteristics of investment and very slow and low profitability. The wholesale privatization as done in some countries has reflected a hasty and ill considered experiment driven by political expediency and not as a model to be followed. The U.K. example of privatization was the worst case which was normally cited against privatization. Indian government policy had been against privatization of the railways and all the successive ministers within a decade had already announced their opinion against this motion.

Railways: Strategic Mode of Transportation

The railway transport has been accepted as a strategic mode of activity and any reform or change should be done within the frame work of this declared national policy. The railways were built in India for national integration, economic development and exploitation of resources and above all for military purpose and support for national defence. The railways continued to be highly visible as a national symbol of unity and solidarity and the role played by them in times of calamities like Maharashtra and Gujarat quake, Orissa cyclone and military operation like Kargil was something that could not be replicated by any corporation. The corporations with their purpose and aim are too short to be accepted as factors to contribute towards the high ideals of national integration and solidarity. Defence services in India are normally linked with other activities like telecommunication network and postal services for getting help at the times of emergency and war but they are fully dependent on the transportation services of the railways. There seems to be no comparison between other infrastructure facilities and the railways when the question of national defence and protection arises. This fact must be kept in mind while deciding or suggesting about 'corporatization' of Indian railways. The Expert Group (2001) was less strategically inspired and exhibited the least defence oriented attitude while recommending 'corporatization' of the railways.

The railways can work better and efficiently as a department of government than a separate body as corporation. In its operation the railway requires cooperation and help from the state governments, on the one hand and central government, on the other. A constant cooperation with both the levels of governments, is needed. How can it get such operative facilities if corporatized? Many studies including Kunzru Committee (1947), The Estimates Committee of Parliament (1955-56), Railway Reform Committee (1981), and studies conducted at IIM (Ahmedabad) have concluded for retaining the departmental status of the railways with a 'Board for the Indian Railways at the top to conduct its activities'. The Railway Reform Committee in 1985 concluded, "From the point of view of financial viability, stability of the organization, the burden that devolves on the organization to face situation like internal and external emergencies, the departmental form is most suited for the railways". It also added, "The present set up wherein the Railways are being run as a department of the central government should continue". The basic advantages of railways functioning as department are as follows:

- By adding a proper attitude and a code of conduct to pursue 'political mandate', the railways can be freed from political and other interference.

- Government procedure of functioning can be made flexible by relaxing rules and developing a new 'mindset'.
- Within a time bound programme advantage from pricing process can be achieved.
- Employees can be made accountable for sharing blame for deterioration and benefit for prosperity.

It needs to be kept in view that corporations are capable of showing illusory advantages. Actually, they are not as free from interference in day to day operation, as their image of freedom is projected. In this light, if railways are converted into corporations one should not expect that they would be free from interference.

A new reform procedure should be adopted to check the 'political and populist mandate' with which the railways are subjected to suffer. A 'definite code of conduct' should be adopted by the minister of the railways as a compulsory procedure, whenever he introduces 'new projects' pertaining to 'populist mandate'. The sources of revenue to such expenditure must be attached in detail for such projects. They should not be adopted without prior exercise to find out resources. The minister should not be allowed to treat the department of railways as a source of distributing 'bounties'. This fact must be ascertained to be followed through Prime Ministers Office (PMO) and a railways wing for such investigation should be established there in coordination with Railway Board. This does not mean pruning the authority but a check over expenses or 'extravaganzas'. How should it take place is still open to debate but a limit and control should be put over 'populist mandate'. For rest of investment and planning procedure the minister and the Railway Board are as free as ever to enjoy flexibility and autonomy.

New Reforms Procedure

There is another point of view to deal with railways' reforms. The authorities should be accommodating to such reforms. They must create room for accepting the political mandate as a part of democratic exercise within the commercial framework of the railways. How can the voice of the people be ignored on the pretext of interference by the minister? Actually, there lies a thin line of difference between the political authority and social commitment known as political interference. The political mandate of the minister costs little in comparison to the totality of investment and resource utilization. It should not be labeled as the activity trying to arrest the growth of railways. In this situation political and 'apolitical' spheres of activities should clearly be demarcated and the railways should continue to operate with greater vigour and force to achieve better results from rest of the projects. A little political margin should be left for the person who is answerable to the Parliament and the people. In this regard classifying and re-classifying works and activities are necessary to find out politically sensitive and non-sensitive areas of operation. The railways' professionals should concentrate on non-sensitive activities. Politically sensitive areas of operation should be left to the minister to decide and act.

Why many reports submitted earlier failed to attract political attention for change and reform? It is because many of them including The Rakesh Mohan Committee Report 2001 harped too much on negative side and politically sensitive approach in proposing changes. The re-inventors must accept the fact that 'corporatization' does not form the part of reform process. In the same way the case of retrenchment and pension schemes do not form the areas of change. As such they have to be kept untouched. Just find other areas of reforms like creating more of rail loads , increasing wagon loads, developing 'Diamond Freight Corridors' (DFC) , improving tare to pay load ratio, producing light weight greater-carrying- capacity wagons, enhancing freight traffic speed and generating more traffic. These are the areas where no minister would like to interfere. As a matter of fact, the concept of interference and non-interference should not be cropped up. The pity is railways' stalwarts and bosses have lost the will to change or reform the organization. Let there be an agenda - a single minded approach - to develop railways into a larger business enterprise by putting them on fast track.

There has never been political constraint over technological improvement. The operational area of the railways is wide open for reform and change. One needs to keep in mind that within five years of operation the sign of technological changes start appearing and one should not wait for long to bring out real technological change i.e., more than a decade. In the fast technological changing world of today, even two-year period seems to be longer to bring transformation. Let changes be recognized as a continuous part of the growing system of the railways. Who is going to stop the efforts of the railway-staff if they are being directed towards genuine change and reform? The fault lies with the human resource of the railways. High or low, they are not truly interested in bringing the change. It is surprising to find that the efforts of the predecessor are being nullified by producing White Paper. What was the need of issuing it at this juncture when several status papers were already lying with the Rail Bhavan? Only a plan of action was needed and the purpose would have been solved by issuing Vision Paper only. But the great minds of the railways never do the work normally. They first stir a problem and then try to find its solution.The present conflict between 'turnaround' and 'White Paper' is the outcome of a 'crack special' - an empty train full of sound and fury carrying nothing substantial to offer.

The Indian railways need to overhaul the managerial and operational system. They are under constant threat by road transport and losing its share of the market year after year. They have to accept this challenge and set their own house in order. The railway as a mammoth organization has so far enjoyed the monopoly revenue, now found it in a competitive environment unable to respond well and manage itself. It seems to be in a state of dilemma leading to considerable introspection over the years. In order to find the real situation one has to examine the track record of Indian railways in managing the change and reform. A normal way is to look at initiative taken to reduce expenditure and increase revenue. An examination of the expenditure incurred by the railways reveals that almost 60 percent of income is spent on its own maintenance and the balance is spent equally between fuel and material management. The other basis is to reduce workforce. A decision has been taken in this regard on the basis of 3 per cent of annual retirement of the staff. It has been decided that only 1 per cent will have to be newly recruited and the rest 2 per cent of vacancies would go unfulfilled reducing the staff till it reaches 1.2 to 1 million total strength of work force. The railways freight services have to be remodelled with greater volume-creation and reduced unit cost. The goods trains have to be heavier, longer and speedier. However, the technical character of rail traffic cannot be changed completely. Freight trains are basically meant for heavier loads and longer distances to cover comparatively at higher speed than road or shipping transportation. As an answer to greater competition the railways have started container services and introduced private public participation (PPP) schemes along with joint ventures to form the norm of future railways traffic system and management. A regular improvement in technical process has to be maintained with better signaling, track maintenance, electrification, developing speed and adopting efficient human management system and control. The 'soft' and 'hard' areas of operation should be covered with equal emphasis to bring a change in style of functioning and to redefine the line of action which railways have to take relating to government interference, regulation and policy framework. It is not a good way to express that the government should be kept at arm's length. Why? Is the government untouchable? Does this distancing mean freedom to railways? It is futile to argue that the authority which empowers the railways to function and maintain their status be asked to keep its hands off. It is directly challenging the authority. Those who remember the situation prevailing during 1980s may easily ascertain the real status of the Railway Board when all its members including the chairman were removed at one stroke and Gujral was installed as the new chairman by the then Prime Minister Indira Gandhi. The railway must know its limits - the extent to which it can demand autonomy or freedom from interference. The only way out is to find the solution by accepting the political mandate of the minister. It requires totally transformed mindset to adjust with such a situation and the railway bureaucracy has to learn this craft. Reforming the railways means crafting the way to provide space for change and adjustment.

Bringing Back the Glory

The railways had ups and downs several times during the long history of their existence but never faced an occasion when they were not able to manage the crisis boldly. They had addressed the grievances and tackled the situation gracefully. However, with the passage of time the fighting spirit, resilience and the force to resist against outside factors affecting railways had weakened. It happened due to the lack of proper understanding, unity and in-house harmony which led them to accept deteriorating situation. The operative, commercial and managerial processes were damaged and the railways virtually came to a halt at the turn of the century. It became normal for them to perform work-as-usual by adding less and extracting more. The results were obvious. The department was brought into disrepute and the grace and dignity with which it used to live so long got reduced. The early years of this century faced financial bankruptcy, managerial deterioration and operational crisis. Some efforts were made by the predecessor during 2004-09 but the railways could not win over the vituperative and damaging tendencies of downgrading the past. The hard earned glory of the department thus started fading away.

Play to Win

The working of the railways is highly technical process and requires all wings to be fully operational and well managed. The lack of proper coordination among them will defeat real purpose of providing transport services. The railways should be accepted as a game to be played purely with sportsman spirit to put efforts to win it. The good player always plays fully determined to win, not to lose the game. It is the spirit behind the game that is important. If you indulge in business not to earn profits, what is the use of such a business? It is another matter that you fail in your efforts, but the purpose and aim should be to defeat your rival, competitor and opponent. A constant focus is required on playing the game; the railways need the same attention, spirit and mindset. The railways is not a single player in the field of transport business; there are a number of other modes of transport which oppose directly and indirectly its move to capture the market. The days of railways' monopoly have gone; that of competition, rivalry, trials and stakes have come in.

How to play this game is the strategy which is adopted to outline the steps and moves necessary for it. To win the game is always strategic. One cannot have a simple walkover. One should not be complacent about entering into the risk. Manage the risk intelligently and play to catch the kill. It is a fight - may be a battle to lose, but a war to win. Strategies, ways and methods are yours; put courage, confidence and inner force to master over them and achieve success. Whether it is change or reform, operational system or business initiatives, it is the will power that motivates all. The Indian railways has fought many a battle in the past: it has to win the war now to bring itself at number one in the world. You have to change unfavourable ratios and deteriorating traffic volume, bring down unit cost and increase the rate of profitability. 'Re structuring and policy imperatives' are no more the issues. The railways are competent enough to achieve success within the existing framework.

To win the game, one has to follow the rules accurately. Playing the foul game gives opportunity to the rival to add up to their score.What are these business rules to follow? What are political games to watch and theoretical aspects to develop?

Winning the game that is being played by the railways means increasing productivity, revenue, the efficiency of the workforce and profitability. It also means to reduce the ordinary working expenses and bring the operating ratio at the favourable level at least less than 80 percent in normal course. Indian railways do not attach any ideological dogma with it and as such it is neither left or right to centre. It is just linear. It has its own philosophical approach to observe operational values and intrinsically what was true to Indian railways during the Raj regarding ownership, functionality, purpose of existence and vision for service still holds good. It consolidates the national life and serves the people far and wide-with profit or even without profit. It is this fact which necessitates laying new railway line in Jammu and Kashmir profitless and developing Dedicated Freight Corridor (or Diamond Traffic Corridor as the new incumbent called it) for easing out traffic movement with an eye over the profits. Has Chinese 'Tibetan Corridor' of railways meant for profits? It is always half way between the strategies and profits that the railways' operational philosophy lies and no 'corporation' has capacity to fathom the depth of purpose and vision behind the railways.

Towards New Turning Point

The new incumbent of the railways or the successor should have taken "turnaround' as a challenge to defeat the predecessor in generating record volume of traffic and earnings rather than making a fuss about it even if it did not appear as sound as she was expecting to be. At least the targets which were achieved during 2006-08 were high in volume and percentage and the year 2009-10 should have been set to achieve higher targets, instead of lowering the whole system calling it unrealistic rather unachievable. This was the spirit which demoralized the railways.

An immediate thrust or pushing up the operation with some induced mechanism was desired for the railways. Pulling it down disturbed the whole system and brought it back at least for five years to recover the lost position. One could cry over the past but on what cost? If one did not want to move ahead, the stand might be tolerated, but if the aim was to acquire high targets, as it ought to be, the analysis of the period of the predecessor (2004-09) became counter-productive as nothing substantial followed from being too critical and vituperative. The best way was to generate a turning point or turnaround again or one might call it as new strategy to bring the glory back. It should have moved in such a way as to cover up an ambitious plan of investment of Rs. 250,000 crore by the end of eleventh five year plan (2007-12). But nothing seemed to have come nearer to such targets as internal, external and budgetary resources (all put together) were far away from their own estimates. In order to achieve a turning point, old or new, the railways needed to know if (a) they were really at the cross roads; (b) what immediate thrust or pushing action was adopted to create a turnaround - financially a major breakthrough was to be created; (c) whether the action taken was capable of sustaining itself for the further years? Such steps were not at all taken up. Instead, a White Paper to please political intent justifying 'below par' achievements of the predecessor had come to highlight and the railways were set to move in slow motion to suit the somnolent bosses and employees showing least concern for development like their new guard who seldom wished to be at Rail Bhavan.

Provide Space for Reforms

The railway needs reforms, not White Papers. The bosses and higher ups should try to create space and opportunities for reforms within the basic constraints they are operating. They should adopt a workable plan for reform. The aim of reform and change should be to generate greater revenues. If one plan fails they should try for the other. But in any case they should not remain complacent about the change.

A blue print of reform has already been presented. What is important here is to work out basic practical approach so that a line of action may be drawn. Besides, this may give a broader spectrum of change and justification for such changes to be retained for longer period. This may also ensure that no reversal of such changes take place either on ideological or flimsy technical grounds. The following theories may give a clear line of action.

1. *The theory of gradual change*

It is not new for railways to adopt a process of change gradually. When the administration during the Raj found that the guarantee system was not working well rather counter-productive, they thought over patiently and brought a modified system along with the old system which continued. It took about ten to twelve years to bring about the change (1870-1882) and again a new phase of reformation was adopted encompassing a long period of about 41 years ranging from 1883 to 1924, known as Reformation Age. When Acworth committee recommended the total nationalization 'to bring English companies to an end', it took 19 years to complete the process— 1925-1944. What is surprising here is to mention and compare how callously, The Rakesh Mohan Committee wanted to bring out the change rather demolish the railways' system to be replaced by Indian Railways Executive Board (IREB), Indian Railways Regulatory Authority (IRRA) and Indian Railways Corporation (IRC) and a road map of railways' reconstruction was prepared to phase out the old system within 3 to 5 years only. The cosmetic touches required at the end were allowed a year or two more. The Expert Committee was in too much of a hurry to become 'immortalized' historically by bringing the 'new face of the railways' which proposed to destroy the old system and replace by the new. While the Railways' of the Raj took nineteen years to nationalize it, The Mohan Committee sanctioned only 3-5 years for 'Re-invention, Re-structuring and Reforming' the railways. We have to learn the principle of gradual change from the railways of the Raj.

2. *The Principle of Time Element*

The factor of time generates dynamic system. When, how and what changes have to be brought about - the timing of action, decision and implementation is as important as the change or the reform. The action which is related to more of 'political mandate' has to be judged by its timing to decide its implementation. The increase in axle load started at the most suitable timing. The railway was searching for new avenues of resources and the idea of increasing the tare to pay load ratio suddenly struck the leader of the turnaround. Although the members of the Railway Board were opposed to it, but the predecessor was adamant to this change. He ultimately succeeded in his fight.

As opposed to the above 'good' timing, the announcement of 'corporatization' of Kapurthala rail factory was ill-timed. It was met with great resistance by the workers and ultimately the ensuing change was dropped. In the same way, the passengers sought a rollback when a new 'side-berth' was added to three tier sleeper class. It was causing more trouble than enhancing revenue. Increasing fare or freight is not a good strategy related to time when elections are to be faced by the person or the party. It is called a populist policy but it is accepted as a strategy. The fare and freight policy is in many ways governed by the time factor. Therefore, some margin should be provided for policy adjustment and time. But when financial system is at stake there is no alternative except to increase freights and fares according to the dynamic price which involves the element of time called slack or lean period when demand is low, and thick or peak period when demand automatically rises. The commodities are also categorized according to their seasonal demand and benefit to such time or seasonal effect has to be taken into account. Such exercise is normally done by revenue and finance section of the railways for increasing freights to earn revenue. But nothing can be done according to text book instructions. Such changes are possible only in a practical way by field studies and work experience.

3. *The Theory of Privatization and Joint Venture*

The railways need to develop more and more private participation and joint ventures in the areas which are known as non-core sphere of activities. Since core activities are difficult to be brought under private public participation on account of stiff resistance from work-force, difficulty of divestment and non-takers for the scheme, the non-core avenues should be made available for private capital investment. There is no opposition for such non-core activities for bringing into the fold of private capital. The areas which do not show real inclination of privatization, may be tried to bring under joint venture. A broad scheme of private public venture should be made and a type of mixed economy in railways should be introduced. The purpose of such scheme is that non-core areas be freed for new capital venture. During the stint of the predecessor (2004-09), container services were launched and railway land and buildings were brought under the pre-view of such activities. It is heartening that a committee under A.K. Mitra has also been set up for bringing out such proposals by the new incumbent but the work is not getting done on the fast track.

The railways have to develop their own approach to privatization and joint venture schemes. The areas of basic operation were left untouched. The private players were asked to participate in bookings, aggregating and delivering freight. The private partners may be allowed to open city cargo booking office. Such schemes are never opposed by labour unions because they do not displace labour. They are employment generating schemes. There are other areas where they can operate like modernization of railway stations, leasing out railway buildings for commercial use, developing hubs for logistics to connectivity to ports. Even the new manufacturing units may be allowed to be worked under joint-venture because new units don't face resistance from the unions. Joint venture therefore is crucial for railways' new projects because they seem to be harmless for workforce and the 'sting on full privatization' is out as a dangerous tool and the state authority still stays in the system, although day to day or managerial function is performed by autonomous private firms on the basis of their percentage of stake in the joint sector organisation.

4. *The Theory of Least Resistance*

It is a lesson plan for railways bureaucracy. The Indian political system and the present economic situation have slowed down the speed of reforms. The methods of change too have been tempered to be rendered ineffective. There are left wing organizations which hamper the progress of reforms if at all adopted and ultimately such changes get reversed and do not see large span of life to exist and operate. On the one side, there is political leadership, with dominant authority to overrule what is done by the bosses at the management level, and on the other side is the rigidity of the railways operators, their bureaucratic temper, trying to exert their influence and pull down the top authority. The old timers must have an episode to remember how B.C.Ganguli and K. Hanumanthaiya clashed over a small issue which took an ugly turn. Not only Ganguly was instantly 'retired', just within six months or so Hanumanthaiya was removed as a minister of the railways. Their disproportionate ego got them involved in such a clash. It is a lesson for the bureaucrats in general and railways professionals in particular to adopt 'a line of least resistance' especially in the case of reform or change. In the most liberalized and democratic set up that is India today, the people who matter always consider their political position, the diction which they use, the period in which they operate and the speed at which they try to function. Thus, a formula of change in the present condition is evolved: adopt a gradual process of change and implement it with an eye on timing, positioning, and use of language while taking a stand of the least resistance during the process of transformation or change. This scheme of action worked well for both – the minister and the railways professionals – who brought turnaround – a historic change in the railways operational and managerial set up.

Fixed the Target High

"Armed with technology, knowledge...I realize small aim is a crime". Thus wrote APJ Abdul Kalam in his book of poems[11] *'The Life Tree'*, p. 3. It is true to individuals as well as the institutions having acquired stake in the progress of the society and the nation.

One may still wonder why the present incumbent of the railways announced in the budget speech (2009-10) - a difference of amount Rs. 4740 crore – an estimate as unrealistic or 'unachievable'. Till the period the predecessor was in office, everything was all right - if not, he could have tried to achieve it or come nearer to it. But downright rejection of the past estimate by implanting a 'small' target (aim) might be called in the language of the Poet-President a 'crime' on the basis of self assessment. The impact of meltdown on the economy or slowing down the rate of GDP was a point to be considered, but what was the meaning behind issuing White Paper? Joining two points to make a line - 'unrealistic estimates' and bringing up 'White Paper' - the linear process seems to generate a suspicion. It was all meant to down size the contributions made by her predecessor.

The Indian railways put up an ambitious Eleventh Five Year Plan (2007-12) with an investment of Rs. 250,000 crore. The railways were to acquire the target of Rs. 100,000 crore to finance by internal resources. It required an additional income of Rs. 20,000 crore or more a year. Has any definite arrangement been made in this regard? What about Rs. 40,000 crore of market borrowings? And how PPP schemes would provide Rs. 50,000 crore? The Eleventh Plan period is coming to a close and the railways are still enjoying lethargically the 'blame game'. White Papers don't generate revenues. They can however, kill the spirit that lead the railway employees to work for the common agenda of achieving high target which is the demand and the purpose of the organisation. They must have high targets to achieve and strive hard to bring the glory back.

The targets have to be set in the light of Vision 2020. This is incumbent's own document. If the predecessor's estimate of Rs. 4740 crore in the interim budget 2009-10, seems to be unrealistic how will she cross the minimum limit of Rs. 20,000 crore extra revenue annually? The only fact which has to be kept in view is: if your targets are low, you can't bring any revolutionary change in the financial system of the railways.

When high growth strategy and massive investments are required for capacity enhancement to the tune of about Rs. 14, 00,000 crore in the next 10 years or Rs. 140,000 crore annually and a step has been taken to project Vision 2020, why then the railway is shy over as little a sum as Rs. 4700 crore of predecessor's estimate and brings out a White Paper? Is it not a contradictory position to present both the documents together? What about the resource mobilization for such a massive programme of capacity creation, network expansion and technological upgradation? It is believed that world-class stations which were being announced since the period of Nitish Kumar – a decade back – will be financed through PPP scheme now because railways failed to persuade the Central

Government to make provision for the same earlier. But what is the guarantee of getting these schemes completed when the picture of PPP itself is not very clear and it is still a scheme on papers? The high speed corridors too may expect to meet the same fate.

Instead of moving on their own strength and getting on to the fast track, the Indian Railways are showing a borrowed strength of 'Gross Budgetary Support' (GBS) in financing about one third of resources i.e., Rs. 500,000 crore in ten years or Rs. 50,000 crore annually. However, the past trends of GBS are not very encouraging and if dwindling support in the past five year plans regarding GBS from 75 percent to 25 percent is of any evidence, it is futile for railways to bank upon a 'steady-flow' of finances in the shape of readily available 'Accelerated Railways Development Fund (ARDF)'. It seems quixotic way of riding and driving the railways.

The Indian Railways must develop their own resources and gradually enter into the high growth scenario. It matters little if Vision 2020 takes a decade more, but it is disheartening if the railway loses courage to cover up as low an amount as Rs. 5000 to 10000 crore annually. The railways have to cross this limit to Rs. 20,000 crore and Rs. 40,000 crore annually more than their previous year's earning in sequence. It is not difficult for Indian Railways with such a devoted work force and world class professional cadre. Only they have to set their mind and plunge into the revolutionary programme of transforming the railway with a vow to achieve success within a decade or two. If the railways of China (MOR) can develop the fast corridor over the hard snow-bound terrain of Himalayas running across the highest plateau on the earth, why can't we bring a miracle to our Indian railways (IR)?

Enhance Technical Base

Indian railways must change it to acquire excellence in operation, finance and management. Living in a subdued state of being called an institution 'below par' and getting degraded to be labeled as bankrupt is a sign showing lack of self respect, grace and dignity. It gets more and more debased when 'insiders' try to bring dishonour to the organisation. It is like attempting to enact a 'stripping' (*cheer haran*) of the railways. If the railways have self esteem, the insiders must stop to play blame game against their own people. What the railways need is technological enhancement, capacity increase and network expansion. By adopting such steps effectively they can bring back the fame and prestige to the railways.

Enhancing technical base requires modernization of the railways. The priority should be given to replace the old and laying the new rails creating standardized track structure with 60 kg, 90 UTS rails. Sleepers should have iron and concrete base with elastic fastening. It should be assured that these tracks remain fit to allow trains with the speed between 150 km. to 200 km.ph. The bridges should be monitored through latest management system and new bridges should have approach slabs. The retrofitting of arch bridges should be taken up. The traction power is important to run the train. High horse power locomotives should replace the old stock for heavy haul freight and high speed passenger train services. Electrical high horse power locomotives (9000hp – 12000hp) should be developed for speedy and heavy transportation. The system of tare to pay load ratio of 22.9T per wagon carrying capacity (CC) has already been developed. It should increase to 25 T (CC) with the aim to improve further up to 30T as tare-to-pay load ratio. Quick and heavy transportation will ensure better service to the consignor and the passenger. It will bring more revenue by increasing efficiency, productivity and better operation. Nothing else, but hard work, higher aim and developing human face of the railways will bring the honour, grace and glory back to the organisation.

Footnotes

1. This relates to the report of the Expert Group titled "The Indian Railways Report - 2001". The report is over loaded with the concepts of financial deterioration, impending bankruptcy, business inadequacy and collapse of the railways economy. It pleads nothing less than re-structuring the railways for recovery from the financial illness.
2. The railways were not only at cross roads, but they had lost almost all points, links and signals making them unable to move any further.

According to White Paper, IR was still far from optimizing the operational and efficiency parameters compared to global standard. The carrying capacity of IR is still low, unable to meet the additional demand generated by rapid economic growth.

3. The White Paper projected the image of the railways as a stagnant sector hovering over its contribution to GDP at 1.18 during the period of study. The IR GDP elasticity is still hovering around only 0.79. According to White Paper the traffic growth performance has been below par.
4. There was a dangerous sign indicating that the rolling stocks were over burdened due to deliberately increased carrying capacity which had a bearing on the wear and tear of tracks and wagons.
5. Comparing to international standards the Indian Railways did not match the benchmarks and their losses were increasing year over year. The White Paper had stated, "In terms of route length IR is fourth in the world. As regards freight traffic, again it is fourth and substantially behind US Railroad, Russian and Chinese Railways.
6. Indian Railways Report - 2001, Vol. 2, Part II page 313. The exhibit 8.7 has given a purpose statement for Indian Railways. The highlighted parts are: to play a central role in India's overall economic growth; to provide customer focused cost effective transport solutions like freight, passenger and suburban passenger and provide the most compelling value to them; to have the objective of integration of strategy, discipline and customer orientation etc.
7. Re-structuring process has been proposed by the Expert Group. It has many aspects starting from capacity building, increase in volume of traffic, greater capital expenditure and investment, generating high growth scenario to create confidence among external investors and bringing out a phased programme of reorganizing administration and management system of IR.
8. The words 'Repairers' and 're-inventers' have been used by the Expert Group in order to create distinction between the two. They actually fail to draw a clear line of demarcation because linguistically and also from the 'usage' point of view, the words do not make such difference as has been conceived by the Expert Group. Perhaps no member of the group seems to be really expert in linguistics so as to derive such a meaning. There exists no such group or cluster as 'repairers' and're-inventers'. Repairing does not mean 'reverting' or showing no alternative that can be proven to be better. The arguments given in favour of re-inventers are not convincing. How one can be sure of re-inventers for not doing face lift but adopt fundamental change? Is there any guarantee? The

concepts derived so are totally confused. The Expert Group goes in length to discuss this matter only to justify the point of re-structuring the railways which can be done by re-inventers and not by repairers or reformers.

9. White Paper has referred to it as the period 1991 - 96 being the best for Indian Railways in the last two decades, forgetting the fact that worst case of railway accident with head on collision occurred during the same period (perhaps to be ranked 'best' accidents don't count in railways according to White Paper).
10. This brought new fame to the successor who remained during 2009-11 at the helm of the railways. People would never forget Sainthia accident and the minister for the railways of that period.
11. Ex-President, A.P.J. Abdul Kalam in his book of poems *"The Life Tree"* writes in the poem titled 'Song of youth':

    "As a young citizen of India,

    Armed with technology, knowledge and love for my nation,

    I realize, small aim is crime."

◆◆◆

11

White Paper and Beyond: Railways in Quagmire

The years that lapsed since the appearance of White Paper have shown damaging effect on the railways - specially their finances. During these years no conscientious efforts were made to establish and adopt any growth process to achieve landmark success in the areas of revenue- increase, traffic enhancement and technological advancement. On the other hand, the railways were allowed to deteriorate further in the sphere of maintaining fund balances, safety measures and modernization programmes.[1]

Indian railways along with White Paper have served a political agenda to undermine the importance of the 'past regime' and establish the supremacy of the 'present' by dismantling the structure of 'turnaround', transportation system and the new mindset created to rejuvenate the railways' economy. The railway politics has played a major role in bringing about stagnation to its finances and revenue system. Since the last decade no fare hikes have been made.[2] The cross subsidization has increased to serve the political ends. Non-plan expenses and ordinary working expenditure have grown limitlessly with the result the operating ratio has touched 95 or more per cent leaving no scope for further growth of the railways. The last three years (2009-12) have shown remarkably high political impact on the railways and have degenerated their functioning at all the levels. The following facts may be noted:

1. The political impact of the railways has shifted the routine functioning of the railways' management and top administration from Rail Bhavan, New Delhi to Kolkata and to the Writers' Building.

2. The Trinamool Congress Chief still holds 'de facto' power of running the railways.
3. Even when she was minister for the railways during 2009-11, most of the decisions were taken from Kolkata 'office' instead of Rail Bhavan and the media had nicknamed her as an absentee minister.
4. Politically, the railway is a much sought after portfolio because of its 'people connect' profile. It provides perfect opportunity to woo the voters and play vote bank politics.
5. Through the White Paper a wrong impression was created about financial jugglery to impress upon the Central Government to provide more funds for the railways.
6. Politically, the minister succeeded in establishing 'Pradhan Mantri Rail Vikas Yojana' to get funds for 'dream projects' (though the plan is still on paper only).[3]

The railway politics has made it possible to divert various rail-related projects to the 'home state' of the minister and to syphon off the funds for using them in their completion.

After issuing White Paper the railways adopted negative approach toward preparing budget estimates and fixing traffic targets to earn revenue and pursuing benchmarks to achieve results. The pace of development was slowed and even below normal than the business-as-usual practice was adopted.

It was practically an unsound decision to discard the activities related to 'turnaround' procedure hitherto practiced. To declare turnaround as fake was a folly. It was a shameful spectacle for railway's financial experts to accept the White Paper and let it go unchallenged by not issuing any 'counter' reply to it. The railways accounting process is a cash-based system. The figures and facts accruing during 2004-2009 were calculated on cash based financial practice of the railways. How can cash surplus so earned be negated on accrual accounting? The peculiarity of railways' depreciation reserve fund (DRF) has not been properly understood and the so called 'consultant' has created a mess of the whole matter. Rail

Bhavan has the best of financial cadre in the country. Why did they keep quiet when the White Paper was out? If they had fear for losing their jobs, why did they not issue a joint statement under their association's name specially when their credibility was at stake? Yes, a retired finance commissioner of the Indian Railways A. V. Poulose has raised his voice against the 'overrated elasticity' used in White Paper to downgrade the past regime. But his was the lone voice which created little impact (See Poulose, A.V. "Vision 2020: A Workable Goal for Railways", *The Indian Express*, January 13, 2010. Poulose adds, "Considerable confusion has been caused by 'White Paper on Indian Railways' released along with Vision document. The railway convention committee could take up the equity of methods adopted in the White Paper and other aspects).

The truth of the matter is that there has been a turnaround, and it has been expressed by 'Iras Times' in 'professional issues' (*Iras Times*, 2009). They declared that there was actual turnaround of the railways (during 2004-09) and the change in accounting system so adopted was better rather than on political consideration. If it was financial jugglery, how could it escape the attention of both the Cabinet and the Lok Sabha Standing Committee concerned? The main dispute was on two entries or head of expenditures i.e., appropriation to depreciation reserve fund and expenditure on Pay Commission pay out. The White Paper doubted on changes made in accounting norms during the last five years which had 'inflated cumulative cash surplus' before dividend by a whopping 55 per cent to the claimed Rs. 88669 crore. If payouts for Sixth Pay Commission demands on accrual basis (Rs. 26306 crore) and appropriation to the DRF (Rs. 22952 crore) are taken into account, the figures fall to Rs. 39411 crore.

The crux of the problem is how can these be done on accrual basis when order of payment on account of Pay Commission itself has come in 2008 and DRF was never taken as expenditure on accrual basis?

The White Paper thus is a flawed report full of contradictions and is fraught with severe evils.

Depleting Fund Balances

When the new minister took over the charge in May 2009, the first step she did was to terminate the process of turnaround. This disturbed the financial progressive ways and tempo of railways' working so meticulously adopted by the earlier regime. Once you disturb the rhythm and the momentum, it is hard to regain it. It was this reason that she could earn an all time lowest surplus in her first year as a minister and never was able to reach nearer to the earlier figures. She started reducing budget estimates out of intrinsic fear that she might not achieve higher targets. She was not ready to put up a fight against the forces hindering the growth and to take the railways on the fast track. She discarded turnaround rather decried it on the wrong advice given by a few of her favourites at Rail Bhavan. This formed the basis of quite a different path chosen by her. She started with low targets and very 'realistic' lower revenues and traffic movements. This pushed railways into back gear, and fund balances started declining much faster than the revenue earned.

Three main budget studies may be cited as examples of such a deteriorating condition. As it has been mentioned earlier in Chapter 3 of the present study where the main budget 2009 and interim budget 2009 have been compared that a deliberate effort was made for a final showdown to the cause of turnaround and in the name of 'realistic' estimates almost all the head of items were reduced considerably. The net result was quite disparaging as expected. Two years later, when actual performance of the year 2009-10 came to light, all the estimates (budgeted and revised) were reduced to a horrible state. There was no surplus/excess generated worth mentioning. The railways could earn only Rs. 0.75 crore net revenue (Explanatory Memorandum — 2011-12, p. 1, Budget at a Glance, Col.1, and Actual 2009-10) as against an estimated figure of Rs. 2642.26 crore. This increased the operating ratio to the tune of 95.3 per cent. In this way, railways cash reserve fell from Rs. 13431 crore to Rs. 75 lakh. The minister of this period — 2009-10 – literally left the railways in a state of financial meltdown as from Rs. 13431 crore in 2008 their cash reserves fell to a paltry sum of

Rs. 0.75 crore or Rs. 75 lakh in 2011. This means between 2008 and 2011 railways lost a whopping Rs.552 crore every month or an average of Rs. 18 crore per day. A down spiral that began towards the end of RJD chief's tenure, as a minister for the railways, primarily due to change over and not picking up the threads left by the predecessor, by the new minister, accelerated during the new regime (2009-11). This decline could be touted as the biggest fall in finances for the railways since Independence.[4]

When we go through the details of the railway budgets 2010-2011 and 2011-12, we find the same story of downfall.

Budget– 2010-2011

The same situation of financial meltdown continued in 2010-11 due to several factors not conducive to railways' growth and development. However, the main factor was the lack of will to pursue higher targets of revenue to achieve and generating more loading capacity to increase freight earnings. A very weak plea was given as a case of 'disruption of train services' for low passenger earnings. On the other hand, loading target was reduced by 20 million tonnes to 924 million tonnes in 2010-11. However, goods earnings were retained on the basis of trends of higher yield per NTKM. Total gross earning was fixed at 94742 crore which was 1277 crore higher than the budget. With the reduced traffic suspense clearance of Rs. 98 crore, gross traffic receipt was a little higher than the budget target by Rs. 75 crore at Rs. 94840 crore (revised estimate). But the actual situation was somewhat different. The railways could attain only Rs. 94535.63 crore as actual gross total receipt which was less by Rs. 304.81 crore than the revised estimate. As regards total receipts the actual figures fell by Rs. 1040.53 crore from budget estimates. The surplus/excess was only Rs. 1404.89 crore (actual) which could be appropriated to development fund and no funds were transferred to capital or railway safety funds. Net revenue fell by Rs. 3435.41 crore at the level of Rs 6346.14 crore as against the budget estimate of Rs. 9781.55 crore. Out of gross revenue earned, the dividend payment to Rs. 4941.35 crore was made, leaving just Rs. 1404.89 crore actual surplus or excess.

Towards expenditure side, hikes in the rate of HSD oil and increased electricity tariff in some states, higher DA rates and excise duty rates, as well as impact of unanticipated higher salary and allowances, raised the requirement by Rs. 5700 crore. After providing Rs. 14500 crore toward depreciation reserve fund and pension fund the revised estimate to total working expenses came to Rs. 87200 crore. However, the actual total working expenses increased to the level of Rs. 89474.22 crore i.e., an increase of Rs. 2274.22 crore from revised estimate. The total expenses increased by Rs. 2394.88 crore from the budget estimate. This increased the operating ratio from 92.3 per cent as budget estimate to 94.6 per cent as actual.

Budget 2011-2012

Budget 2011-12 which presently provides the figures relating to budget estimates and revised estimates does not give a rosy picture. It cannot generate surplus/excess more than the previous year. The revised estimate of the surplus shows just Rs. 1492.15 crore i.e., only Rs. 87.26 crore extra. If trends set any example, the actual excess would be even less than the previous year or in no case cross the revised figure as estimated. When there is no or little surplus, what else can we think of development or capital fund?

According to estimates of Rs. 106239.00 crore for the financial year 2011-12 under the head Gross Traffic Receipts, the revised estimates have fallen by Rs. 2322 crore at the level of Rs. 103917.00 crore. The total receipt thus fell by Rs. 2746.35. crore at the level of Rs. 106646.78 crore.

Towards expenditure side, the budget estimate of total working expenditure was Rs. 96450.00 crore which was increased in revised estimate to Rs. 98610.00 crore- a net increase of Rs. 2160 crore. The total expenditure in this respect increased from Rs. 97400.00 crore of budget estimate to revised estimate of Rs. 99502.39 crore i.e., an increase of Rs. 2102 crore. When such is the case of total expenditure, how can we expect a favourable operating ratio? According to revised estimate the operating ratio is 95 percent - an alarming situation for railways financial performance.

It seems that the railway is moving a at snail's pace (Misra, R.N. 2011a) ultimately to come to a grinding halt. The situation of fund balances has become precarious. The depleting fund balances and shortfall in surplus/excess have been shown as below:

Table– 13 Depleting Fund Balances (Rs. in crore)

Years / *Balance*	*2007-08*	*2008-09*	*2009-10*	*2010-11*	*2011-12*	*2012-13*
Opening	16694.35 Actual	20483.21 BE	15661.26 BE	7698.39 BE	3102.55 BE	2005.93 BE
	16529.78 RE	26027.90 RE	15654.71 RE	5032.06 RE	342.51 RE	-
Closing	22279.35 Actual	19706.76 BE	8360.88 BE	5063.73 BE	1367.64 BE	-
	20483.21 RE	15661.26 RE	7698.39 RE	3102.55 RE	2005.93 RE	-

Source: Compiled from Explanatory Memorandum on budgets of various years.

Table- 14. Successive Shortfall in Surplus/Excess and Increasing Operating Ratio (Rs. in crore)

Years	*2007-08*	*2008-09*	*2009-10*	*2010-11*	*2011-12*
Surplus/ Excess	11449.45 BE	11786.74 BE	2642.26 BE	3173.09 BE	5258.41 BE
	13534.08 RE	6355.56 RE	551.03 RE	4104.50 RE	1492.15 RE
	13431.09 Actual	4456.78 Actual	0.75 Actual	1404 .89 Actual	-
Operating Ratio	75.9%	90.5%	95.3%	94.6%	95%

Source: Compiled from Explanatory Memorandum on budget of various years.

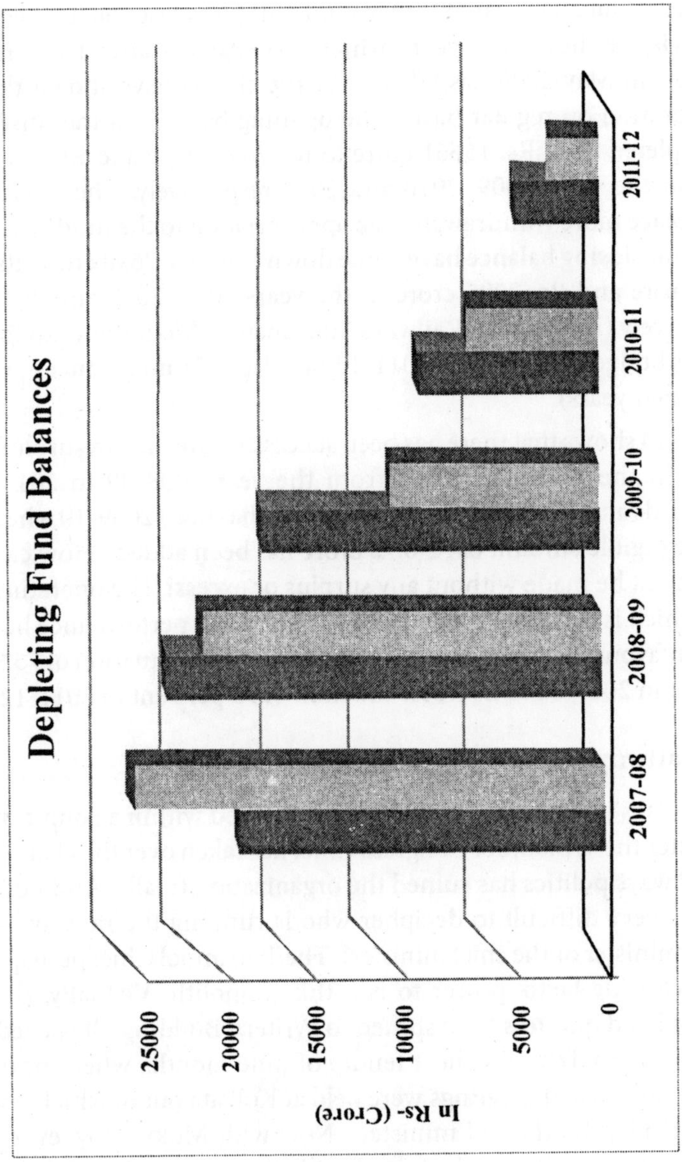

Figure. 6 : Depleting Fund Balances

T-13 shows how rapidly the fund balances have depleted year after year. Since last year of turnaround, this phenomenon has been quite visible. But three years which have lapsed after the new minister in May 2009 has taken over the charge have shown the deterioration on regular basis. The opening balance of the funds has depleted from Rs. 15661 crore to Rs. 7698 crore and Rs. 3103 crore in the years 2009, 2010 and 2011 respectively. There have taken place more withdrawals than appropriation to the funds with the result closing balance have come down from Rs. 7698 crore, Rs. 3103 crore and Rs. 2006 crore in the years 2009, 2010 and 2011 respectively (Ministry of Railways, Explanatory Memorandum for various budgets, 2007-08 to 2011-12, see Page - Fund Balances - of concerned years).

T-14 shows that there has been successive shortfall in surplus/ excess in the revenue earned from the year 2008-09 to 2010-11onwards and the worst year in this period has been 2009-10 when only negligible amount of Rs 0.75 crore has been added. How can investment be made without any surplus or excess? The operating ratio which is the best to judge the efficiency and performance has been unfavourable and has increased from the best situation of 75.9 per cent in 2007-08 to its worst situation of 95 per cent in 2011-12.

The Railways in ICU: The Roll Back Drama

This is how the railways have deteriorated within a couple of years after the Trinamool Congress Chief has taken over the charge. The railways politics has ruined the organization finally. And now it seems very difficult to decipher who is running the railways – the rail minister or the chief minister? The Trinamool Chief perhaps still wields 'de facto' power to run this monolith. Virtually, the railways head quarters have shifted to Writers' Building. It started during Dinesh Trivedi's short tenure of nine months when more than 16 rail-related meetings were held at Kolkata out of which six were attended by the rail minister. Now with Mukul Roy, every policy related matter is discussed with the party chief and the distance between Rail Bhavan and Writers Building has been narrowed through fast tracks by railway professionals attending the meetings almost daily held at Kolkata on government expenses.

Indian railways have come under a severe grip of fast deteriorating condition and have been put on ventilation. Financially, the railways have been completely ruined. They have become sterile and do not generate any surplus/excess worth the name. No appropriation to funds is possible for development activities. Most of the funds have been used for non-plan and ad-hoc schemes during these years and it becomes difficult to manage ordinary working expenses and salary and pension bills. Every now and then new committees are formed for submitting the reports which aggravate the problems by their suggestion to arrange more and more funds to solve the problems. The Amit Mitra Committee, The Sam Pitroda Committee and The Anil Kakodkar Committee – all such committees have added to railways woes more than solving the problems. After all, Dinesh Trivedi ultimately has to lose his job by accepting such hi-fi recommendations of the committees to transform the railways over night! The only way to railways' reform is to go slow. We must take lessons from the past – the railways of the Raj. They were wise enough to shift the guarantee system in phases and took 19 years to nationalize the railways (Misra, R.N. 2009d p.13). We want to do every thing in haste. Even the much talked about - Indian Railways Report 2001– recommended restructuring the railways by dismantling the whole system, diluting the authority, power and prestige of the Ministry or the Railway Board and bringing out the roadmap for railways reinvention by disintegrating the whole system and replacing it by IRC or BRaiN, IRRA, IREB and what not within a year or two! (See The Indian Railways Report 2001, NCAER, (pp. 321-28). This hasty process is ruinous. The railways minister must keep confidence in his own professionals. The financial and accounting experts of the railways are competent enough to calculate how much funds are needed for a particular activity. They know what priorities are to be given. But first things must come first. When the patient is in ICU, he does not need 'vitamins' to rejuvenate the body. He requires immediate treatment through life-saving medicines. Let

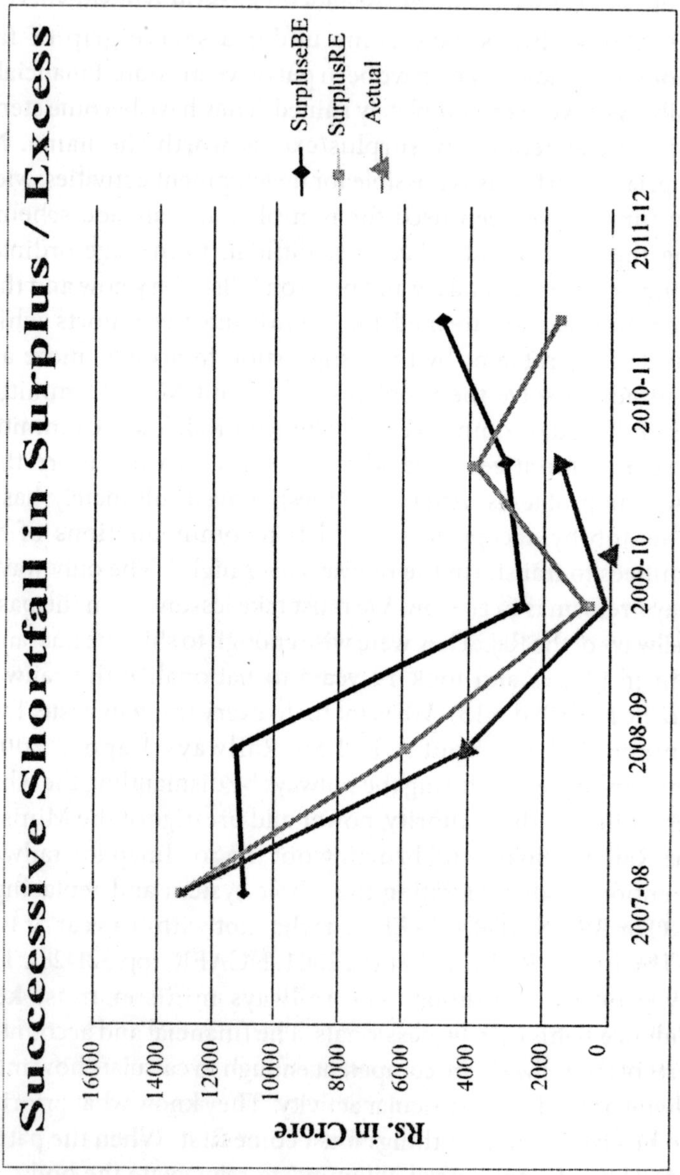

Figure. 7 : Successive Shortfall in Surplus /Excess

all the non-plan and ad-hoc projects be dropped immediately. Why to lay new line from Singur to Nandigram? Why to have new connectivity between Salboni – Jhargram via Lalgarh, Belpahari. All such projects must be scrapped. What is the use of re-laying of the railway tracks to Jayanti from Rajabhatkhawa, cutting across the core forests of tiger reserve and disturbing the whole eco-system?

The railways need urgent help to keep their vitals intac· and functioning. No long term project should be taken up immediately. It is enough for the railways to create more traffic and earn more revenue as a first step. Fare hike for premium classes are necessary and that is not a politically sensitive factor. It should start to create new turnaround by adopting minor innovative practices. The performance efficiency of the railways should be increased. It requires only good leadership to establish such practices and to develop new mindset. Let the 'will to change' be created first. The second step is to generate confidence among the workers and the staff. The volume of traffic should be increased by all means including increase in loading capacity by adopting simple traditional methods which do not require more funds. Working expenses should be reduced by adopting austerity measures. These are the steps immediately required for the railway to save it form sudden collapse. The next step is to sustain the process which has been adopted earlier. Once the volume of traffic is increased, it is time to think about reduction in cost and increasing productivity. This will stabilize the railways' finances and after that more stringent action may be taken. Pulling out railways from ICU is not an easy task. Unless railways cross the self consuming economic barrier and become self sustaining in generating normal profits, no adoption of higher schemes of modernization and technological advancement is possible. A patient in ICU can not think of joining a health-club or a gym. The railway has to regain some strength first to resume strenuous activities. Therefore, 'go slow' is the only workable principle for the 159-year old organization of the railways.

The roll back drama staged by the Trinamool Congress Chief in March, 2012, ("Mamata Tells Trivedi to roll back fare hike or resign, Business Line, 15-03-2012) had caused quite a sensation through political and academic circles. They called it good, bad and ugly. Dinesh Trivedi, the then railway minster, tried to perform a long jump championing the cause of the railways over night! He thought he would win half the battle by providing a kick-start to the railways. But in doing this acrobatic he got injured and lost his job. It was to create serious problems for the railways too. Once you accept Trivedi-Formula there seems to be no end to hike fares and freights and the railway would again come to a grinding halt as it was in the year 2000-2001. Indian railways need funds, reforms and modernization but only in slow process. The minister must understand that it is not an 'expert group' that runs the railways, but the group of engineers, Rail Bhavan professionals and workers at large who manage and run them. The railway is an organisation of great potential provided the minister listens to Rail Bhavan people. He should not act whimsically – either not to hike fares or freights at all or hike them limitlessly and across - the - board. Both the extremes are dangerous. They would not serve the purpose essentially for which the railway is meant.

It was an ugly situation to ask the minister (or fax to the Prime Minister) to roll back the fare hike or sack the railway minister. "Roll back or resign" was the Napoleonic order issued in a democracy in 21st century-India.[5] But the nation took it lightly like a joke and set it aside calling it as an 'internal matter'. However, history will not forget this incident - the drama played as an insult to the person who hiked the fares, on the one hand and who asked for the roll back in the name of the poor (living in Nandigram?), on the other. She assured the gathering at that place that she would roll back the hike and did it at the cost of democratic and human values. There were other soft ways to do that. But populism and human values don't go together. It was the day of Jackal. The 14th March 2012 will go down in the history of Indian railways as a day when the drama of extreme love and hate was staged, when party's own man was asked to quit immediately. Such extreme situations do happen in an individual's life, but in case of organisation or at governmental level such behaviour is rarely seen. It will have a long range effect and create greater repercussions. Only time will tell -

let us wait and see. Trinamool Congress Chief has had her way. The fare hike and other reform measures announced in the railway budget 2012-13 were rolled back on March 22, 2012, (IANS Live, Mukul Rolls back fare to please Mamata - March 22, 2012) by a trusted lieutenant, the new railways minister – fifth in three-year period – Mukul Roy. The roll back would mean a loss of Rs. 3500-4000 crore to the budgeted gross traffic receipts of the railways. As against Rs. 5700 crore expected to be made from the first increase in passenger fares in eight years, the national transporter (Railways) will now be able to mobilize only less than Rs. 2000 crore from this head. Under such conditions how can one expect the railways to be pulled out of ICU? On the other hand, it is time to be prepared to hear greater mishaps, if things are not properly managed.

There is a hidden agenda behind the process of fare hikes and roll back affairs. This 'fare hike' has been neither genuinely meant for railways' growth programme nor the 'roll back' dictate really designated for the poor. As the leader of the Trinamool Congress keeps a hidden idea behind her every move, so is the case with the minister of the railways who has hiked the fares. Both have their ulterior motives. As is clear by the fact that Dinesh Trivedi is an MBA, he shows his competence as CEO of an undertaking and forgets that he represents a constituency, the people, and is responsible for every action taken and is answerable to them for any wrong decision made. A railway minister has a double role to play. He is head of an organisation but also speaks on behalf of the people who use the railways. In this way, his role is difficult and he can not side always a failing undertaking or deteriorating institution like the railways. What about the people – the passengers or the consignors who use the railways? Who will speak on their behalf in the Parliament? Dinesh Trivedi failed in this respect as a true leader and a responsible representative of the people. His MBA training only taught him to work like an executive officer and he lost the track that was really required by the leader. He imposed an across-the-board hike in fares regardless of the class and the people who use the railways. His lack of grassroots level contact with the people has led him to this situation. Even his management text-book approach was wrong. Which MBA school teaches that telescopic pricing of transport service is incorrect? Why the fair hike has not maintained the principle of 'higher the distance, lower is the ratio of price of the trasport service. His approach to per-km hike in passenger service has remained practically and academically imperfect. Why he forgets the theory of increasing returns or diminishing cost which applies to the transport services quite effectively?

The truth of the matter is that he has been ill advised by his fair weather friends. Why he approached Pitroda or Kakodkar? Why he appointed such committees which have a different agenda than the real policy makers of the railways. They have actually misguided him. They are the same old faces, with the same ideology and reporting the same material. They always play a double game. Take for example, Prof. G. Raghuram. He was included in the Rakesh Mohan Committee and reported against the railway set up, tried to dismantle the total railway structure – rather signed the death warrant of the railways in 2001. And when 'his' report was discarded, he came in another garb propagating quite an opposite philosophy than he pleaded for 'Indian Railways Report 2001' and started writing in favour of the 'turnaround' to woo the new minister during 2004-2009. Now he is again the member of the 'Expert Group' of modernization of railways! He has a double role to perform - from looping the noose around the neck of the railway and to bring it to the modernization! Why this duplicity of activity adopted and appreciated? These expert groups have only one hidden agenda-restructuring the railways and bulldozing the organization by privatizing it ultimately. Dinesh Trivedi became the victim of this hidden policy. In this respect the Trinamool Congress chief is quite clear in her approach. The railway as PSU will remain intact in her hands as per declared policy, but you can't be sure of others who are bent upon restructuring the railways by hook or by crook.

The railways worker's unions - the federations of the unions – must take note of this fact and should come out to protect their organisation. The functioning of the railway is the responsibility of the workers – the staff and the bosses at Rail Bhavan. They are the real functionaries – the stake takers. They have to serve the passengers and the consignors of the goods. It is their duty to see that in the name of 'fare hike' the outside people may not be able to serve their own agenda and dilute the powers of the workers at the lower level and the bosses of Rail Bhavan at the top. How and why the proposal of 'Tariff Regulatory Authority' - an intermediary - has been made to infiltrate when the railway has power to present the budget and the Parliament has authority to amend or replace any provision - financial or otherwise - not found fit in the national interest? The expert groups have a different aim than the railways. When they fail to get their ideology accepted through their 'flawed' reports, they adopt indirect methods to infiltrate into the administration in the name of 'regulatory' or 'advisory' bodies and try to influence the minister or the policy as such. This has happened in case of Trivedi's proposals for hiking the fares and taking the railway to an altogether different track.

The Trinamool Congress chief has a significantly unusual role to play as far as the railways is concerned. She has a political stake in retaining railways' portfolio. She has strived hard for it; supported UPA government only on the condition that she would have railways portfolio and this has been her 'modest' demand. She could have asked for finance or home portfolio. The Manmohan government would have provided that had she insisted for it. One can see how fragile is the government at the centre and how strong is the Chief of the Trinamool Congress. It was no wonder that she faxed the message to the PM for roll back of the hike in fares immediately. She had shown such strong preference, interference and dominance at several other occasions like Teesta water dispute, hike in petrol prices and home ministry's gimmick of NCTC just to mention a few. It has been 'number' game which has brought her to a higher pedestal and the PM also wants to drag on with the government to have the distinction of pulling on with the lame government for two terms almost in continuation. Who knows he might play the hat-trick?

The Chief of the Trinamool Congress has displaced the 34-year old CPM rule in West Bengal by her comparatively new and inexperienced party. It is this elevated feeling that is dominating her sense of achievement, confidence and self esteem. Her critical but at the same time strong equation with the centre has generated a new power-position in her mind and she is out to compare herself with no less than the Chief of the ruling Indian National Congress. When asked, "Why she dictates the centre to appoint railway minister of her choice"? She abruptly replied, "Why Sonia ji appoints PM of her choice"? One can judge by the tenor of her exalted tone, how much power she wants to hold and how powerfully she behaves.

She has 'de facto' power of the railway minister for all practical purposes. And she is right in retaining this position. When three years earlier she had opted for this office, she had a blue print in her mind, how the railway-projects would be established in West Bengal. There was nothing wrong in such preferences if she has a lion's share of railways for her home state. Many other minister's had done so. But her case was going to be different. She had an eye over the office of chief minister even at the time when she became the railway minister in 2009. So the story of the railways and West Bengal politics was inter-woven in such a way that it was difficult to separate them. And this bond is still working in a much stronger manner. So when Dinesh Trivedi did not consult her while preparing railway budget 2012-13, it was a shocking experience to the Trinamool Congress Chief and it was no wonder that she shot at the singing nightingale in the mid-air.

She had brought several railway-related projects to West Bengal. At least she has something to show to her rivals – the CPI (M) and others - that she had been a step forward in establishing new rail projects to the state of West Bengal. There was nothing wrong in doing so as long as new projects were generated and established inside the country – States matter little - unless the investment became too skewed. West Bengal is well connected by railways with 4151.98 km of railways tracks of which 2227.3 km run on electricity. This state has the distinction of running first Metro in the country. A new railway link from West Bengal to Sikkim has been proposed. A new rail axle manufacturing factory has been finally set up at Jalpaiguri (West Bengal) for Box N Wagons. An AC Container and

Bogie manufacturing factory has been established at Budge Budge (near Kolkata). It is all "Advantage West Bengal" because the Trinamool Congress Chief has strived hard to retain the railways portfolio with her. How can one think of getting this prized portfolio separated from her? The railway as a PSU is intact in her hands and the 'expert groups' can't demoralize her by suggesting hike in fare and freight. Dinesh Trivedi as ex-minister should realize his mistake by playing in the hands of such camouflaged groups that have kept the Rakesh Mohan Committee Report alive for all practical purposes which has been referred to at several places in their reports to influence the policy towards greater divestment and de-nationalize the railways. The railway worker's unions and their federations must read this hidden agenda that surrounds the railways.

Footnotes

1. Mamata Banerjee joined as the minister for railways in May 2009. In July 2009, she submitted the budget with reduced GTR and Total Receipts claiming that earlier budget (Interim, presented by Lalu Prasad) was unrealistic. The maximum variation existed was in the head 'Sundry and others'. This implied two factors: first, the commercial utilization of railways land and second, creative accounting or shift in accounting system. Mamata wanted to hit here and make out the case for White Paper. She submitted White Paper in December, 2009 only to reduce the estimates and scale down the benchmark so that she might not be compared with earlier achievements. This brought Indian railways to the edge of dying a slow death.
2. Officially speaking, there was no fare hike in the railways. Although in the name of readjustment and rationalization some changes were made, but taking passenger services and pricing as a whole, the fare hikes were not done by the railways. Last time it was during Nitish Kumar's regime that some structural changes and hikes in rates were adopted in the year 2002-03. The relativity index for sleeper class (mail/Express) was increased from 155 to 160 and AC Chair Car from 300 to 350. For AC First Class reduction in relativity index was worked out from 1440 to 1400 to make it more competitive with air travel. No change in relative index for other classes of travel was done. Regarding passenger services minimum fare for Second Class (Mail/Express) was increased from Rs. 15 to 16. At longer distances up to 341 kms, the increase ranged from Re

1 to 6. Minimum fare for Second Class (ordinary) increased from Rs. 3 to 4. Maximum increase for any distance upto 100 kms was only Rs. 3. At certain distances fares were lowered by Re. 1 to 2 due to rationalization. The fares of distances beyond 100 kms for Second Class (ordinary) were fixed 55 percent of the Second Class (Mail/Express) fare. The fare for Second Class MST was fixed equivalent to fares of 15 (single) journeys by Second Class (ordinary). This exercise was done by Nitish Kumar while presenting the railway budget on 27th February 2002. Since then no fare hike was done by the Indian Railways.

3. When the railway budget for the year 2011-12 was presented, Mamata Banerjee indicated that a new scheme known as 'Pradhan Mantri Rail Vikas Yojana' was launched. This was done at her behest in the name of 'Pradhan Mantri' for the railways benefit. Her equation with the Prime Minister was so good set that he had no way to refuse her. This scheme would ultimately be used by the railways minister for those projects which were socially desirable or in other sense which are desired by the railway minister. The scheme has yet to take a clear shape as it is under formulation, lakh of crore rupees might be sanctioned under this scheme by the central government with railways having no stake. To take care of socially desirable railway projects a fund under the name "PMRVY" was established. It was a non-lapsable fund for socially desirable scheme of 'minister's choice' fully supported by the Ex-chequer. Mamata Banerjee had proposed an increase of Rs. 771 crore to connect the underdeveloped areas of Orissa, Jharkhand, Chhatisgarh, Bihar and Maharashtra - but first the scheme was to be launched in West Bengal. The ultimate aim of the present scheme was to connect all State capitals with railways except Sikkim. Perhaps this scheme would remain in existence till UPA and Trinamool Congress coalition continues in sharing the fruits of power. The additional funding assistance under the scheme was required to be about five lakh crore according to the railway budget 2012-13.

4. There had been ups and downs in the railways finances, but it was perhaps the biggest fall during 2009-11 since independence. The cash reserves fell to a paltry sum of Rs. 75 lakh as against the proposed amount of Rs. 2642.26 crore. There was a sharp decline in surplus/excess from Rs. 13431.09 crore to Rs. 4456.78 crore and to Rs. 0.75 crore in the years 2007-08, 2008-09, and 2009-10 respectively. Never such a sharp decline was experienced in the history of the Indian Railways. The operating ratio was also unfavourable which increased from 75.9% to 90.5% and to 95.3% for the years 2007-08, 2008-09 and 2009-10 respectively. The fund balances declined from Rs. 22279.35 crore to Rs. 15661.26 crore to

Rs 7698.39 crore to Rs. 3102.55 crore and to Rs. 2005.93 crore in the years 2007-08, 2008-09, 2009-10, 2010-11 and 2011-12 respectively.

5. Mamta Banerjee still holds de-facto power of the minister for railways. Her ego is higher than her size and she exercises her authority like Napoleon. Her order "roll back or resign" smacks of Victorian authority practiced in 21st centuary. In this respect she has surpassed all the dictators of the past and even her rivals - the CPI(M) people. Only God will take care of her. Her sense of Ma, Mati and Manush has a native bias. A Gujarat Manush is unfit for her. Dinesh Trivedi had no alternative but to resign. It would have been better had he resigned from Trinamool Congress also. Human dignity is greater than politics, power and position. In this case Gandhi - the father of nation - should have been Trivedi's role model. Mamata's utterance "roll back or resign" is a slur on the face of democratic process and values of India.

◆◆◆

Conclusion

At the time when the railways in China - our neighbouring rival in progressive benchmark - zoomed over the hard terrain of the Himalayas snaking through the highest plateau on the earth keeping their tracks with a speed covering 1000 Km in less than three hours, we in India preferred down playing our story of railways' transformation by presenting White Paper to the Parliament, on 18th December,2009, supposedly a dispassionate study of the preceding period by the new incumbent of Rail Bhavan (2009-11), in the most desperate style, obviously to lower the scale against which her own progress report would be judged after she might leave the office.

This was how we managed our railways progress - one step forward, two steps backward. As if it was not enough, the then incumbent presented another document – Vision 2020 – a Utopia creating capacity and modernization of the railways including the details of backlog projects requiring no less than Rs. 1400,000 crore. This was a dream document promising the railways an Eldorado with an outlay three times more than their annual budget. The Vision document dreamt so big that the entire budget of government of India in 2009-10 which involved about Rs. 9.5 lakh crore failed to come at par with the railways estimates of nearing double the amount to be invested in 10 years. An imaginary Accelerated Railway Development Fund (ARDF) was created with a provision of Rs. 500,000 crore from Central Budgetary Support. The rest of the amount would be mobilized through internal sources, public borrowings and other PPP schemes.

Presenting two documents of different nature – high and low; vibrating and stagnant; healthy and sick – only suggest that the railways were caught in the process of great contradiction, controversy and conflict. It was ridiculous to find that hot and cold streams were allowed together to merge and the scheme relating to them got fogged and looked hazy, unable to show a clear picture of new plans and programmes. If the railways were showing negative aspects during the predecessors' stint, how could robust achievement be possible within a short period of a decade or so? It was this inherent contradiction which made the Vision Paper hazier and put a question mark also on the dispassionate character of the White Paper.

In a democratic set up, healthy criticism is always welcome to keep the administration in proper working order. The procedure of checks and balances keeps the system well controlled, organized and effective. However, when the motive is to pull down the past regime by fixing a different benchmark to judge, it is a degrades the whole system and lowers the prestige of the department in the eyes of the people. In the present political scenario of India, it rarity that the successor agrees and carries forward the initiative of the predecessor. Doubts were raised on the eve of the (former) minister's departure from his office at Rail Bhavan, in May 2009, regarding the sustainability of turnaround, if the new incumbent of the railways refused to move the relay baton fast-forward. The suspicion came home to the roost.

The progress of administrative procedure is like a relay race. It may go well only if the parties involved in the race respond quickly in a cooperative effort to win the race. The new player must accept the past, put renewed energy and hand over the baton (symbol of power) to other player to generate further energy to move the baton even faster than before. It is an act of creating synergy for moving fast, faster and the fastest – step by step and stage by stage - to win the race at the end. But there seems to be lack of cooperation between the past and the present regimes of the railways with the result that what was earned earlier went down the drain as an act uselessly performed.

The White Paper issued in December 2009 tried to prove that the predecessor (2004-09) of the then incumbent of the Rail Bhavan was full of odds and manipulation and did nothing positive for the railways. The path chosen by the new regime (2009-11) to downgrade the image of her predecessor had created an internal rift between the believers and non-believers of the turnaround. The successor knew it well that every accusing finger had an equally accusing counter finger and there was no use of creating a controversy over turnaround process of the railways. But she took a controversial step and would equally be accused of malfunctioning as and when she would leave the office or power. The figures did not tell lies and all the achievements of the predecessor could not be the product of manipulation. The figures which showed surplus were generated by the railways staff in consultation with finance commissioner and the revenue so collected was deposited with the RBI (Reserve Bank of India). It was an internal matter to judge if there was any conceptual difference of putting an item from one particular pocket to another and that did not require a White Paper.

It was lack of magnanimity on the part of the successor to have withdrawn the prestigious Railway Chair from IIM Ahmedabad. As a matter of intellectual propriety, honesty and integrity the chair could have been kept intact for benefit of both the parties.

The railways should have learnt the lessons from the West where government and corporate work together for the betterment of the society. The corporate has the duty towards society and the government too has an intellectual debt to be paid to the academics. At times when internal assessment failed to bring results, one had to consult outside experts. The railways got a consultative service by the creation of the Railway Chair at IIM - A. It was easily possible to get the facts and figures verified through analytical studies at IIM - A. The institute would have provided expertise on marketing and managerial services whereever needed by the railways. Market mechanism, pursuance of profit and methods and ways of increasing productive efficiency were tricky routes to be followed by experts and the advice of a super specialty B - School would not have been out of place, had the railway-chair been maintained as meaningfully as it was established. Its scrapping was a loss to the railways.

One might find it debatable whether the 'turnaround' study submitted by Prof. G. Raghuram of IIM - A was a genuine or just a paraphrase of the railways' own study material, statistical statements and analysis, but the highly trained and qualified cadre of Indian Railways Services did not appreciate Prof. Raghuram's intrusion into railways' 'internal affairs' because it would silently and craftily try to corrode and vitiate the functioning of the railways, converting it into a 'private concern' much like a worm in the bud eating softly from within. The mystery of corporate capitalism is that what they can't achieve directly, they try to acquire through intrusion and infiltration. IIM– A is the cauldron of capitalism in India much like Harvard Business School (HBS) in US. What they teach and don't teach form the main basis of their ideological thrust and intensity. A person from such a committed school of thought would be more a 'corporate man' than an exponent of public policy measures of government sector as the railway is. The presence of such a person would not benefit the railway as a public sector in any form. Perhaps Prof. Raghuram's focus on 'organizational structure' and The Rakesh Mohan Committee Report 2001 ran parallel in contents and he very subtly tried to keep the Indian Railways Report 2001, alive for all practical purposes. The railways cadre therefore sharply reacted and attacked the very purpose of the study and the ministry said, "Productive ideas have not come. The chair has been scrapped as the Railway can ill afford such wasteful expenditure". However, it was a hurried decision because in the globalized world no institution could survive in isolation and one of the causes of railways deterioration was that it had developed a habit of making an island of its own, just living in a 'make-believe world'.

The predecessor had accepted that there were three changes made in accounting process by the railways during the period 2004-09. They were the parts of their ongoing reforms in financial standard. They were: (a) changes in lease charges payable to Indian Railways Finance Corporation (IRFC); (b) changes in interest accounting in railways fund balances; (c) changes in calculation of losses on strategic lines. The Indian railways had adopted the process of accounting reform and addressed them according to the needs. The railways had adopted a consortium including French Railways SNCF, and Ernst and Young, among others to work on its accounting reform programme. The government of India needed service-based revenue and cost data from the railways to support existing government reporting requirements, according to Economic Survey. Thus, the railway had to address various issues for business orientation including changes in lease payment accounting process, rate of interest according to fund balances and concessions of loss making branch lines. A great change took place all over the world in lease accounting system. So the Indian Railways was not alone in adopting such a change. There were two approaches to lease accounting – risk based and reward based. The lease obligation might appear to meet the definition as a 'liability' under operating lease if it was a risk lease. Similarly, right to economic benefits under operating base might appear to meet the definition as an 'asset' if it was reward base lease. When such changes were internationally (IFRS – International Financial Report Standard) adopted, how could Indian GAAP (Generally Accepted Accounting Principles) remain away from these definitive changes? In 2008 out of a total Rs. 2153 crore lease changes, the principal or income part was only Rs. 1677 crore and was added to the receipt or surplus and so was the case in 2007 when only Rs. 1720 crore of the principal amount was added. But it should not be said that all surpluses were due to shift in accounting policy or they were not legitimate surpluses. Since IFRS had adopted a change, the modified lease policy in Indian railways had come to stay as an approved accounting principle. Similarly, there was little depth in arguing against the case of deciding interest on fund balances to be brought into miscellaneous' receipts as well as loss on strategic line be deducted from working expenses. Why the re-imbursement of losses should go to reduce excess of expenditure and not to reduce dividend liability? In 2008, Rs. 637 crore amounted to this head and interest on fund balances amounted to Rs. 1175 crore. As a result of such changes the railways income increased to Rs. 3489 crore in 2008 and Rs. 2690 crore in the year 2007 in which Rs. 1720.90 crore, Rs. 660 crore and Rs. 309 crore had been shown as the lease charges, rate of interest and losses on strategic lines respectively. But one should not have felt that there was stoppage of turnaround process as substantial surpluses were created year after year.

The White Paper on Indian Railways issued by the incumbent of the Rail Bhavan was an attempt to thwart the turnaround created by the predecessor during his regime 2004-2009. Without understanding the concept, strategy and purpose of the turnaround, the new guard of the railways started refuting it fiercely immediately after the leader of turnaround left the railways. What were those distrustful conditions prevailing behind the move? Was there lack of transparency in ex-minister's ways and methods? Did the predecessor not take the workforce into confidence? Did the professionals inside the Rail Bhavan feel insulted or found themselves side tracked? But this was not the case. The leader of the turnaround had taken all the employees into confidence. What was the real cause behind the tirade against the leader then? It was an invisible factor, a human weakness that created clash of personalities – a political rivalry between the two stalwarts - which may be described as 'the war of Roses' for showing the supremacy over the empire of the railways. The ex-minister had played his share of the innings with the railways. It was the then incumbent's turn to start afresh and she desired that the pitch should be cleared without any hangover of the past. According to her the turnaround had unnecessarily hyped the situation and kept the benchmarks quite tough to reach, perhaps unrealistic in estimates. A few of the prominent advisors at Rail Bhavan too had an occasion to add fuel to the fire. They started scripting new CV of the predecessor by dismissing his approach to turnaround and soaring figures of 'surplus' to please their bosses. It was here that the ex-minister's (predecessor's) achievements were decried and the incumbent of the Rail Bhavan tried to abort 'turnaround concept' already conceived, nurtured and sustained by the railways.

When the White Paper was presented to the Parliament, the then incumbent of Rail Bhavan (2009-11) was in hyper agitated mode. She got her inner self engrossed in destructive creation of bringing the railways past achievements to such a demolished state that the White Paper emerged as a part of her own personality to show that she had generated antithetical view to what her predecessor called a 'turnaround'. But contrary to her thought process, belief and attitude, so maliciously construed, the White Paper neither proved itself true in real terms nor did it bring a fair assessment of the railways' finances to visualize the future course of action. It resembles a mischievous bundle of odd conclusions based on misrepresenting the facts to prove the fallacies of the railways.

It was the complexity of financial system of the railways which was difficult to understand. The process was so developed as to be made for themselves to use, understand and apply in accordance to their need and purpose. Their items of accounts had different uses and special interpretations. In this line of action, their oldest account for depreciation had different meaning. It was used as depreciation and replacement cost; it was also used as investment for new schemes and revenues. This created a great rift in understanding its special status and the corporate world came heavily upon its differing roles. Moreover, the railways had got so many pockets. It could add or subtract the amount from one pocket to another to prove their point in question. The predecessor was not wrong in declaring the 'turnaround' or his estimates. He was insisting upon the same estimates. But the successor was misguided by the babus at Rail Bhavan who wanted to prove a right point wrong. The new incumbent of Rail Bhavan had admitted the fact that during 2004-2009 the freight earnings had increased, but she expressed the view that this had happened because of the better environmental conditions of growth of national economy and GDP. How strange was the logic? When the predecessor failed, it was his fault; but when the predecessor succeeded, it was not his victory: it was environment that favoured him to win - the GDP growth that pushed the railways economy. It was a peculiar way of interpretation. The new incumbent of the period 2009-11 did not want to give any credit to the former minister (the predecessor). The achievement of railways was not the outcome of just booming economy but it was due to the clear gains in capital and labour productivity, increase in labour market share, profit margin, the quality of service provided and above all the predecessor's political will to bring a change and give leadership acceptable to the workforce. It ill behoves the new incumbent to decry the turnaround of the railways which is a historical fact that cannot be denied.

It is a ritual with the railways to issue White Paper without following it. It is perhaps the seventh time that such a document has been released. The White Paper appears to be a merry-go-round for the then incumbent to while away time. In this way, the attention of the railways and the people in general would be diverted to discuss endlessly the merits and demerits of the railways' finances and she would find enough time to spend and nurse her constituency with the basic objective to oppose land acquisition for the industries. Who bothers for the railways? She has already wasted a year accusing others, providing nothing for the railways except a White Paper. It is a fact that the predecessor who ruled the railways during 2004-2009 has lost much ground in Bihar only because he had devoted all his time and energy for the railways creating a turnaround situation. The nation recognizes his services and Bihar too would not remain behind in showing him the gratitude. Serving the government at the centre is a full time job and responsibility and piecemeal efforts will neither benefit the nation nor the ministry.

The White Paper has damaged the psyche of the work-force of the railways and majority of the people serving at Rail Bhavan. They are surprised by such type of critical assessment about their previous guard – leader of turnaround. But they are silent because they can do nothing. How long their silence would work? They will ultimately come up to give a fight to such an evil design if it hampers their interest in 'bonus', pension calculations, or degrading their efficiency and delaying promotion prospects. How could they get bonus without surplus? Such doubts have set deep into their minds. The White Paper is silently corroding the fruits of growth, development and the turnaround achievement by piercing, destroying and devastating the economy from within. In this respect, the White Paper and The Rakesh Mohan Committee Report have served the same purpose - 'Killing the spirit of the Railways'. The White Paper has a startling resemblance to the ideological tautology of World Bank's study, on the one hand and The Rakesh Mohan Committee Report on the other. The working and the impact of both the studies are quite in tune with their aims and purpose and it seems as if the same think-tank has been used to produce them. In fact, both the documents – White Paper and The Mohan Committee, Report, have the same genus and both technically produced by hired consultants. Both the reports are the outcome of their respective ministers. The Rakesh Mohan Committee Report has based its major financial findings on the expert group of the company called M/s Rangaraju and Associates and the present incumbent has hired the services of S.S. Kothari Mehta & Co to create financial bungling and faulty calculations to bring out White Paper just to malign the previous administration including its leader.

It took about six months for the railways to work out a document, highly biased and distorted, with the help of a hired consultant, in support of some spicy material against the predecessor, known to be a status paper or as it is generally called White Paper. A genuine White Paper is normally not a subject matter of criticism. But the present White Paper on Indian railways (2009) is unique in approach and unparalleled phenomenon, in the 'series of railways' White Papers. This White Paper needs a proper mending, a better overhauling with an equally vengeful treatment which it really deserves. The period of analysis chosen by the White Paper is quite intriguing and the report submitted is retrograde, disastrous and offensive. Why only the period 2004- 2009 has been taken into account? Does it not relate to a particular person? It does fall into a graceless situation as it speaks of the malice where naming a person matters little. What matters is the conscious effort of creating an antithetical account of turnaround. It deals with the situation where the work done does not matter, but what is undone, creates greater challenge not only regarding publicity but for the assessment of the real purpose for which the White Paper is normally issued. However, contrary to all established norms and values, the White Paper on Indian Railways, 2009, emits wrong signals for the person concerned - the leader of the turnaround who considers the railway as a business unit and thinks in terms of the health of the railways. Here the parametres of judging the transport growth are wrongly chosen, misrepresented and negatively construed. The White Paper does not help organizers or the planners to understand the real maladies afflicting the railways and the oppressive ways that stunt the growth of its finance and businesses. This White Paper clearly prompts to draw the opaque conclusion against the turnaround process. The White Paper is basically unjust, intuitively weak and detestably irrational and no healthy or decisive step can be taken on its fumbling foundation and distrustful treatment of the subject which it takes into account.

By keeping the study confined especially to the period 2004 - 2009 and still calling the White Paper as an account of dispassionate reporting is a fallacy. The study seems to have included the information on growth of traffic in frastructure and financial performance, apart from many other aspects, to make it look like an annual report of statistics and accounts. However, the factors of analysis, including the framework, have not been fully justified and do not give a clear picture of growth when a concluding remark has been made by it that "traffic growth performance has been below par for the entire period (of the predecessor)". Here the single parameter used is the 'growth rate of transport elasticity' in relation to GDP. This concept is not fundamentally suitable to assess the potential growth of the railway GDP. It has overrated the growth pattern to falsify the earlier achievement, specially in the form of 'turnaround'. The process adopted in calculating the growth potential is also crudely applied. How can an 'absolute' transport growth elasticity bring a clear picture of a relative term or single mode of transport i.e., the railways? The railway is one of the modes of transport. There are other modes of transport like roads, coastal shipping, air, inland water and pipelines etc. How has the White Paper applied the total transport elasticity of growth as a measure of a part i.e., railways' elasticity? All the modes of transport have varying degrees of growth elasticities. Even if the differences are minute, the methodology applied to measure it is weak, crude and unconvincing. The calculation of potential growth of railways' GDP is unsatisfactory, unreasonable and incomparable. The growth elasticity of railways is not the same as growth elasticity of transport sector as a whole. Hence the analysis of White Paper needs to be reworked and revised.

No absolute transport growth elasticity as multiplied to GDP growth rate can bring out a clear picture for comparative study i.e., GDP×1.25 =Potential growth of railway GDP, as applied to White Paper (p. 4). It is erroneous unless it brings into its fold differential elasticities belonging to other modes of transport and their mutual relationships. The potential rate of growth of railway GDP should be calculated differently, not on the basis of transport elasticity, but in accordance to demand forecasting and the traffic calculation for the Indian railways should be done separately and not mixed with other modes of transport (as the World Bank has done), like road, shipping and airways etc. It is because Indian railway has peculiar characteristic regarding demand for traffic. The railways 'loss' in traffic is 'gain' for road transport and railway lags behind in competing with the road in the present scenario and perhaps the trend may continue in future too. The peculiarity of Indian railways as linked with its competitor - road transport - brings it to acquire the characteristic of a class of cross elasticity of growth i.e., with the change in growth of road transport elasticity, the rail transport growth elasticity changes in negative form. All this happens because elasticity of growth of GDP and transport elasticity are positively related and the railways and road transport are highly competitive in the race of acquiring traffic share. This race of mouse and cat seems to be everlasting unless transport coordination policy is formulated and practically adopted.

The turnaround has been seen by the White Paper as a process of halting the sustained campaign of 'privatizing' the railways through piecemeal methods. Wherefrom she got this idea? Which theory stipulates turnaround going against liberalization? On the other hand, one should realize that the very concept of turnaround is 'corporate oriented'. It is an exceptional way which was applied by Prof. Raghuram to the public sector economy like the railways for the first time. This was the reason that many of the professionals at Rail Bhawan could not understand its real import and perhaps due to lack of knowledge they brought this wrong idea that 'turnaround is a process of halting privatization'. The new incumbent of Rail Bhavan (2009-11) has accepted "the operational as well as financial performance of the railways in the past five year period has been satisfactory; doubts have been expressed about the quantum of cash surpluses. Therefore the issue is not that no progress has been made, but 'abounding surplus has not been created'. The turnaround has been fallen short of her expectation which is why she cries, 'where are the funds and the surpluses'? All that is available is growing expenditure of Pay Commission expenses and insatiate desire of increased pay, pension and appropriation of amount to various funds created by the railways".

The concepts – surplus and investible surplus-were meant to serve railways own purpose to justify that like other corporate units, it also generated surpluses reflecting railways finances in commercial accounting terms and could be presented as cash surplus before dividend and investible surplus. The railway as a public sector was least bothered for the payment of dividend because it was a nominal amount and based on railways own interpretation of various concepts like operating losses on strategic lines, interest on pension fund and payment of deferred dividend. These Items were subtracted from cash to arrive at investible surplus. In this connection the most disparaging was the 'missing' page no. 2, table 1 (a), in the 'explanatory memorandum on the railway budget 2010-11' which used to be there for the last three years. The concept of cash surplus and investible surplus had been done away with and a new concept of 'excess' had been introduced almost signifying the same thing but in a different and less impressive manner.

The concept of surplus is a cash expression loosely adopted by the railways which means cash left after ordinary expenses. It will create confusion to those who judge it on the basis of accrual accounting. The concept of surplus for railways creates an understanding and purpose of amount that they have to earn after meeting the expenses. By keeping surplus in mind they target increased earnings, on the one hand and try to reduce expenditure, on the other. It is a relative concept and the outcome of the difference between income and expenditure which are changing variables and the railways strive hard to achieve them in the best possible way. They know the amount of dividend to be paid on the fixed basis to the ex-chequer. Therefore, they calculate surplus before dividend. The target fixed by the railways is not the payment of dividend but earning minus expenditure i.e., surplus.

The White Paper conceals more facts than what it reveals. It deals only with specific situation and a particular period of study. It conceals the real health of the railways by putting unimportant facts and avoiding the real financial and managerial syndrome which directly hits the railway and its functioning. A true study must observe the condition prevailing for the smooth running of the railways or the factors which obstruct its financial and managerial growth and development. But the White Paper does not go beyond the predecessor's regime. Such studies have a definite purpose and aim and they cannot provide a proper platform for bringing about holistic treatment of the subject. The White Paper, thus, has a shortsighted approach to view the railways' finances and management.

The main impediment to growth of railways finances is the lack of independent authority to control and manage the system which looks after funds availability, functionality, investment and allocation of resources. This may further be attributed to flexibility in free pursuance of business and decision making.

The Indian railways is a controlled system under the public authority and as such it cannot have the benefit of a corporate sector with independent working, implementing programmes and adopting plan of actions. Nevertheless, one must not forget that the railways had survived historically a long past as a public sector, dashing out various constraints and critical junctures which came in the way to thwart its progress. It was believed that the railways suffered losses due to their social obligation factor. But it was not every time and everywhere the same. It had been researched that in most cases it was the wrong policy which was the cause of despair. About 80 percent of railways commercial activities were 'apolitical'. Again, the factor of cross subsidization had been cited for losses whereas the price policy was found to be the main culpable offender. It was also viewed that the dichotomy of railways' status as a commercial organization, but operating as a public sector, had created an impasse in its financial management as a business concern. It was a symptom supposed to generate railway's deteriorating financial condition. Earlier, there used to be equilibrium between railways as a government department and a commercial undertaking - both balancing each other - a complete harmony and understanding in financial matters was observed. However, this equilibrium was disturbed by the government in way of withdrawing the budgetary support and providing investment capital on affordable rate of interest. This compelled railways to borrow at unbearable market rate of interest. The financial stability and strength of railways thus immediately came under great stress and strain.

The railways have changed their total perspective. They have changed the ways of looking at problems and adopted new style of learning to adjust with times. The predecessor's regime has brought a change in the mindset of the railways employees, the top bosses and the workforce in general to look towards their organisation as a competitive unit. The old concept of monopoly power has vanished. In the present globalised economy, the railways have to interact with market forces, their rivals and find opportunity to pursue profit, create surplus, and invest to generate further capital on the competitive lines and innovative practices. The predecessor brought turnaround and enhanced the prestige of the railways. The glowing image of the railways has been brought about by untiring efforts put up by 14 lakh employees, working round the clock, pursuing a national agenda for railways' development, growth and social justice. However, those who are opposed to this objective have brought out White Paper (2009) out of sheer defeatism and despair.

The Indian Railway is one of the oldest institutions which has established industrial revolution in the country. But being old and revolutionary, it too has its saddest thoughts and experiences. They may be regarded as its 'happiest songs' also. Nevertheless, the casting shadow of the old age on the railway has rendered it more rigid, slow and apathetic to the new ways, system and life. It has become stagnant, hard and resistant to change. But it has not been so for the period which is accounted in White Paper i.e., the regime of the predecessor. The railways intermittently have shown the periods of slow down activities when it has not been possible to do better managerially and administratively as is desired. It is this framework of railways' management and organisation which is sticky, sick and has suffered from various ailments. There are three important factors responsible for this stalemate. Firstly, it is 'aversion to change'. After the British departure the railway has continued its role as a public sector unit. It has worked quite gracefully; has revamped its style and functioning. But its bureaucracy – the professional cadre of the railways – is hard to change its attitude in accepting the organization as a 'business enterprise'. The world of business is different from government system. Business demands quick pursuance to profit, alertness to market forces and acceptance to change with times. It is this aversion to change which has started dwindling the railways performance in the sphere of finance, administration and economy. It has created a type of 'managerial syndrome' which has greatly affected the railways. Secondly, its weakness has been seen in the form of railways' departmentalization which has kept it aloof from the real national agenda, strategy and purpose. While the railways is an integrated identity, its departments have followed separate action, programme and process. They have hardly shown any interaction with each other and know their future plan of action and strategy. Thirdly, the railways is lacking business acumen. It lacks managerial initiative, organizational process and programme of action which are responsible for the failure of railways on administrative and financial fronts to attract profits and larger share of transport market. The railways are not well managed inherently to analyze profitability and execute their affairs to improve yields, margins and efficiency. The railways' declining spirit of competitiveness is supposed to be an administrative weakness and suggestions like control and 'price regulation' or creation of 'Tariff Regulatory Authority' are meant to generate negative impact on the working of the railways. The symptoms of deterioration and decrease are being reflected in the form of failure to pay dividends, reducing market share, even of bulk commodities, lack of initiative to face competition with immediate rivals and above all, various operative deficiencies including decades old corruption, unearthed during predecessor's regime - 2004-05, exposing loss of more than Rs.5000 crore every year.

It was observed how the financial and managerial system has created a weak front to fight against the forces responsible for railways deteriorating condition. It is symptomatic of the failing health – a syndrome – generating low esteem, skepticism and timidity which prohibited any kind of improvement for the organisation. This situation has to be properly diagnosed, examined, identified and effectively treated to eradicate the symptom and the disease. The railways have failed on different fronts and the predecessor – the leader of turnaround - has tried to treat the railways well through his own ways and methods and has generated unprecedented profits. However, instead of taking the process forward, the then incumbent of Rail Bhavan contradicted the efforts of the predecessor and to the astonishment of everybody has issued a White Paper – a visionless approach – to mar the turnaround progress and demoralize the workforce and the staff for taking any further steps in this direction. Even the budget estimates of the predecessor have been declared unrealistic and the railway is compelled to run on reverse gear. It is pertinent to make a diagnostic analysis of the White Paper in the light of turnaround, on one hand

and Vision 2020, on the other. Such study would bring a clear picture of the inherent contradiction prevailing within the approach of the new incumbent (2009-11) regarding the railways system, working and procedure followed.

The White Paper is self contradictory and provides an example of double speak; talks two voices; projects two faces. In dealing with growth of traffic and financial performance, it lauds year over year (YOY) growth for freight loading and passenger originating but keeps an option open for judging these improved YOY traffic against the 'shortfall' of achieving the expected growth based on 'self approved' transport elasticity. Why this duplicity of judgment? There has been a remarkable achievement in financial performance during the period 2004-09 regarding freight and passenger earnings and given this as benchmark it will be difficult for the new incumbent (2009-11) to achieve the YOY growth rate in her own period as the declining trends show for the year 2009-10. The White Paper projects two faces: a 'masked' face for destroying the image of turnaround and another face, accepting the changed pattern and achievement of turnaround. It is blowing hot and cold in the same breath.

The Swot analysis in the White Paper presents a confused scenario. Swot analysis is primarily a tool of corporate world. It is being applied to public sector – a square peg in a round hole! This study is used in private economies to find out how much resilience is there to fight with the rival forces and what strategies need to be followed. But the public economy system is based on targets and the process of planning adopted to achieve them. Therefore, when the public economies fail they produce White Paper to justify their plan of action – the conditions under which they fail and the steps which they would take to save their organisation. The corporate sector doesn't produce White Paper: it creates Swot analysis. Why the successor has used Swot analysis for 'the first time' when it is not a part of analytical tool of public sector? It is a mismatched exercise and providing a confused scenario by putting all contradictions together. Swot analysis is seldom used as a tool of public-policy studies. Nevertheless, this study became the part of

White Paper to find out where the weakness lies. The strength of the system should have been provided with greater emphasis but only traffic with operational and commercial strategies along with infrastructure, renewal of replacement and safety measures have been dealt with. It has avoided to mention the strength of 'freight earnings' and 'turnaround' and the credit of unprecedented growth during 2003-04 to 2007-08 has been given to GDP growth and other sector-wise development of the economy. The study does not belong to complete SWOT factors, but it has been made lopsided - a WT - analysis representing only an odd bundle of 'weaknesses and threats'. How strange is it that the 'turnaround' was declared as a threat to 'liberalization' of the economy by the new incumbent of the railways? On what ground and theoretical base this aspect has been projected?

The Indian railways became 'vision minded' soon after the critical assessment by the Expert Group indicating that 'currently they do not have a vision'. The bosses at the Rail Bhavan suddenly changed their attitude like a nursery child who obeys his teacher more than his parents. Not only the railways have strived hard to compose a paragraph as a 'vision statement', appearing on page 1, Vision 2020, they on every step and stage have found a workable vision like a burden line of a poem. So the smart railways now has an accumulated 'stock of visions' for every occasion like a cosmetic laden lady keeping various hues and shades of lipsticks in her vanity box suiting her dress for every event or celebration. The railways has 'Vision Statement' (Vision 2020, p.1), 'Vision for Freight Services' (p. 20), Passenger Service Vision' (p. 22), and Five Critical Visions' (p. 25) etc. The visions seem to be important and are testimony of Indian railways modified and improved pattern of business and traffic services.

The new incumbent of the Rail Bhavan - 2009-11 - has mesmerized everybody by issuing White Paper and Vision 2020 on the same day; at the same time. It is a like laughing open throatily and at the same time ballooning the cheeks. It is a difficult exercise, rather impossible to do so unless one happens to be an inmate of a high profile Russian Circus or has crafty talent like Raj Kapoor who used to cry and laugh together in 'Mera Nam Joker'. But the present guard of the railways has performed this magical effect of producing contradictions together - issuing White Paper and Vision 2020 on the same occasion. Vision 2020 has visualized an Eldorado for the railways. It provides an attractive theoretical framework with inspirational philosophy and innovative ideas. It highlights railways' special position and role to be played in the Indian economy. It explains its mission, motto and measures needed to be adopted. It tries to discover new areas of application of services to be rendered by the railways. It also projects to apply new technology and operative system so as to achieve excellence in production, sales and profits. A document of great hope and potential, Vision 2020 brings new life and thinking to Indian railways transport system. But how much it is workable and feasible is yet to be seen in the present context of the railways' economy where, on the one hand it issues White Paper showing its terrific weakness in the areas of financial and managerial processes and, on the other generates a robust dream of achieving excellence through Vision 2020 just within a decade. Is it not creating a contradictory situation? It seems to be - a Utopia – a make believe world of railways' dream and imagination.

Historically, railways seem to have enjoyed the luxury of issuing White Papers. It is like preparing an action plan without putting any efforts to follow it. But this phenomenon has appeared only after Independence. The railways of the Raj never tried to adopt such an exercise. They had problems which they dealt with responsibly. When for instance, during the Raj, the situation was so precarious that companies were earning profits at the expense of recurring loss to the railways, they did not issue White Paper, but boldly faced the unprecedented situation, pondered deeply over the problem and took decisive action to stop 'guarantee system' in a phased programme. Again, they had administrative and financial problems and two important facts emerged in this connection. These facts were: first, the emergence of the concept of inevitability of the 'total state management' and second, the concept of formation of The Acworth Committee. They took an appropriate decision without any refuge in White Paper. It may be said that the advent of White Paper is a democratic ideal and so the government or its department makes it a point to bring to light the infirmities and accumulated problems before the public. But it must be viewed that the process of White Paper should not form a ritual as it is in the case of the railways. It should not be followed as a routine exercise but only in emergent conditions the White Paper may be issued with the deeper sense of responsibility to fulfil it, point by point, step by step.

A number of White Papers were issued from the time of George Fernandes to the present incumbent of the railways. A. V. Poulose, a retired finance commissioner (Indian Railways) had expressed the views that there had already been 'a surfeit of Status Papers' in Indian Railways, and still two more papers were added including the present White Paper (2009). If one wished to take the stock of such papers, including special studies, occasional papers and other position papers with suggestions and observations, one would find that there was no limit to issue these papers. George Fernandes issued the Status Paper on March 1, 1990. Nitish Kumar issued these papers thrice: in May 1998, July 1998 and in 2002 in various forms and style. Poulose had suggested including one more study entitled, "Bombay Suburban Railway System – Suggestions and Observations". There had been two other studies of the same nature – one, "Electricity Safety – Perspective in Rail Transport", July 2007 and second, “Position Paper on the Rail Sector in India” – a Status Study of Private Public Participation (PPP) – October 2009. There has been a glut of White Papers. The railways now need firm action and determination to bring about a change in financial and managerial functioning so as to earn more revenue by generating higher productivity, efficiency and cost effectiveness.

However, the railway presents a peculiar phenomenon of turning into a reverse gear after achieving a great landmark of success for the past five years (2004-09). Presently its operative mechanism seems to be failing at different levels. The new incumbent of the railways opted to move backward to change the track in the hope of finding some better opportunities. But she could not find any quick remedy. Her new role was seen as the reversal of goals and strategies. In this respect the years 2008-09 and 2009-10 were decisive. Her first reaction was shown on the interim budget when it was called unrealistic and second when sluggish market conditions prevailed during the last few months of the predecessor's stint and no appropriate steps were taken to control the situation. On the other hand, it was allowed to deteriorate further. A stage of boom to bust had arrived and the railway budget for 2010-11 had confirmed that it had gone haywire. The operating ratio was sharply raised and no further investments were made.

If one tries to judge 'White Paper' and 'turnaround' by placing them face to face, one may find that the former has a tricky scheme and faulty intention and the latter has the sincerity of purpose and prompt action. The turnaround is the natural corollary of the recovered state of financial strength whereas the White Paper is the outcome of downsizing the past achievements. Turnaround is innovative and creative in action while White Paper aimed at image-destruction and demolition. They stood just opposed to each other. The White Paper made faulty revelations of the deteriorating condition of the railways. It is an expression of the deficiency of human behaviour that does not care to establish relationship which grows along with the growth of the system. The White Paper calls the predecessor's achievement of turnaround as 'so called' - a derogatory term to downgrade the image of the leader of turnaround. The White Paper brought about a plethora of deficient programmes and levied unfounded charges of financial, accounting and administrative nature against the predecessor.

The changes brought about during 2004-09 regarding the finances were the consequence of the turnaround conquest of the bankrupt railways. A battle against the deteriorating finance was fought. The damaging forces against freights and fares were won over. A sense of fighting spirit was infused and the railways was armoured with competitive business to acquire the lost share of transport-market. This was called the battle of change and transformation. The railways was rigid in its approach to business earlier to the predecessor and its old mindset did not encourage any change. Somebody was needed to invigorate the new spirit and work culture. A new programme of action was required and a new mindset was needed. The predecessor did both the programmes of changing the finances and developing a mindset for bringing 'turnaround' of the railways. He targeted the finances and toned up the system. It was known as the system-control which turned the loss making railway into a profit generating force. The quality of service was improved. Freights and fares adopted a dynamic policy. The productivity and carrying capacity were enhanced. The new technology of rail-laying and maintenance of old rails, sleepers and bridges was adopted. This brought the victorious scenario for the railways showing growing economy with the benefit accruing to the areas of pricing, costing, loading and revenue etc. The turnaround remodelled the railways' system and provided new concept of change and transformation.

With turnaround, the railways learnt and experienced how monopolies failed to attract business. It was a changing process from monopoly to monopolistic competition and to perfect competition as well. The railways related profit to their organizational set up, technological innovation and market conditions. One should be aware of these facts and strive hard to pursue them. The modern economy of the railways believed in volume-production, cost-reduction and sales-promotion. On this basis the profits followed as a natural consequence of volume-cost relationship. The increasing rate of surplus generated year after year between the year 2004 and 2008 demonstrated how Indian railways had focused productivity, market share and margins as their business strategies. All these achievements were the natural outcome of the turnaround saga of the railways.

However, the White Paper foiled the efforts of sustained growth as it was set well in action by the predecessor. The evidence of the growing economy of the railways could be seen during the past five years 2004-09 which came under attack from the White Paper. The compounded annual growth rate (CAGR) during that period for freight loading was 8.4 percent and for passenger kilometres was 9.14 per cent. The railways total traffic earnings during that period increased by 13.26 per cent while the freight and the passenger earnings grew at 14.11 per cent and 10.52 per cent respectively. This was a remarkable progress achieved. However, contrary to this situation during the present incumbent's period 2009-10, the achievements shown by revised estimates were dismal. There had been a diminishing trend in GTR and passenger earnings. The total expenses had also shown an increasing trend. As a result net revenue fell down considerably and operating ratio ultimately went up. The present incumbent, thus, foiled the sustained growth of turnaround which was earlier maintained progressively well within the system.

It was accepted that brooding on infirmities and events of the past was obnoxious for the positive thinking and transformation. The railways required reforms, not White Papers. The White Paper had left a depressing note. This journey through White Paper was a journey from bad to worse conditions. It had induced downfall of the railways rapidly. The railways thus came to halt at the junction that had almost lost its points, links and signals. It had desperately demanded a real change and transformation.

The White Paper had shown a biased view of the problem and the study was neither holistic nor dispassionate. It had a limited scope of analysis circumscribed by a short period with the particular emphasis to find faults with the person or the regime. This narrowed the horizon of the White Paper. It became a part of self mortifying factor of a diminishing power unable to provide a change. The White Paper regarded the railways as stagnant, below norm and a business unit hovering around less than expected elasticity of traffic demand, showing even lesser degree of performance. Its tracks and rolling stocks were extremely saturated; its operational efficiency did not match the international standard and its losses increased year after year. 'Restructuring' was no answer to the railways' woes. It was suggested various times but there was no scope for its acceptance. The railways were too old to take the 'lessons in transport from the neo-managerial experts' and their operative strategies which were comparatively less experienced to withstand the vagaries of an old institution. It was a sad commentary by the railways classical cadre of professionals who opined that they could not get anything substantial from the railway-chair at IIM – A. The railways kept itself aloof from all such forces which try to dominate it or come nearer to its matured status. The railways had developed their time tested principles of operation and control which they gained through their long experience of traffic work and activities. The railways operate on the basic engineering principles of linear movement in relation to time and distance along with weight, gradient and frictional approach. It governs the basic principle of railways' 'operation'. The land, rails and the rolling stocks make their precious possessions and these in general are actively associated with national or state authority. It makes a risky business to transfer this possession in the hands of private individuals. It generates the principle of railways' 'ownership'. The railways are meant to serve the land and its people and in return to this service, the railways win the loyalty and goodwill of the people. This explains the principle and purpose of their 'existence'. The railways have developed the basis of their growth and betterment of traffic services and it has led to the principle of 'efficiency and productivity'. The railways don't work in parts or in isolation. It is an integrated force and as such it is governed by the 'principle of holistic approach'. All such principles converge to one aspect i.e., reform, change and flexibility. The railways, thus, can't exist without technological change and development.

The reforms in the railways mean bringing the glory back. It requires initiative, strategy and will-power to bring the change. It needs coordination, courage and confidence to move things in proper direction. It has to establish well organized operational system and business activities. It has to generate sporting spirit to play and win. But this has to be alerted and seen that divisive forces have to be done away within the existing framework of railways as public authority. Restructuring the organisation will disturb the whole system. The wholesale privatization is also not a possible proposition. What is needed is to bring changes within the same set up. It is therefore difficult to do so. However, it is possible with great determination and combined efforts put up by the workers, employees and bosses of the railways pursuing a common national agenda. The railways have to find a new turning point by generating record volume of traffic and earning, without creating any fuss about the past achievements or issuing White Paper. It requires immediate and long term changes depending upon the strategies adopted. The turnaround process was an immediate step for change. It created a new mindset for further development. In the long run approach to change, improvement in technological aspects and capacity creation were to be tackled. The railways should bring both the systems on fast-track. It must have a blue print of such changes and reforms i.e., steps to be taken within public sector status of the railways; workforce should develop a new attitude of a work culture; the changes be brought within political and democratic set up with the acceptance of rights and duties at every level; the railway professionals and bosses should be given due recognition; the principle of ownership and management should be maintained on 'one hand and one place' basis; the integrated character of the railways be kept intact without any 'spinning off' functions known as non-core activities; and above all the railways should learn to live on their own resources.

The railways must be accommodating to provide space for reforms. It means that the opportunities for reforms be created within the basic constraints which the railways are facing. The changes must develop the basic theoretical approach to expand the spectrum of reforms. Such reforms should not be based on any ideological tautology or whimsical grounds. The theory of gradual change is a time tested phenomenon and the railways should adopt it as the first principle. The second most important principle is the time element generally accepted as a dynamic factor for railways reforms. It may be applied in different spheres including 'dynamic' price policy. The theory of privatization should be handled with care and where it is not directly possible, joint ventures with other state authorities be created. In order to be practical and successful in organizing reforms, it is important to obey the principle of least resistance. The railways is capable of bringing reforms and changes by keeping their targets of traffic and revenues high and by regularly enhancing the technological base to the level of world class railways.

The years that lapsed since the appearance of White Paper were crucial for the railways development. These years were to be utilized for setting right what was supposed to be "below the par' according to the incumbent of Rail Bhavan who remained in office during 2009-11 as the minister for the railways. But contrary to all expectations the railways were moved into reverse gear. The period (three years – 2010-2011) had shown damaging effect on the finances of the railways. No conscientious efforts were made to establish and adopt any growth process to achieve landmark success in the areas of revenue increase, traffic enhancement and technological advancement. On the other hand, the railways were allowed to deteriorate further in the sphere of maintaining fund balances, safety measures and modernization programmes.

It was easy to criticize the past regime (2004-09), issue a White Paper and undermine the achievement of the leader of the turnaround, but to come to the same level of attaining 75.9 per cent operating ratio was an impossible task for the Chief of the Trinamool Congress who had obliged the Rail Bhavan by her occasionally rare presence during her stint. Her pre-occupation with West Bengal politics left little time for her to look into the railways' affairs seriously. The years 2010-12 had witnessed remarkably high political impact on the railways and degenerated their functioning at all the levels. This was evident from the fact that Rail Bhavan activities were shifted to Kolkata and ultimately to Writers' Building as the Trinamool Chief held 'de-facto' power to run the railways. The issue of White Paper was also a step to politicize the railways.

The budget studies (2010-12) may be cited as the evidence to the deteriorating condition of the railways. The budget 2009-10 boasted of very 'realistic' estimates but it had underplayed the performance. The actual results shown were quite disparaging. There was no surplus /excess generated worth the name. The railways could earn only Rs. 0.75 crore net revenue as against estimated figures of

Rs. 2642.26 crore. The operating ratio was increased to 95.3 per cent. The same situation of financial meltdown continued in 2010-11 and 2011-12. The railways could earn a meagre amount of surplus/excess of Rs. 1405.00 crore and Rs. 1492.15 crore (revised) during 2010-11 and 2011-12 respectively. But these figures are still not final. If trend sets any example, the actual excess would be far less than the previous years. The operating ratio has set the trend to be at 95 per cent or above. The situation of fund balances have also became quite precarious. The closing balances have been Rs. 3103 crore and Rs. 2006 crore in the years 2010 and 2011 respectively whereas the balance has attained the level of Rs. 22279.35 crore in the year 2007-08 during predecessor's period (2004-08).

The railways have deteriorated within a couple of years after the Trinamool Congress Chief has taken over the charge. The railway's politics has ruined the organisation financially. The railways has now been put on ventilation and is admitted to ICU. The doctors like Mitra, Pitroda, and Kakodkar all have come to its rescue but the situation remains unchanged. It is not easy for them to pull railways out of ICU. Their diagnosis was correct but treatment was ineffective. Unless railways cross the self consuming economic barrier and become self sustaining in generating normal profits, no adoption of higher schemes of modernization and technological advancement will help them. Didi's Napoleonic diktat 'roll back or quit' has added fuel to the fire. The history of the railways will not forget this incident – the drama played as an insult – to the person who has hiked the fares and to the railways and their employees – their unions and the federations and the bosses at Rail Bhavan – who have prepared the budget and who actually run the railways.

The following points give in nutshell the assessment of the White Paper in relation to turnaround with a clear explanation of the problems involved in it:

1. The White Paper is neither a dispassionate nor an academically profound analysis of railways' present status of finances and management. It is a politically motivated document based on consultant's own approach to the problems who has used even

non-operative criteria to justify his case to downsize not only the past five years but the last two decades without any sense of proportion, judgment and historical relationship. The White Paper fails as railways' own study because an outsider has influenced it at every stage including the drafting of the report. Therefore, the workers, the staff, the trade unions and remaining high ups of the railways should disown it as a tainted report for not justifying their hard contribution for the last five years.

2. The White Paper misses a lot specially the good part and the achievements which the past regime has created. The paper intentionally avoids mentioning about a corrupt practice being followed by the railways staff and officials for the past several years in the form of overloading the wagons unofficially and sharing the booty so received. This evil prevailed as a system which was unearthed by the predecessor in 2004-05 especially in the iron ore traffic route. When the predecessor tried to regulate it in favour of the railways, a lot of hue and cry was created, even by the Board members. These members along with other staff seem to be the main culprits in suggesting, drafting and ultimately finalizing the White Paper. How tricky is the matter? If you pin point a mistake, rectify it and create a favourable situation, you are opposed after you leave the office; your contribution is nullified by the White Paper. Is it the meaning and purpose of issuing the White Paper? Why did this fact not find a place in the White Paper? Instead, it was reiterated that the system had a bearing on wear and tear of tracks and rolling stock. But what was happening to wagons and tracks when corrupt practice was regularly followed in the form of overloading?

3. Why the authorities remained silent for not accepting the fact that the White Paper was issued without the approval of the cabinet? It was a matter of breach of privilege because what had happened during UPA's first regime was a joint responsibility and how a direct 'disapproval' of the five-year period of the

railways was done by issuing the White Paper? The convention committee on the railways has every right to reopen the case to bring the whole matter to proper investigation and justice.

4. The White Paper has wiped off a useful page which used to be there as page no 2 table 1 (a) in Explanatory Memorandum on the Railway Budget. One can go through this memorandum for the year 2010-11 to see that the page is missing without any explanation. The page contained the statement of cash and investible surplus. This surplus concept was the outcome of the facts and figures which appeared in the budget itself. Only some items were added, regrouped or subtracted to explain the basis of the surplus. If the then incumbent of Rail Bhavan (2009-11) has thought this concept to be useless – an explanation to this effect should have been added. It should not have become a part of her whimsical decision making. Moreover, the concept of elasticity used in calculating the expected rate of growth of railways traffic demand has been wrongly adopted in the White Paper. Not only that the elasticity is overrated (1.25), but the very concept is fraught with severe evils as it does not indicate railways traffic demand elasticity but reflects the traffic elasticity of the mixed sample including other modes of transport. The real measure of transport elasticity of developing countries cannot go beyond unit elasticity and for purely railway's traffic demand elasticity it will remain less than unity - somewhere 0.8 to 0.9 at its ideal form (see chapter 4 for more explanation).
5. When a new budget day arrives, it becomes a part of bounty-distribution by the minister for his/her political gain. This adds to a lot of unfeasible and uneconomic projects and a backlog of such proposals goes on piling up and ultimately finds a place in White Paper as a point to cover up. Such practice must be stopped and the railways should prepare their own 'Five Year Plan Document' instead of being a part of general Five Year Plan. In this way, the project work would be based on the plan with resources clearly mentioned instead of based on budget

projects added year after year. Whenever a new project or proposal is announced it must be accompanied by resource mobilization process and become a part of the planned economy. No unplanned proposals should be allowed to become a part of budget or bountiful distribution. The Planning Commission must put a restraint on it. This practice should form a part of general reforms of the railways.

6. It becomes an issue of RTI regarding the money paid to the consultant and terms and conditions fixed for providing spicy material against the performance of the predecessor. What was the need of outsourcing the study? The railway cadre is competent to find its own fault and even find a short term solution too. For better organized services and traffic activities a long term planning programmes may be adopted. But why the need of a consultant was felt? It was natural; a professional cadre could not help in fault finding mission to the extent as a paid outsider would have done. Most of the insiders were thus kept away from this work and the White Paper became a handy-work of a few persons. It did not represent the soul of the railways.
7. The White Paper though laments on the Sixth Pay Commission expenses but the fact which it misses to mention is that as long as the Keynesian macroeconomic system of financing prevails, the Pay Commission one after the other with a gap of ten years would be constituted to offset the inflationary impact on pay and pension. After every decade a new or a peculiar situation would be developed. For the railways, it is very important to plan this expense in advance because unlike the general exchequer it can't create a 'deficit financing' although it has a power to present a separate budget. The Pay Commission expenses are to be met by the railways own earnings and here either they dwindle or fail to meet the expenses. It is therefore, recommended that a shadow accounting should start immediately after the old account of Pay Commission is settled.

8. The aftermath of White Paper has been seen in the form of successive meltdown of the finances of the railways. It has been a down fall from boom to bust. Once you accept the belligerent path and politicize the railways, there seems no end to it. The railways started deteriorating much faster within a couple of years after the new regime in 2009 has taken over the charge. The financial condition of railways has become so precarious that it seems it has no other way but to be admitted to ICU for immediate treatment.
9. A highly contradictory statement appeared at page no. 1 para 8 of the White Paper and repeated at page 16 para C (V) in contrast to the statement appearing on page 59 para 5 indicating that 'pay load to tare ratio' of wagons needs to be improved significantly even in the main business of bulk cargo transportation. How have these two contradictory approaches appeared? When the predecessor increased the pay load to tare ratio from 20.32 T to 22.9T, he was criticized vehemently and this was one of the reasons that the period of study of past five years was confined to the predecessor's regime (2004-09) so as to pull him down. What made the White Paper to contradict its own concept? Perhaps, if one reads in between the lines, the whole White Paper seems to be camouflaged, projecting a false image of the period under study.
10. The White Paper concludes its study only in two sentences appearing on page 70 para 5.1 as if it has nothing to say on its own as 'the issues ... and options are not new to the railways' and that they have to be 'addressed boldly'. If there was nothing new to add why such a fuss was created? Why the White Paper was issued at all? It only reflects that it has no clear idea better than what has already been explained in previous status papers and similar studies. What is there to repudiate the preceding regime in the garb of a White Paper?

In the end one can draw a line by joining two points – the first point from where this study started and the last point where it concluded. "No successor carries forward the initiative of the predecessor" and that "White Paper has nothing new to add" but to repudiate the preceding regime. The railway as a glorious institution must rebuff the White Paper, and other factors and tendencies which mar the railways and come out clean without malice to one and all.

◆◆◆

Bibliography

Agrawal, V.K. (2004). *Managing Indian Railways - The Future Ahead*, Manas Publications, New Delhi, pp. 45-318.

— (2010). "Towards Greener Transport", *RITES Journal*, July 2010. New Delhi.

Alivelu, G.and K. Siva Prasad. (2008). "Managing the Human Face of Indian Railways", *GI TAM, Journal of Management*, Vol. 6, No.1, Orissa (India), pp. 177-187.

Aurora, Bhavna Vij. (2006). "U Turn on a Train", *Outlook*, Vol. XLVI, No. 24, June 19, 2006, New Delhi, p. 8.

— (2007). "Was It All Track II?" *Outlook*, September 24, 2007, New Delhi, pp. 18-22.

— (2011). *Indian Railways Bankrupt under Mamata*. Web-link. http://www.india to-day.in/story/indian-railways-bankrupt-under-mamata-banerjee/1/127266.html

Bannathan, Esra et. al. (1992). *Demand for Freight Transport, Infrastructure* and Urban Deptt, World Bank, 1992, pp. 1-29.

Banerjee, Mamata. (2009 a). Budget Speech, 2009-10 (Main), July, 2009, Rail Bhavan, New Delhi.

— (2009 b). Railways Were Below Par During Lalu - Era. Web-link.http://www.news.oneindia.in/2009/12/18/html

— (2010). Budget Speech, 2010-11, February, 2010, Ministry of Railways, New Delhi, pp.1-30.

— (2011). Budget Speech, 2011-12, February, 2011, Ministry of Railways, New Delhi, pp.1-35.

Bartwal, H. Singh. (2006). "Prof. What Was Wrong in Bihar"? *Hindustan Times*, December, 28, 2006, p. 8.

— (2007). "Farely Good Lalunomics". *Hindustan Times*, February 26, 2007, p.1.

Bhardwaj, P.K. (2006). "I Rescued Railways: Lalu", *The Hindu*, December 28, 2006, p. 12.

Brigin Shaw, David. (2007). "Boom Times in India" *International Railway Journal*, May 2007, Paris, pp. 47-51.

Business Line. (2003). White Paper on Safety of Railways - Little Cause of Alarm. Web-link.http://www.thehindubusinessline.in/2003/06/02/stories.html

Business Standard. (2009 a). Mamata Dismisses Lalu Prasad's Claim on Indian Railways Tur naround. Web-link. http://www.business-standard. com/ india/news/mamata-dismisses-lalu-claim-on-indian-railways-turnaround/html

—— (2009 b). Mamata May Have Embarrassed Lalu, But… Web-link. http:// www. Business rediff.co./column/2009/dec/22/column-mamata-may-have-embarrassed-lalu-but… html Statistical Abstract, Indian Railway, Ministry of Statistics and CSO. (2005-06 a). Programme Implementation, New Delhi, pp. 251-261. Also Years - 2006-07 to 2009-10.

—— (2005-06 b). *Statistical Abstract*, Roads, Ministry of Statistics and Programme Implementation, New Delhi, pp. 267-277. Also Years - 2006-07 to 2009-10.

CARE. (2009). *Impact of Railway Budget 2007-08*, Credit Analysis Research Ltd., New Delhi, pp. 1-4.

CAG. (2006). *Union Audit Report:* Railways Report No. 5, 2004-05, New Delhi.

Chobe Sudha. (2008). "Indian Railways and its Financial Progress", *Indian Railways*, April 2008, pp. 29-30.

Dalal, Sucheta. (2009). *Indian Railways* White Paper May Expose True State of Finances. Weblink. http://www.suchetadalal.com/november7.2009.

Das, M. (2006). Lalu Flags Off Double Track Container Train. Web-link.http:/ /www.blonnet.com/2006/03/24/stories/2006/03202901100.html

Dayal, Raghu. (2009). A White Paper Previewed. Web-link. http://www.indian express.com/news/a-white-paper-previewed/493267/July 24,.2009.html

Dutta, A.K. (2007). Status Paper on Electrical Safety Perspective in Rail Transport, SE Railways, Ranchi pp.1-5.

Emee. (2006). "Lalu Prasad's IIM Lecture". *Business World*, September 11, 2006, p. 56.

Expert Group (Committee). (2001). *The Indian Railways Report 2001: Policy Imperatives for Reinvention and Growth*, Vol. 1 and Vol. 2, NCAER/IDFC, New Delhi. (Expert Group on Indian Railways, popularly known as The Rakesh Mohan Committee Report, Vol. 1, pp.1-75 (Executive Summary), Vol. 2, Part.1, pp.1-155, Part II, pp. 157-352.

Fernandes, George. (1990). Status Paper on Indian Railways: Opinions and Issues, Ministry of Railways, New Delhi.

Ghose, Arbinda. (2007). Dedicated Freight Corridor in Standard Gauge, *Indian Railways,* October, 2007, Rail Bhavan, New Delhi, pp. 36-37.

Ghosh, Dwalayan. (2010). "Cag Raps Mamata for Losses", *The Times of India,* 26.4.2010. New Delhi.

Goel, Anjali. (2007). Dedicated Freight Corridors and High Speed Rails: India's Ultra Low Carbon Mega Rail Projects, Ministry of Railways. Web-link.http://www.siteresourcesworld bank.org/goel/india.html

GOI. (2007 a). *The Report of the Committee of Infrastructure Financing,* May 2007, Ministry of Finance, Department of Economic Affairs, Infrastructure Division, New Delhi, p.1.

—— (2007 b). Report of the people 2004-2007 (Hindi Edition) of UPA Government I, Issued by The Prime Minister, May 22, 2007, New Delhi, pp. 58-59.

Gupta, Dr. Desh and Dr. Milind Sathye. (2007). Financial Turnaround of Indian Railways: Good Luck or Good Management, University of Canberra, Australia, Canberra, pp.1-22. Web- link.http://www.crawford. anu.edu. au/acde/asarc/pdf/papers/2007.

Hashim,S.R. (1967). "Transport Coefficient and Transport Input Vector (goods transportation, railways)", Edited in, Economic Analysis in Input Output Framework, Vol. 2, Pune, pp. 92-108.

Ibnlive. (2010). Mamata's White Paper Paints Lalu Black. Weblink.http://www.ibnlive.in.com/news/mamatas-white-paper-paints-lalu-black/107351-37.html

Indian Express. (2006). "Nitish oversaw fall of (railways) 29% and Mamata during her stint brought it still further by another 28%". (Indian Express, April 2006, New Delhi), as quoted in Raghuram, G. Turnaround of Indian Railways… Strategies and Processes, IIM, Ahmedabad, p. 48.

Irastimes. (2009). White Paper on Indian Railways. Web-link.http://www.yuku.com/topic/130/>professional issues (12/25/09000:44:09). pra shant73.white paper on indian railways waste of nations resources (01/05/1011:17:45). vijay.white paper or white wash. (01/23/1001:53:08).

Jain, Ashis Kumar. (2009). *Railways: Indian and Global Perspective,* ICFAI, University Press, Hyderabad.

Jaruhar. R.R. (2006). "Great Turnaround of Indian Railways - Role of Civil Engineers". *Indian Railways,* Vol. 52, No. 1, Rail Bhavan, New Delhi.

Jeena, K.C. (2008). "IR—Growth on Fast Forward Mode". *Indian Railways,* April, 2008, pp. 25-26.

Joshi, Rashmi. (2007). *Indian Railways Changing Tracks for Better,* ICFAI, University Press, 52, Nagarjun Hills, Hyderabad.

Kalam, Abdul APJ. (2005). *The Life Tree — Poems* Penguin/Viking, New Delhi, p. 3.

—— With S. Rajan. (1998). *India 2020: A Vision for New Millennium.* Penguin Viking, New Delhi, 1998.

Khare, Vivek. (2009). *The Turnaround Story of Indian Railways,* Ameya Prakashan, Pune.

Kumar, Nitish. (1998 a). Status Paper on Indian Railways: Issues and Options, May 27, 1998, Ministry of Railways, New Delhi.

—— (1998 b). Status Paper on Railway Projects, July 28, 1998, Ministry of Railways, New Delhi.

—— (2002). *Status Paper on Indian Railways: Issues and Options,* (Revised). 2002, Ministry of Railways, New Delhi.

Kumar, Sudhir. (2005). "Indian Railways Turnaround", Presentation made in ASSOCHAM Seminar on Rail Freight Corridor, June 30, 2005. (memeo).

—— (2008). "Turnaround Story: Moving from Bankruptcy to Billions". The Times of India, February 27, 2008, New Delhi.

Kumar, Sudhir and Shagun Mehrotra. (2009a). *Bankruptcy to Billions - How Indian railways transformed?* Oxford University Press, New Delhi pp 1-207.

—— (2009b). "Excerpts on Sustainability", Budget Speech, Part I, February 26, 2008, Appedix 9A, Vision 2025, as cited in, Bankruptcy to Billions, p. 195.

Mathur, P.N. and R. Bhardwaj. (1967). "Input Output Economics — A Resume", Edited in, *Economic Analysis in Input Output Framework,* Vol. 1, Pune, pp. 1-44.

Mattoo, Ajita. (2000). "Indian Railways Agenda for Reforms", *Economic and Political Weekly,* March 4, 2000, p. 771.

Ministry of Finance. (2009). *Position Paper on the Rail Sector in India -Public Participation A Status Study of Private Public Participation (PPP),* October 2009, pp. 3-61.

Ministry of Railways. (2001). *Response to The Rakesh Mohan Committee Report,* Rail Bhavan,New Delhi, pp. 4-8.

—— (2001-11). *Explanatory Memorandum on Railway Budget,* 2001-02 to 2010-11, GOI, New Delhi.

—— (2001-10 a). *Year Books,* 2001 to 2010, GOI, New Delhi.

—— (2001-10 b). Annual Reports and Accounts. 2001-02 to 2009-10, GOI, New Delhi.

—— (2004). *Integrated Railway Modernization Plan* (2005-2010), Rail Bhavan, New Delhi, pp. 1-23.

—— (2005). *Agenda Note on Running of Heavy Axle Load Trains of Indian Railways,* Rail Bhavan, New Delhi, pp. 1-113.

—— (2006 a). "Signing of MoU Between Deutsche Behn A.G. and Indian Railways". *Indian Railways,* June 2006, Rail Bhavan, New Delhi, p. 6

—— (2006 b). "Director HEC School of Management Meets Railway Minister", *Indian Railways,* September, 2006, Rail Bhavan, p. 7.

—— (2007-11). *Annual Statistical Statements* 2007-08 to 2010-11, GOI, New Delhi.

—— (2008). "A New Chapter of Cooperation Begins Between World's Two Great Railways". *Indian Railways,* February 2008, p. 7.

—— (2008). *Outcome and Performance Budget of Railways* for 2008-09, Rail Bhavan, New Delhi, pp. 1-72, Appendix C1 - C50 and D1 - D2.

—— (2009 a). GOI, Indian Railways Vision 2020, December 18, 2009, pp. 1-62.

—— (2009 b). GOI, *White Paper on Indian Railways,* December 18, 2009, pp. 1-70.

Misra, R.N. (2008). "Intra-Sectoral Inequalities of Growth of Transport in India (after liberalization)", *Chintan, IILM Journal of Science, Technology and Management,* Vol. 1, No. 2, (2008), Greater Noida, 201308, pp. 38-43.

—— (2009 a). Lalu, Mamata and Railways. Web-link.http://www.worm in a bud.blogspot. com/2009/11/lalu-mamata-and-railways.html

—— (2009 b). Lalu's Men to Counteract White Paper. Web-link.http:// www.worm in a bud.blogspot.com/2009/11/lalus-men-to-couteract-white-paper.html

—— (2009 c). Mamata's White Paper - An Attempt to Abort Turnaround. Weblink.http.://www.worm in a bud.blogspot.com/2009/12/Mamatas-white-paper-an-attempt-to-abort-turnaround.html

—— (2009 d). Indian Railways Turnaround: A Study in Management, Explores Lalu Prasad's Influence on the Resurgence of the Railways, Jaico Publishing House, A-2 Jash Chamber, Phirozshah Mehta Road, Fort, Mumbai - 400001, pp. 1-305.

—— (2010 a). Mamata — An Absentee Minister.Web-link.http://www.worm in a bud. Blogs pot.com./2010/05/mamata-an-abentee-minister.html

—— (2010 b). Mamata - The Minister of Derailways and Collisions.Web-link.http://www.worm in a bud.blogspot.com/2010/07/mamata-the-minister-of-derailways-and-collisions.html

—— (2010 c). Mamata's White Paper - How Black Is It? Web-link.http://www.worm in a bud.blogspot.com/2010/03/mamatas-white-paper-how-black-is-it.html

—— (2010 d). Mess Of The Railways — Thy Name Is Mamata. Web-link.http;//www. worm in a bud.blogspot.com/2010/01/mess-of-the-railways-thy-name-is-mamata.html

—— (2010 e). White Paper on Indian Railways. Web-link.http://www.worm in a bud.blogspot.com/2010/07/white-paper-on-indian-railways-mamata.html

—— (2010 f).White Paper On Indian Railways - Mamata At Her Worst. Web-link.http://www. worm in a bud. blogspot.com/2010/07/white-paper-on-indian-railways-mamata-at-her-worst.html

—— (2011 a). Mamata's Budget 2011-12: - Snail's Pace Railways. Web-link.http://www. worm in a bud. blogspot.com/2011/03/mamatas-budget-2011-12-snals-pace-railways.html

—— (2011 b). The Indian Railways Running in Losses. Web-link.http://www.worm in a bud.blogspot.com/2011/01/indian-railways-running-in-losses.html

Misra, R.N. and D.M. Mahapatra. (2008 a). "Indian Railways: Strategies Adopted by Shri Lalu Prasad Yadav", in the Proceedings of National Conference On Emerging Business Strategies, ITS, Ghaziabad, pp. 329-337.

—— (2008 b). "The Indian Railways Turnaround: Genesis and Development". Vol. II No. 1, Fall 2008, Apeejay Journal of Technology and Management, Greater Noida - 201308, pp. 40-50.

Money Control. (2011). State of the Railways: Are its Finances in Mess? Web-link.http://www.amoneycontrol.com/news/cnb-tv-comments/state-of-the-railways-are-its-finances-in-mess.525960.html

Narain, Shanti. (2007). "Long Term Sustainability of Indian Railways. *RITES Journal*, March 2007, Gurgaon, NCR, Delhi, pp.16.1 – 16.10.

Network 3i. (2006). *Infrastructure Report: Urban Infrastructure,* Oxford Univerrsity Press, New Delhi, pp. 1- 6.

—— (2007). *Infrastructure Report: Rural Infrastructure,* Oxford University Press, New Delhi, pp. 1-6.

Nilakant, V. and S. Ramnarayan. (2009). *Changing Tracks Reinventing the Spirit of Railways* Harper Collins Business New Delhi, pp. 52-85.

Poulose, A.V. (2009). "Evolving Methods of Funding Projects", RITES Prasad, Lalu. (2006 a). Journal, January, 2009. "Fully Airconditioned Garib Rath",

Budget Speech, Indian Railways, Vol. 51. No.12, Ministry of Railways, New Delhi, pp. 22-23.

— (2006 b), "Record Breaking Output in Freight Business", Indian Railways, New Delhi, pp. 22-23.

— (2008). "No Risk No Gain", *Outlook Business*. Budget Speech, March 22, 2008, New Delhi, pp. 4-8.

— (2009). *Budget Speech*, 2009-10 (Interim), February, 2009, Rail Bhavan, New Delhi.

Raghuram, G. and N. Shukla. (2007). "Turnaround of Indian Railways: Increasing the Axle Loading", Working Paper, Number 2007-05-03, *Vikalp*, Vol. 99, No. 2, April - June, IIM, Ahmedabad, pp. 87-96.

Raghuram, G. and M. Ravi Babu. (1999). "Alernative Means of Financing Railways", *Infrastructure Development and Financing*, (Ed). Raghuram, G. et. al. Macmillan, New Delhi, pp. 356-380.

Rao, Raghavendra. (2009). "Mamata's White Paper Won't Be All Lalu Bashing", *Indian Express*. Web-link. http://www.indianexpress.com/news/mamatas-white-paper-wont-be-all-lalu-bashing/555710/Dec18.2009.html

Sinha, M.K. (2008). "Security on Railways: Emerging Challenges and its Role". *Indian Railways*, April, 2008, p.19.

Sopan, Kasinath. (2011). Human Resource Management - A Study of Indian Railways. Weblink. http://www.free patents on line.com/article/review-business-research/ 272484937.html

Srinivasan, Roopa et. al. (Ed). (2006). *Our Indian Railways*, Fountain Books, New Delhi.

Satyawadi, (Dr.) N.C. (2007). "Economics, Transport Economics and Engineering: Challenges Galore for the Economists". *RITES Journal*, March, 2007, Gurgaon, NCR, Delhi, pp. 10.1 - 10.11

Tandon, P. (1994). *Organizational Structure and Management Ethos of Indian Railways, Ministry of Railways*, GOI, March (1994), New Delhi.

The Hindu. (2009). White Paper on Indian Railways Financial Status Likely on December 21. Web -link. http://www.thehindu.com/news.national/article64388.december13.2009. New Delhi.

Thomson, L. and J. Fraser. (1993). Infrastructure Note: World Bank's Railway Database. Weblink.http://www.siteresources.worldbank.org/inttransportresources/33629175973157/td-rw6.pdf

TRAI. (2008). *The Indian Telecom Service Performance Indicators, October-December, 2007.*

April 10, 2008. Web-link.http://www.trai.gov.in/trai/upload/report/41/preport/10april08.pdf

UIC. (2006). *International Railways Statistics 2006* (UIC Leaflet) Paris, International Union of Railways (UIC).

World Bank. (1994). *World Bank's Railway Database.* Web-link httpl://www.worldbank.org/ transport/rail/rdt.html

—— (2006). *Highway and Railway Development in India and China, 1992 - 2002,* Transport Notes, Rural Transport Thematic Group, Washington DC: The World Bank Group, May, 2006, Washington.

Index

P

R